Travel and Tourism

A North-American - European perspective

Patrick Lavery   Carlton Van Doren

TRAVEL AND TOURISM

A North-American-European perspective

Travel and Tourism
a North American — European perspective

An overview of the characteristics and operations of the tourism and travel industry and the role of private and public sectors in developing tourism.

Tourism is new to the curricula of many schools of higher education in the U.S. and Canada — this book fills the need for a short introduction for use in beginning courses as well as a supplementary book for courses in recreation and leisure behavior, geography, economics, business and hotel administration. It focuses on three main areas:-
— the study of tourism and its social, economic & environmental components
— operations of the private and public sectors & interactions between them
— behavioral aspects: tourists' motivations, perceptions & group characteristics.

Contents
The nature of the tourist industry
Domestic and international tourism
Development of the tourist industry
Sectors of the tourism industry - demand and supply
International tourism
The retail travel sector
The passenger transport sector
The lodging sector
Federal, State and regional roles
Planning & development of tourism
Tourism marketing
Economic impact of tourism
Environmental impact of tourism
New developments in tourism

isbn 1 85450 125 9 $ 17.95 (UK £11.95) Sewn paperback (245x185) 224 pp.

ORDER FORM

Please send ......copies of **Travel & Tourism** at $ 17.95 a copy to:-

NAME............................ SIGNATURE..

ADDRESS   ....

                    ....

                    ....

State Mutual Book & Periodical Service Ltd, 521 Fifth Avenue,
NEW YORK CITY 10017.

Please send me a copy on 28 day approval .... tick here & return to
ELM Publications, Seaton House, Kings Ripton, Huntingdon PE17 2NJ, England
Tel. England 04873-254 Fax England 04873-359

Travel and Tourism

A North-American — European perspective

Patrick Lavery

Carlton Van Doren

Elm Publications

© Patrick Lavery and Carlton Van Doren, 1990

First published June, 1990 by ELM Publications,
12, Blackstone Road, Stukeley Meadows Industrial Estate,
Huntingdon, Cambs., PE18 6EF (0480 414553) who hold the
copyright on behalf of the authors Patrick Lavery and
Carlton Van Doren.

Apart from critical assessment or review, no part of this
publication may be copied, reproduced, broadcast or
transmitted, stored electronically in an information retrieval
system or issued in part or in full in any other binding than the
original without the prior, written permission of the publisher.

Printed by the St Edmundsbury Press, Suffolk.

ISBN 1-854501-25-9

CONTENTS

List of Tables
List of Figures and Maps
Introduction
About the authors

Chapter	Page
1 The tourism industry	1
2 The development of the tourist industry	19
3 The tourism product – attractions	37
4 International tourism – an overview	57
5 The retail travel sector	67
6 The passenger transport sector	81
7 The lodging sector	105
8 Federal, State and regional roles	119
9 Planning and development of tourism	135
10 Tourism marketing	151
11 Tourism impact studies – 1. The economic impact of tourism	163
12 Tourism impact studies – 2. The impact of tourism on the environment	173
13 New developments in tourism	185
Glossary	199
References and further reading	201
Index	207

LIST OF TABLES

Table Number   **Page Number**

Chapter 1
1. Characteristics of total trips and vacation trips — 9
2. Person trips by primary mode of transportation — 10
3. Profiles of overseas visitors to the United States and to the United Kingdom, 1984 — 12

Chapter 2
4. Changes in United States market composition — top 12 countries — 31

Chapter 3
5. Standard industrial classifications related to travel and tourism — 40
6. Recreation visitor days in leading National Park areas — 45
7. Caribbean destinations of United States visitors, 1987 — 55

Chapter 4
8. International tourist arrivals, 1965-1987 — 59
9. International tourist receipts, 1965-1987 — 59
10. International tourist receipts as a proportion of national income — 63
11. Share of tourist activity in total economic activity — 63

Chapter 5
12. Travel agency turnover — 73

Chapter 6
13. Hours of recreation per year provided by National Parks, roads and streets — 87
14. Growth of Channel/North Sea ferry traffic — United Kingdom — 92
15. World scheduled domestic and international air traffic — 96
16. Scheduled traffic of commercial air carriers — 96
17. Aircraft operational characteristics, 1940-2000 — 97
18. Estimates of commercial jet aircraft requirements, 1985-1995 — 97
19. IATA members' rankings — top scheduled airlines, 1987 — 98

Chapter 7
20. Trends in performance measurements — worldwide hotels — 106
21. Main hotel chains — United Kingdom — 108
22. Hotel marketing consortia operating in Britain — 109
23. Top 25 United States lodging chains, 1986 — 114
24. The United States hotel industry, 1986 — 116
25. Market share of United States hotels — 116

Chapter 9
26. Forecasts of peak capacity at main sites on the Roman Wall — United Kingdom — 147

Chapter 11
27. A transactions matrix — 165
28. The tourism multiplier in action — 167

Chapter 12
29. Suggested Space Standards for Environmental Capacity — 174
30. Growth of timeshare ownership, 1975-1985 — 191
31. Major companies developing timeshare in Europe — 192
32. Airline computer reservation systems in the United States — 195

LIST OF FIGURES AND MAPS

Figure Number	Page Number

Chapter 1
1. Employment related to tourism and leisure — 4
2. Foreign visitors to the United States — 5
3. Number of visits by overseas visitors to the UK — 6
4. Total trips and vacation trips, 1972-1986 — 8
5. US receipts from foreign visitors in the US for 1986 — 13
6. Top 20 States in total visitation — 14
7. Bureau of Census Regions used by the National Travel Survey — 17

Chapter 2
8. Schematic diagram of a 'typical' seaside resort — 23
9. Evolution of resort hotels and areas in the United States — 27
10. Trends in international travellers to and from the United States — 33

Chapter 3
11. Top 20 States ranked by total number of visitors, 1986 — 38
12. Resource dependency of attractions — 42
13. Classifying attractions — 43
14. Vacation centers in the United States — 46
15. National Parks, and Seashores and lakeshores in the United States — 47
16. National Parks, areas of outstanding natural beauty & stretches of Heritage Coast in England & Wales — 48
17. Resort hotel centers of the United Staes — 52
18. Coastal zone scenarios — 54

Chapter 4
19. International tourism demand — 60
20. Growth of international tourist expenditures — 61

Chapter 5
21. Travel agencies in the United States, 1986 — 68
22. Links in the retail travel sector — United States — 71
23. Links in the retail travel sector — United Kingdom — 71
24. Growth of United Kingdom business travel 1978-86 — 74

Chapter 6
25. The main British Rail Inter-City network — 83
26. Amtrak's National Rail Passenger System — 84
27. Intercity travel modes — United States — 86
28. Sealink route map — United Kingdom — 93
29. Growth of international and United States air traffic, 1974-86 — 95

Chapter 7
30. Location of Center Parcs Development in Holland & Belgium — 118

Chapter 8
31. Travel generated employment, 1985 — 121
32. United States — domestic travel expenditures for all trips — 123
33. Tourist Board structure in the United Kingdom — 126
34. England's Regional Tourist Boards — 128

Chapter 9
35. Three kinds of destination zone 137
36. Resort development in the Languedoc-Rousillon region 144

Chapter 10
37. The product life cycle 155
38. A typical 'Z' graph 159

Chapter 11
39. Contribution of tourism to the Balance of Payments:
    United States and United Kingdom 170

Chapter 12
40. An environmental impact matrix 178

Chapter 13
41. Location of major theme parks in North America 188

Introduction

This book provides an overview of the characteristics and operations of the tourism and travel industry and the role of private and public sectors in developing tourism. Tourism is new to the curricula of many schools of higher education in the United States and Canada. The authors felt that there was a need for a short introductory book for use in beginning courses as well as a supplementary book for courses in recreation and leisure behavior, geography, economics, business, and hotel administration.

The original edition from which this edition was modified, used primarily British examples, but still included a large number of international sources to aid in the recognition of the world-wide nature of tourism. This edition focuses on North America, primarily the United States, and includes much of the British orientation. We have attempted to compare and contrast the tourism industry in these two nations for a number of reasons. First, the early development of the North American leisure travel industry has roots in the United Kingdom. Secondly, for many North American students their first foreign travel experiences include a visit to the United Kingdom. If their professional interests and aspirations are to work in this growing industry, the United Kingdom provides them a laboratory to analyze the industry with a minimum language barrier (See Glossary). Thirdly, both authors forsee the day when students enrolled in higher education courses in tourism on both continents will be exchanged as an accepted part of their educational development. It is logical to assume that this exchange will take place between the English speaking nations. Fourth, we wrote this book because we wanted to do so. It was a challenge and admittedly a first approximation with both strengths and weaknesses. Our students and peers will be the severest critics.

The book focuses on three main areas:

— the study of tourism and its social, economic and environmental components;
— the operations of the private and public sectors and interactions between them;
— the behavioral aspects of tourism--tourists' motivations, perceptions and group characteristics.

We accept all responsibility for any errors and omissions.

About the Authors

Dr. Carlton S. Van Doren Professor of Recreation, Tourism and Resources Development at Texas A&M University. He has taught at the University of South Dakota, Michigan State University, and Ohio State University. During two summers he was a guest professor at the University of Hawaii and the University of Wyoming. During his faculty development leave he was a Visiting Senior Lecturer at the Dorset Institute of Higher Education. His publishing career includes articles in the *Journal of Leisure Research, Leisure Sciences, Journal of Travel Research,* and the *Annals of Tourism.* He has served as editor of the *Journal of Leisure Research* and *Leisure Sciences.* He has co-edited two books, *Land and Leisure* and *Statistics on Outdoor Recreation.*

Dr. Patrick Lavery is Deputy Director, Humberside College of Higher Education, formerly he was Professor and Head of Tourism at the Dorset Institute of Higher Education. He has taught at the Universities of Liverpool and London and for several years was responsible for tourism planning with a Metropolitan County Council. He has published extensively over the past 20 years and has written many articles on several aspects of tourism research and development. He has also acted as a Consultant on Education and Training for Tourism and has worked for the European Economic Community and the English Tourist Board. He has also presented papers on tourism management at Conferences in Britain, Europe and the United States.

Acknowledgements

No one takes steps forward without the assistance and encouragement from others. For this edition my willing right hand was Mrs. Marguerite Van Dyke, the 'executive' secretary for several professors here at Texas A&M. I respectfully and affectionately refer to her as 'M'. She has the ability to make our work and our goals her avocation. I will forever be very grateful. On the other side of the Atlantic, I acknowledge a secretarial staff in the Department of Tourism at Dorset Institute whom I got to know during my sabbatical. The original book would not have been possible without Mrs. A. Gifford and Mrs. L. Drew and the skilled illustrations of Pam Griffin. I thank my colleague and friend Pat Lavery for the opportunity and challenge to undertake this modification of his initial work. Lastly, I owe a special thank-you to my wife Sharon for continued encouragement, tolerance, and stimulation. There were times when her strength energized my own.

Chapter 1

The Tourism Industry

Learning Objectives: After reading this chapter and some of the references and tackling one of the assignments you should have a clear idea of:

(i) the nature of the tourist industry
(ii) some data sources about trends in domestic and international tourism.

Introduction: What is Tourism?

Although tourism has existed in a limited form since the Middle Ages, the first definition of the term 'tourist' was made almost 50 years ago by the Council of the League of Nations, (L.N., 1937) and subsequently ratified in 1963 by the United Nations (IUOTO, 1963). The term 'tourist' was taken to mean any person travelling for a period of twenty-four hours or more in a country other than that in which he or she usually resides, for the purpose of leisure, business, family, friends, meeting mission. To this was added the term 'excursionist' to cover people staying less than twenty-four hours in the country visited (Lickorish, 1958).

However neither definition covers domestic tourism and for this reason the phenomenon should be best described using the National Tourism Resources Review Commission's definition in 1973:

> A tourist is one who travels away from home for a distance of at least 50 miles (one way) for business, pleasure, personal affairs, or any other purpose except to commute to work, whether he/she stops overnight or returns the same day.

In the United States the U.S. Bureau of the Census conducts a National Travel Survey every five years. Vacation, weekend, and recreation 'trips' are included with other types of travel in this census. Unfortunately, this survey only includes trips of 100 miles or more away from home. These census surveys understate national tourist travel. In Canada, a country that is very dependent upon tourism income, a tourist is anyone who travels 25 miles or more away from home. Unlike other countries the use of the words tourist and tourism are not widely accepted in the United States. The industry that serves the traveler (transportation, lodging, food, and travel agencies) refers to itself as the travel industry. A tourist using these same services is frequently considered to be synonymous with any traveler.

Tourism then is a unique phenomenon. Unlike other products the tourism product has to be consumed on the spot and the industry is designed to move the market to the product; and in this regard is quite unlike any other form of economic activity. However, tourism is not just an economic phenomenon. It can have social, political and environmental consequences. So tourism is not a simple phenomenon and the types of 'tourist' and the reasons for them being tourists are not always readily apparent. Tourism is rather like the elephant. It is easier to recognize than to define.

What then are the characteristics of tourism? It involves travelling to a destination away from home for the purposes of leisure and pleasure. Tourists may stay in their holiday destination for days or weeks or hours — but in general their activities on arrival are similar — for example sight-seeing, relaxing on a beach, sport, shopping, enjoying the local cuisine or similar pursuits. Often it involves buying a 'package' and this may cover everything from the return journey home from the resort as well as accommodation and meals and organized activities during the stay there.

The industry has developed to meet all the needs of the tourist, and in sequence these are:

(i) Developing tourist destinations/attractions;
(ii) Promoting and selling these?
(iii) Transporting tourists from their home area/country to the tourist resort;
(iv) Providing them with accommodation during their stay;
(v) Developing additional leisure activities and tours during their stay;
(vi) Making goods and selling souvenirs of their visits, local crafts, and produce;
(vii) Transporting them home again.

The Tourist Industry

The tourist industry then can be divided into four main sectors each of which has some responsibility for part or all of these activities. These sectors are:

(i) **Travel:** including travel agents, tour operators, airlines, cruise companies, coach companies, railways, taxis, tourist guides, reservations and sales staff.
(ii) **Accommodation, food and related services:** Hotels with all their staff from receptionist to chambermaids, chefs and cooks, waiters/waitresses, bar staff, porters, caravan site/camping site staff, self-catering enterprises, restaurants, cafes, bars.
(iii) **Leisure facilities and entertainment:** These will include theatres, museums, art galleries, theme parks, zoos, wildlife parks, sports centers, gardens, historic houses, country parks, cinemas.
(iv) **Tourism organizations:** whose aim is to market and monitor the quality and development of the tourist region. These will range from national and regional tourist organizations to staff at local tourist information centers.

It is already clear that the industry is a complex one and includes many different kinds of occupation — all designed to meet the particular needs of the tourist. As well as being complex, tourism is a major industry. For example, in 1987 it was estimated that in Britain some 1.4 million people worked in jobs directly or indirectly connected with tourism. There are also many temporary and seasonal jobs connected with the industry. The following facts give some guide to the scale of the industry:

* The American Automobile Association has a membership over 29 million. No other association in the world services such a large travel population.

* There are 30,000 travel agencies in the United States.
* An airline buying a new wide-body plane will probably spend about $40 million.
* Travel and tourism in America generated 5.2 million jobs in 1986. Industry employment has increased 56% since 1976 (**Figure 1**).
* 10 million Britons took package holiday trips outside of the United Kingdom in 1986.
* 11 million Americans purchased week-long tours in 1986 from the 500 companies belonging to the National Tour Association.
* U.S. citizens spent $28.1 billion and Canadians spent $4.1 billion for foreign travel in 1985.
* The 1800 passengers on the Cunard liner QE2 are looked after by a crew of more than 1200.

Although the industry employs large numbers of people, in Europe it mainly consists of small firms, for example family-run hotels, guest houses or restaurants, small travel agents on the high street, craft shops, taxi services, often supplemented by seasonal staff. At the other end of the scale there are a limited number of very large companies with many thousands on their payrolls. Large travel oriented corporations are the rule in the United States and Canada.

To sum up, the industry is a complex one and contains many small firms; it covers both the public and private sector and is very much the mixed economy in action. It is one of the world's major industries. In 1986 the World Tourism Organization's preliminary figures indicated that 340 million trips were made worldwide and receipts from tourism were $115 billion excluding international fares for transportation. In the United States earnings from tourism through spending by foreign visitors rose from $7 billion in 1978 to $11.7 billion in 1985. During this same period the number of foreign visitors to the United States increased from 5.7 million to 7.5 million, a growth of 32% (*Survey of Current Business*, 1982 & 1986). Foreign visitors to the United Kingdom increased 85% between 1978 and 1985. The size of the two countries and the proximity to a densely populated travel conscious populous in Western Europe partially account for the foreign visitor growth of the United Kingdom compared to the United States. There have been fluctuations in earnings and visitor numbers in both countries during this period, as Figures 2 and 3 on pages 5 and 6 illustrate, but the overall long-term trend has been one of growth. Although on the evidence...tourism has been a success story in both countries, it has never been fully recognized.

Domestic Tourism

In 1986, 1,121 million person trips were taken in the United States, and travel expenditures by U.S. residents amounted to $273 billion. Travel and tourism was the nation's third largest retail industry: sales of conference-appointed travel agencies reached $54 billion, (62% of this total was for airline sales); sales revenue of leading car rental firms was $4 billion and sales in lodging places reached $44 billion. The industry directly employed 5.2 million persons. The U.S. Travel Data Center estimates that travel and tourism generate more than $33.6 billion annually

Figure 1:
EMPLOYMENT RELATED TO TOURISM & LEISURE

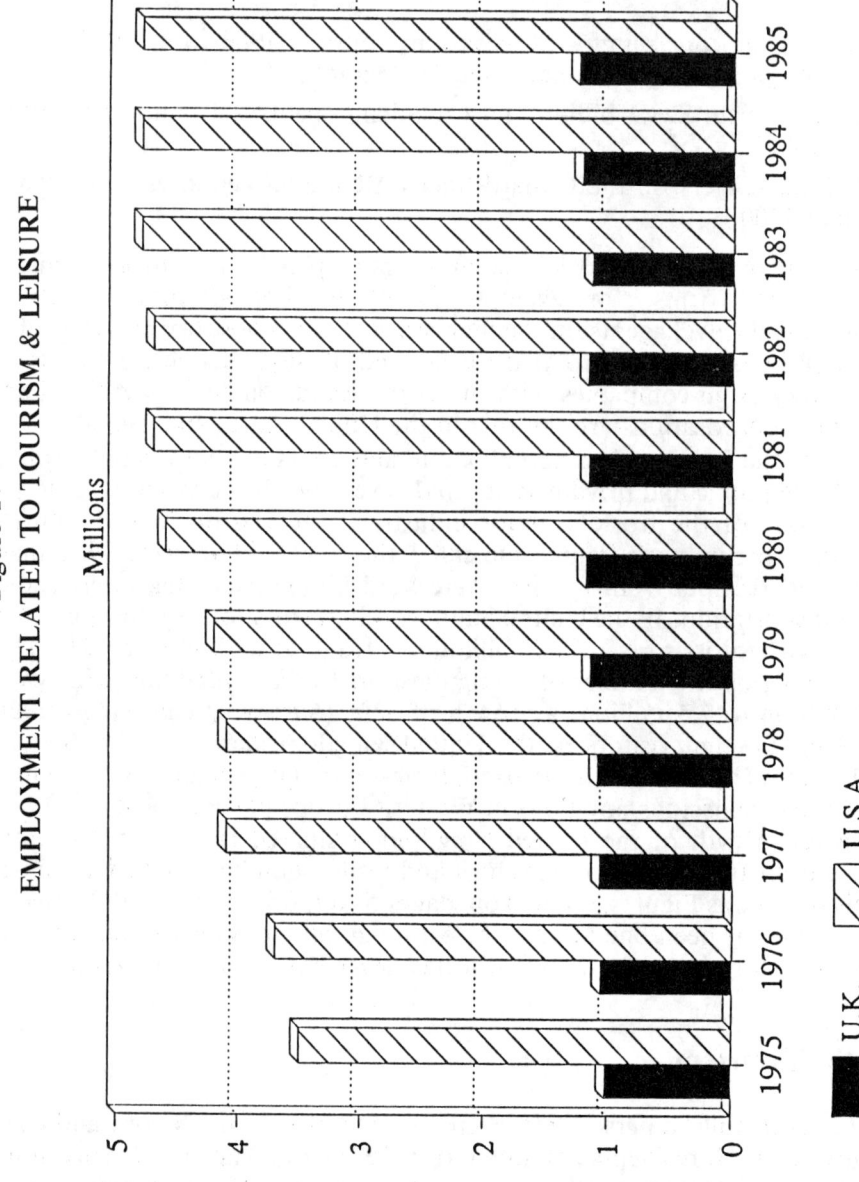

Millions

■ U.K.   ╱╱ U.S.A

SOURCE: British Tourist Authority and
U.S. Travel Data Center

Figure 2:
FOREIGN VISITORS TO THE UNITED STATES

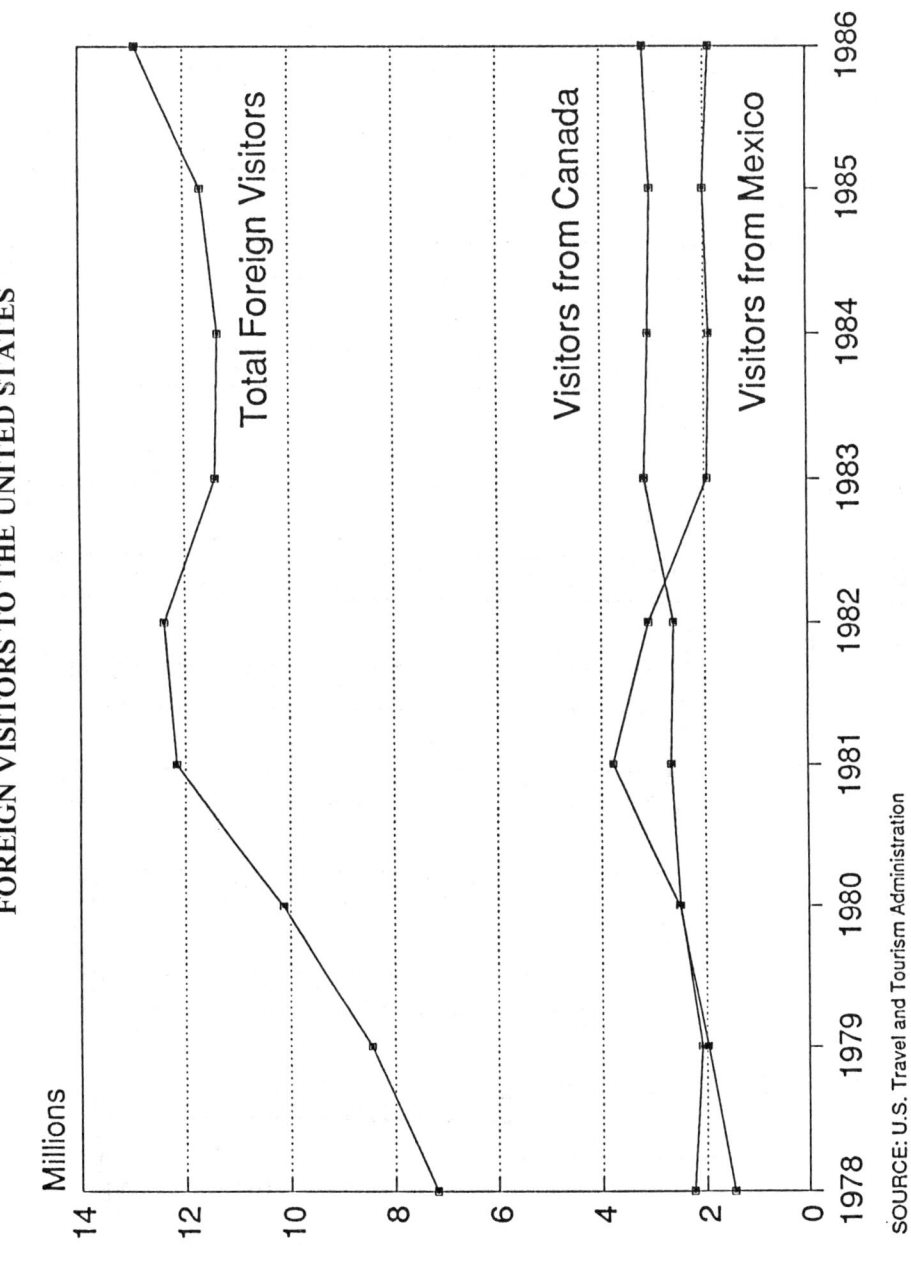

SOURCE: U.S. Travel and Tourism Administration

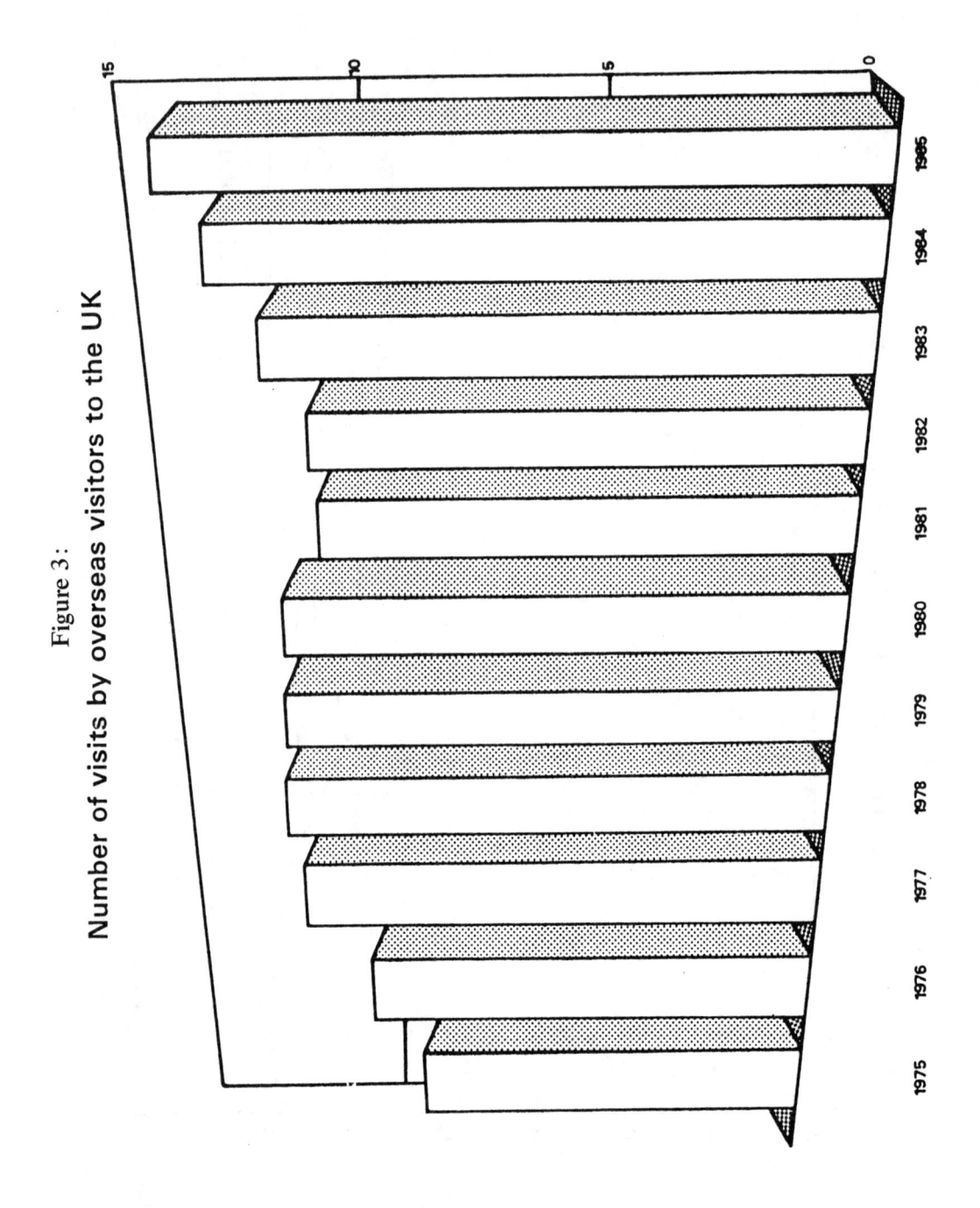

Figure 3:
Number of visits by overseas visitors to the UK

in federal, state and local tax revenues and, partly for this reason, the 1986 average state travel development budget was $4.3 million. Most of the state travel development budgets are aimed at luring domestic vacationers from one state to another.

Governments tend to think only of tourism travel to and from their country with natural concern for balancing trade. Tourism is an export. Instead of a tangible product being transported for sale to another country and the money for that product returning to the country of manufacture, the tourist comes to a nation with money to pay for a travel experience, an intangible product. In most developed nations domestic tourism far exceeds the importance of international tourism in terms of the number of travelers and the amount of money spent. For example in 1986 the U.S. Travel Data Center estimated that only 4.6% of all travel expenditures were made by foreign visitors. In spite of several recessions and fuel crises since the early 1970s travel expenditures in the United States have increased significantly from $50 billion in 1974 to more than $270 billion in 1986. Vacation travel as a percent of total person trips increased from 39% in 1972 to 67% in 1986 (U.S. Travel Data Center) (**Figure 4 on page 8**).

In Britain domestic tourism has also grown significantly over the past 10 years, from 114 million visits in 1974 to 140 million in 1984 (BTA, 1981), though again with some peaks and troughs. Earnings from domestic tourism grew over the same period from $4.2 billion in 1974 to over $8.7 billion in 1984 (BTA, 1981).

For British holidaymakers staying in the UK the seaside has remained the big attraction over the past 30 years and about two-thirds of these holidays are taken at the seaside (BTA). However, the nature, timing and duration of these holidays has changed.

Popular destinations in the United States for vacationers include the ocean but equally important are major cities. Combined these two types of destinations account for 57% of all vacations. Small towns and rural areas are third in importance (22%) while mountains (10%), lakes and reservoirs (5%) and state and national parks (6%) are other desired trip destinations (U.S. Travel Data Center, 1986). In the United States the theme amusement parks are also very popular family destinations. Unfortunately, the data above does not include theme parks, but since most theme parks are located in large cities we can surmise that they are a part of a city's attraction. Favorite vacation pursuits or motivations for leisure travel are: sightseeing 41%, rest and relaxation 28%, swimming, water sports and sunning at the beach 19%, visiting friends and relatives 14%, tennis, golf and other sports 10%, fishing and hunting 10% and camping and hiking 9% (*U.S.A. Today* Poll, May 5, 1986).

Unlike their holidaymaker counterparts in the United Kingdom, North Americans can vacation on a large continent in the family automobile or recreation vehicle without the need to ferry across the English Channel. Nor do North Americans have to be concerned with language communication or money exchange unless they visit Canada or Mexico. Europeans on the other hand can quickly be stimulated by changing cultures in a short travel time. Domestic vacation travel in the United States, due to the great distances between popular destinations, can be a long and tedious family experience for the ritual middle class cross country automobile trip. In the United States vacation travelers have become accustomed to inexpensive gasoline for the family automobile, and when visiting a European country, are surprised at the cost of gasoline. Americans can

Figure 4:
TOTAL TRIPS AND VACATION TRIPS 1972-1986

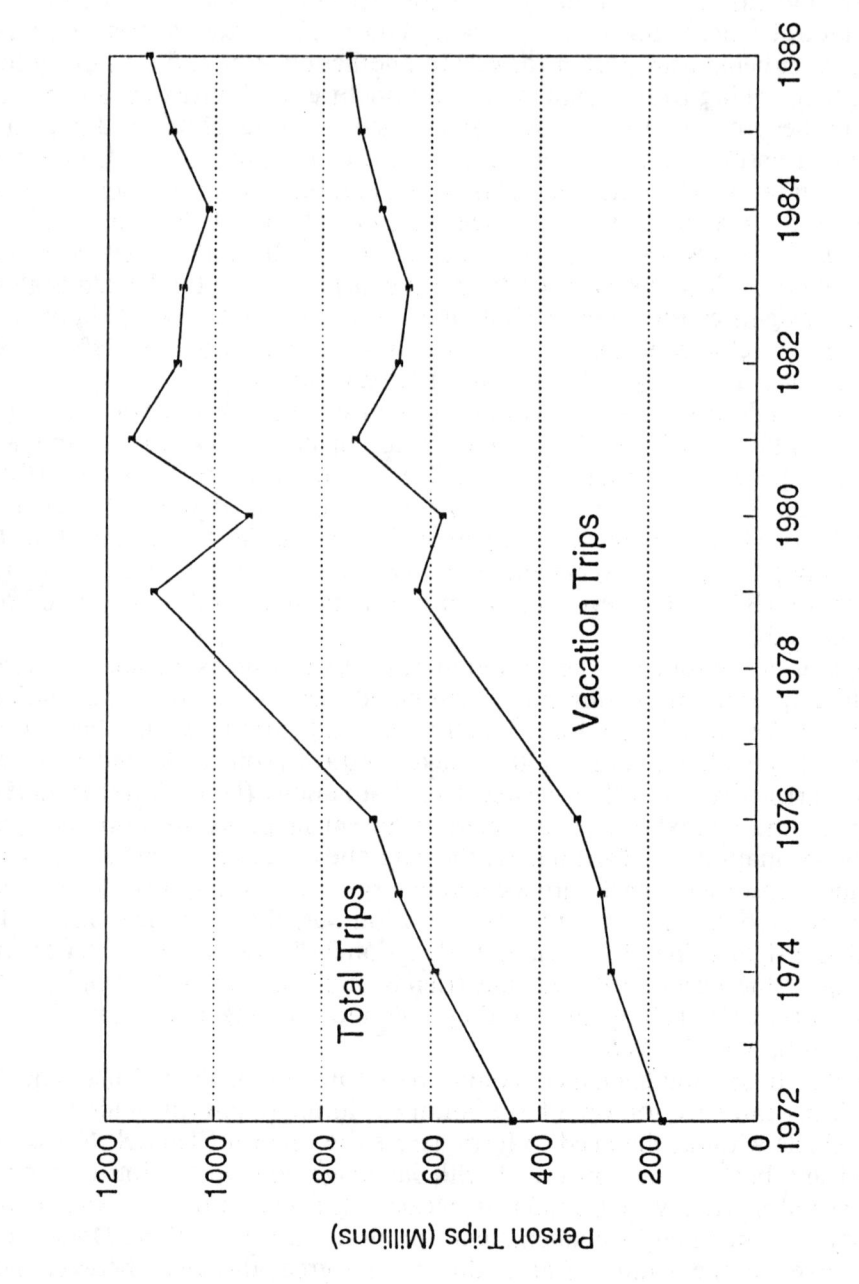

SOURCE: U.S. Travel Data Center

appreciate Western Europe's mass transport systems by rail and motorcoach. In 1987 a gallon of gasoline in the United States cost 94 cents while in the United Kingdom a gallon of gasoline cost $2.39 (*Chicago Tribune* Graphic, April 18, 1988). Inexpensive private transportation even over long distances is a luxury few other countries experience. It has encouraged a growing domestic vacation market in the U.S.A. and the growth of large travel-serving corporations.

Although the citizens of the United States do not have as many vacation days as people in Western Europe (U.S. average 16 days per year versus 26 days in the United Kingdom, *Travel Industry World Yearbook,* 1987), the U.S. work week is on average shorter (35.6 hours compared to 42 hours in Germany and 44 hours in the United Kingdom *U.S.A. Today,* Dec. 5, 1984). A shorter work week encourages weekend trips. In 1986 51% of all vacation trips were day trips of up to three nights duration. A majority of these trips were within 300 miles of home (Frechtling, 1986). Week long trips were one-third of all vacations and averaged 550 miles from home. Long vacation trips were of ten nights or more and varied by year from 14% to 17% of all domestic vacation trips of U.S. travelers. Long trips have averaged between 950 and 1000 miles in recent years and account for 40% of all vacation nights (U.S. Travel Data Center, 1986) (Table 1). About

Table 1: CHARACTERISTICS OF TOTAL TRIPS AND VACATION TRIPS
1972 – 1986

	1972	1976	1979	1980	1981	1982	1983	1984	1985	1986
Total Person Trips (millions)	450	706	1110	935	1152	1069	1058	1012	1078	1122
Vacation Person Trips (millions)	174	329	624	578	737	660	642	690	729	752
% Trips Vacation	39	47	56	62	63	61	60	68	68	67
Total Persons per trip	1.94	2.00	NA	2.09	1.96	1.99	1.96	1.92	1.93	1.89
Vacation Persons per trip	2.29	2.24	NA	2.23	2.14	2.10	2.09	2.07	2.14	2.12
Total Nights per trip	3.88	4.06	NA	4.8	4.6	4.5	5.2	5.2	5.4	5.2
Vacation Nights per trip	6.2	5.9	NA	5.8	5.6	5.3	6.2	5.9	6.0	5.7
Total Miles per[a] trip	806	862	NA	790	740	790	800	830	960	970
Vacation Miles per[a] trip	1056	1096	NA	880	800	860	900	850	980	1010

Source: U.S. Travel Data Center, *National Travel Survey,* Full Year Report, Various Years.

[a]Round-trip Mileage for Domestic Travel Only.   NA = Not available.

Table 2: PERSON TRIPS BY PRIMARY MODE OF TRANSPORTATION
1972 – 1986

	1972	1976	1979	1980	1981	1982	1983	1984	1985	1986
Total Trips										
Auto/Truck/R.V.	85%	84%	83%	81%	83%	82%	79%	78%	75%	75%
Air	12	11	14	15	13	14	18	17	20	21
Bus			2	2	2	2	3	2	2	2
Train	3	4	1	1	1	a	1	1	1	a
Other			1	1	1	2	1	1	1	2
Vacation Trips										
Auto/Truck/R.V.	84%	82%	82%	81%	84%	83%	79%	81%	76%	77%
Air	12	11	14	15	11	14	17	15	18	19
Bus			3	2	2	2	3	2	2	3
Train	4	6	1	a	1	1	1	1	1	1
Other			1	a	1	1	a	1	3	1

Source: U.S. Travel Data Center, *National Travel Survey,* Full Year Report, Various Years.

a = Less than 1 percent.

40% of all vacationers stayed in hotels or motels, 47% with friends and relatives, 5% in rented cabin or condominium, and 6% camped out.

Seventy-five percent of vacation trips were taken in the family automobile or recreation vehicle in 1985 (Table 2). The advent of airfare discount wars for domestic U.S. airlines has made strong enroads into the vacation trip scene. Before deregulation of airlines in 1978, 11% of the person trips for vacation were made by air. In 1986, 19% of vacation person trips were made by airplane travel.

The most popular destination regions for vacation trips are the South Atlantic states, particularly Florida; the Pacific states including California, Hawaii and Alaska and the East North Central states particularly Michigan, Wisconsin, Illinois and Minnesota, all adjacent to the Great Lakes. Florida has become premier vacation state in recent years. It is larger than England and Wales and only Alaska has more coastline. According to *The Big Picture, 1987,* Florida received 30 million visitors from other states and 4 million from foreign nations in 1985. A warm winter climate, air conditioning in the summer and a complex of attractions such as DisneyWorld have combined to create one of the world's popular destinations.

International Tourism

This refers to travel across National boundaries and may involve visits to one or several other countries. If we analyze the pattern of tourist flows on a world scale it is clear that the industry is a major economic activity. International traveler arrivals amount to 336 million and world spending for international travel amounted to over $115 billion in 1986 (Waters, 1986). In the developing countries international tourism accounts for about one-third of their service trade. It is one of the fastest-growing industries in the world, and between 1974 and 1980 international tourism trade grew faster than world trade generally. Between 1961 and 1981 the world total of international tourist arrivals quadrupled. However, although the rate of growth of the international tourist has been dramatic, the potential for growth is still substantial. The reason for this is that most of this activity is confined to Europe which accounts for 70 percent of international tourist arrivals and North America which attracts 20 percent (WTO, 1986). The rest of the world accounts for only 10 percent of international tourist arrivals. Tables 8 and 9 on page 59 and Figure 19 on page 60 show the recent trends in international tourism.

The development of international tourism has produced two types of country — the generating country who provide the tourist and the receiving country who attract and play host to the tourist. A few countries, like Britain and the United States, fall into both categories, but most are clearly one type or the other. Generally, the tourist generating countries are those with advanced economies, high standards of living, available disposable income, greater spending power and a general system of paid annual holidays. The most important tourist generating countries are the United States, West Germany, Japan and the United Kingdom.

The host countries have a low cost of living, attractive scenery and climates, are readily accessible and have a good public image. As the host countries, such as Spain, Italy and Greece have developed their tourist industries over the past 20 years, so the beaches and main resort areas are reaching saturation point and more developing countries are turning to tourism as a major source of income. Recent years have seen the development of new tourist areas outside of Europe with lower price levels and less tourist saturation.

Given that international tourism is the largest single item in foreign trade, the balance of trade between tourism generating and receiving countries can be a significant element in encouraging economic development. Table 11 on page 63 shows international tourist receipts and expenditures based on figures supplied by the Organisation for Economic Cooperation and Development (OECD). In Europe, Austria, France, Greece, Italy and Spain, all have net surpluses in their balance of payments, while West Germany, the Netherlands, Belgium and the Scandinavian countries have the most marked deficits. Outside of Europe, Japan has the most substantial net deficit and North America has a marked imbalance in its tourist trade.

Trade is a key word in that all countries can use the income from international tourism to create jobs and to buy additional goods and services. In the United States more than 510,000 firms of all sizes provide goods and services for the vacationer whether domestic or a foreign visitor. In 1986 foreign visitors spent $16 billion in the United States. As Figure 5 shows, Canada and Mexico provide the largest number of foreign visitors while the largest number of overseas visitors came from Japan, Germany, United Kingdom and France (U.S. Travel and Tourism Administration, 1986). Visitors from overseas countries contribute 49% of total receipts including amounts paid for transportation on U.S. airlines to reach the United States.

The pattern of visits was much the same as in recent years with vacation holidays accounting for 49 percent of all visits, business 35 percent and visiting friends and relatives 19 percent (Table 3). Like visitors to the United Kingdom 29 percent of visitors to the United States came on an inclusive tour (Table 3). Visitors to the United States stay longer on the average than visitors to the United Kingdom where the lure to visit other European countries is large. Expenditures in the United States by foreign visitors include lodging 26 percent, gifts and souvenirs 22 percent, food and beverages 21 percent, and domestic transport 16 percent. The average expenditure per visitor in 1984 was $1,155 (U.S. Travel and Tourism Administration, 1986).

Table 3: PROFILES OF OVERSEAS VISITORS TO THE U.S. AND U.K.
1984

	United States	United Kingdom
Business	35%	21%
Vacation, Holiday	46%	21%
Visits to Friends and Relatives	31%	20%
Pre-Paid Package Tours	29%	29%
Type of Accommodations		
Hotel, Motel	80%	32%
Private Home	39%	50%
Camping	27%	5%
Nights Spent (Average)	22	12

Sources: U.S. Travel and Tourism Administration and British Tourist Authority, 1984.

The most popular destinations for foreign visitors to the United States are New York City, California, Florida, Washington, D.C., and Hawaii. The most popular natural attraction is the Grand Canyon in Arizona while the Disney theme parks in Florida and Southern California are the most popular man-made attractions. Unlike many European countries the size of the United States limits use of a visitors package tour to one and at the most two regions. In Britain the typical package tour itinerary might include London-Oxford-Stratford-Chester-the Lake District and/or Scotland with perhaps York and Cambridge on the return leg to

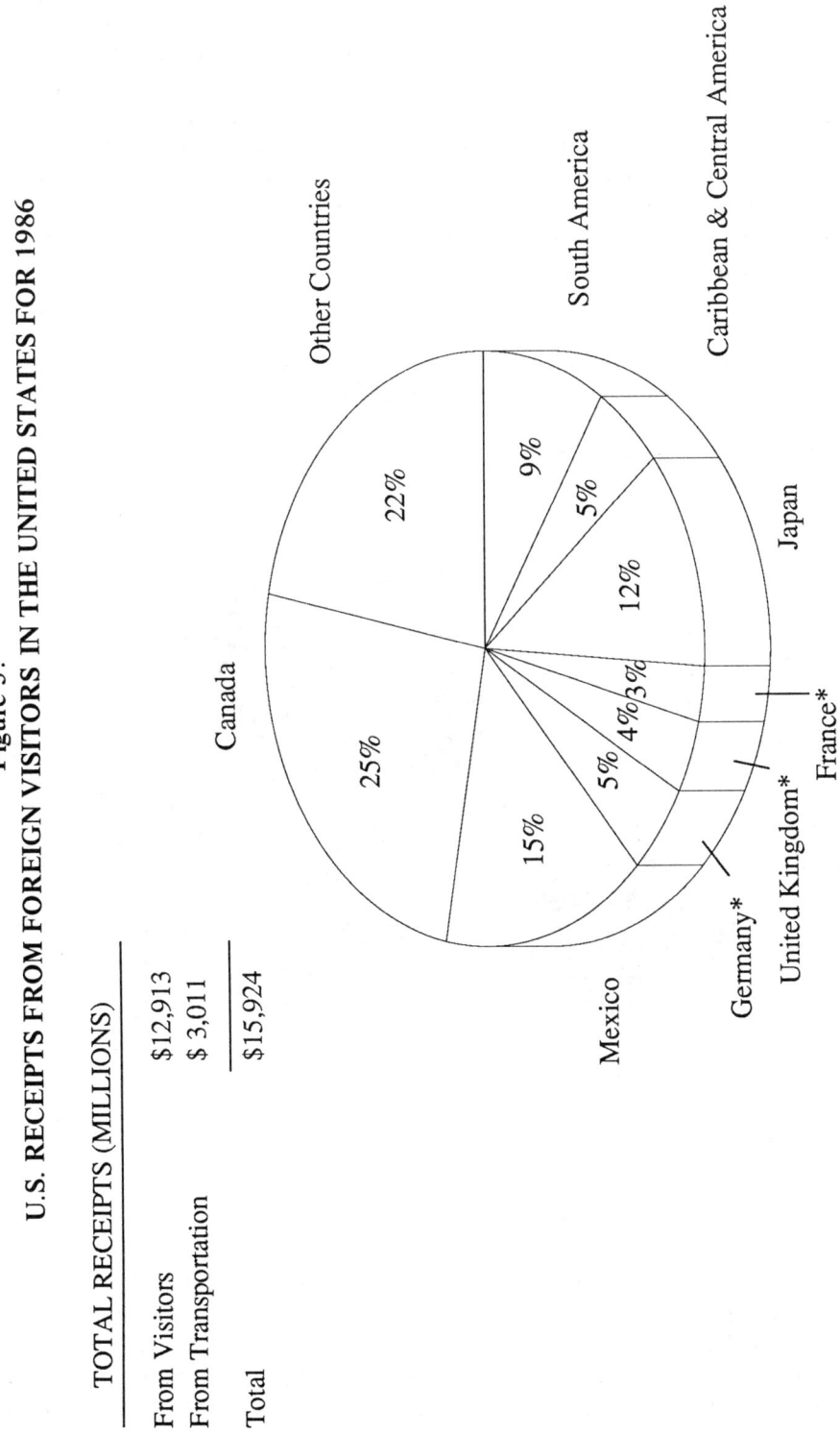

Figure 5:
U.S. RECEIPTS FROM FOREIGN VISITORS IN THE UNITED STATES FOR 1986

TOTAL RECEIPTS (MILLIONS)

From Visitors	$12,913
From Transportation	$ 3,011
Total	$15,924

Pie chart segments:
- Canada: 25%
- Other Countries: 22%
- Mexico: 15%
- Japan: 12%
- South America: 9%
- Germany*: 5%
- Caribbean & Central America: 5%
- United Kingdom*: 4%
- France*: 3%

*Estimated

Source: U.S. Travel & Tourism Administration

London. A similar tour of this type in the United States might be limited to a circular route from New York-Boston-Montreal, Canada-Philadelphia-Annapolis and Washington, D.C. On the west coast a tour might include Los Angeles-San Francisco-Yosemite National Park-Las Vegas-Grand Canyon National Park-San Diego and return to Los Angeles. Unless a visitor flies between major cities in the United States it is impossible to see most major points of tourism interest in the country in the same time frame as a visitor to a Western European country.

Relative to other countries the United States government does not spend a great deal of money to promote travel to the U.S. But each state government does invest in the promotion of a travel industry. Promotion expenditures will be discussed in Chapter 8.

Figure 6: **TOP 20 STATES IN TOTAL VISITATION BY TOTAL NUMBER OF OVERSEAS VISITORS 1986**

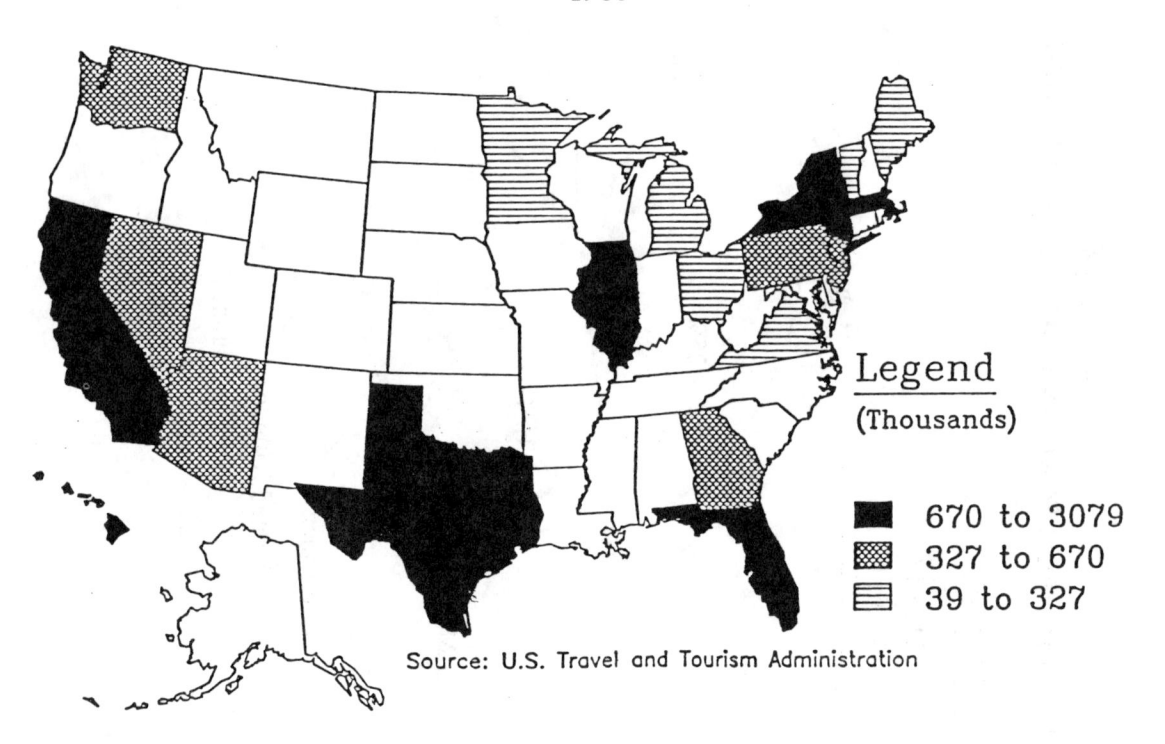

Legend (Thousands)

- ■ 670 to 3079
- ▦ 327 to 670
- ☰ 39 to 327

Source: U.S. Travel and Tourism Administration

Data Sources on Tourism

Clearly, the movement of people between countries and within countries generates a demand for tourism which consists of a range of goods and services provided by both the public and private sectors. The income from the sale or purchase of these goods and services may be a major source of foreign or domestic revenue. When many industries or economic activities are examined, detailed statistical data are available on the production, export and import of hundreds of physical goods, often on a monthly basis, yet data on tourism are scarce, often unreliable and not consistently compiled. Part of the reason for this is the substantial time lag which exists between the initial expansion of a sector and the collection of adequate data for that sector. For example, it was not until well into this century that detailed statistics on manufacturing industries became available in many developed countries, although the industrial revolution had transformed the manufacturing sector during the 19th century.

In 1982 White and Walker highlighted the dearth of reliable statistics on tourism, even on an aggregate basis, in some of the more advanced economies (White, 1982). They claimed that some countries may not even be able to tell whether they have a surplus or deficit on their tourism income. Yet, given the importance of tourism as a source of income and employment, it is clear that both the public and private sector need to have detailed statistics on many aspects of tourism. For example, national governments need data on tourist arrivals, countries of origin, visitor spending, mode of travel, purpose of visit, length of stay and places visited. All of this data, analyzed over time, is used to provide forecasts in the growth, stability or decline of the tourist industry. Similarly, private firms need such data to plan their marketing strategies and to measure the effectiveness of their existing policies. With this knowledge the public sector will improve road/rail links, plan airport and port expansion schemes and the private sector may develop more hotels or new resort complexes.

International Tourism Surveys: The main sources of data on international tourist flows and the characteristics of international tourism are the annual reports of the Organisation for Economic Cooperation and Development (OECD), and the World Tourism Organisation (WTO).

The OECD was set up in 1960 and its members consist of the countries of Western Europe, Scandinavia, North America, Australia and Japan. The importance of OECD data is that it provides a reliable, standardised and comparable set of statistics for a range of countries who between them account for over 90 percent of all international tourism. Each year the OECD publishes an annual report containing five main sections:

— recent trends in government policy towards tourism;
— international tourist flows by member country including length of stay, accommodation used and main tourism generating countries;
— the economic importance of international tourism in member countries;
— main types of transport used;
— changes in the accommodation sector.

The WTO publish annually the *World Tourism Statistics Annual Yearbook* (WTO Yearbook), which has a wide range of data on trends in international tourism. It includes data on country of origin, arrivals by month, accommodation, transport, purpose of visit, tourism receipts and hotel accommodation capacity.

In addition to these reports, the *Travel Industry World Yearbook* (Waters, 1988) attempts to provide an overview of trends in world tourism, albeit with a marked North American perspective. It provides a commentary on a very disparate range of tourism data covering all the main centers of tourism activity. Although many of the data sources cited in this yearbook are not directly comparable, it does provide a useful and wide-ranging commentary on trends in international tourism.

The Economist Intelligence Unit publishes four invaluable sources of tourism data. Each quarter the EIU publishes *Country Reports* which provide a business-oriented analysis of the latest political and economic developments in 165 countries worldwide, together with a review of their short term prospects. This data is collated in an annual report which provides a *Country Profile*. On a monthly basis the EIU also publishes a *Business Update* for the ten largest OECD countries. A separate page is devoted to each country and data is provided as industrial trends, financial indicators, consumer demand and related economic indicators. Every three months the EIU publishes the *World Trade Forecast* which provides an integrated view of the world's economic prospects. Finally, the Economist Intelligence Unit publishes the *Travel and Tourism Analyst* on a monthly basis. This contains several in-depth analyses of the main sectors of the travel and tourism industry and topics can range from timeshare to forecasts for long haul travel from Europe to the Caribbean.

National Tourism Surveys: In the United States in recent years the main source of international travel data have been surveys by the U.S. Travel and Tourism Administration. Arrivals and Departures and estimates of expenditures are garnered by a variety of methods with the assistance of the U.S. Immigration and Naturalization Service, Statistics Canada, and the Secretaria de Turismo of the Direccion General Politica Turistica and Banco de Mexico. To obtain better information the U.S. Travel and Tourism Administration instituted an In-Flight Survey of International Air Travelers in the early 1980s. This survey provides data on visits and spending by country, purpose of visit, mode of travel, length of stay and places visited in the United States.

The U.S. Travel Data Center conducts quarterly telephone surveys of U.S. residents to determine travel characteristics. This information is published quarterly with the annual summary, the National Travel Survey (Table 2 page 10). In 1986 the survey included 18,240 telephone interviews. The survey questionnaire includes questions on household size, nights spent away from home, purpose of trips, type of transportation used, lodging and household income. The Data Center's surveys are privately supported and are not a part of public documents but nevertheless provide the single best source of domestic travel information. Many of the state tourism offices purchase the Data Center information and contract with the Center to conduct general surveys as a part of the Center's ongoing surveys. Some states do from time to time conduct their own surveys, some with a high degree of sophistication and cost.

Using and measuring tourism data: Although a wide range of both aggregated and disaggregated data exists on international tourism in the developed countries, this information must be used with care, especially when making comparisons between countries. For example, the OECD data which is collected for 19 countries has almost as many different methods of measuring tourist flows. Thus Austria and Belgium have records from all registered tourist accommodation; Finland records hotel registrations only; while the Netherlands have records for hotels, motels and inns, but not self-catering or other forms of accommodation. Some countries such as the UK and France, base their estimates on frontier checks, supplemented by other surveys such as IPS in the UK. However, it is possible to provide a picture of overall trends in tourism and to determine the order of magnitude

Figure 7: BUREAU OF CENSUS REGIONS USED BY THE NATIONAL TRAVEL SURVEY

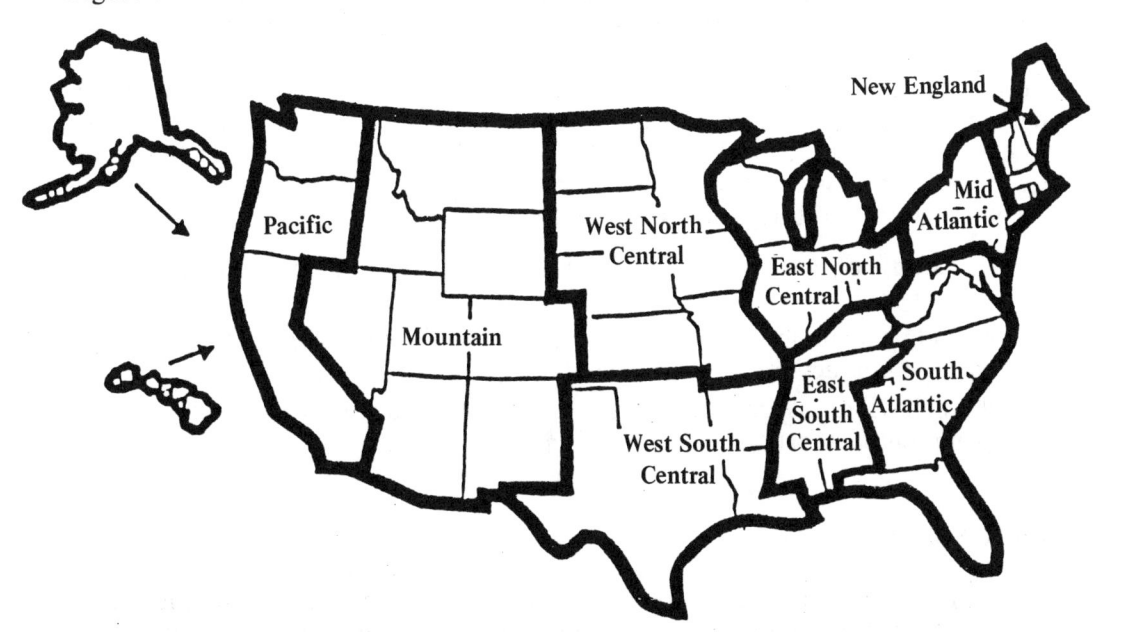

Regional definitions: **New England**: Connecticut, Maine, Massachusetts, New Hampshire, Rhode Island, Vermont; **Mid Atlantic**: New Jersey, New York, Pennsylvania; **East North Central**: Indiana, Illinois, Michigan, Ohio, Wisconsin; **West North Central**: Iowa, Kansas, Minnesota, Missouri, Nebraska, North Dakota, South Dakota; **Mountain**: Arizona, Colorado, Idaho, Montana, Nevada, New Mexico, Utah, Wyoming; **South Atlantic**: Delaware, District of Columbia, Florida, Georgia, Maryland, North Carolina, South Carolina, Virginia, West Virginia; **East South Central**: Alabama, Kentucky, Mississippi, Tennessee; **West South Central**: Arkansas, Louisiana, Oklahoma, Texas; **Pacific**: California, Oregon, Washington; Alaska and Hawaii as destinations (not origins)

of tourist activity. Thus, even for Europe which has been collecting statistics on tourism for over 30 years, there is no common standard or agreed source for tourism data.

There is a great shortage of data on domestic tourism, and the annual reports of the OECD on *Tourism Policy and International Tourism* (OECD) indicate that among the member countries only the United States, Canada and the UK carry out annual surveys of their domestic tourist market. Most of the remaining countries either carry out periodic market research, directed at either the domestic industry or their major foreign markets, or sectoral studies of the tourist industry, usually on a one-off basis. The limitations of data on domestic tourism are particularly significant when we consider that about 90 percent of world tourism is domestic tourism.

The purpose, scope and function of this book

The overall aim of this book is to provide a broad foundation course in tourism studies. It is intended to provide an overview of the operations and characteristics of the tourist industry and the role of the private and public sectors in developing tourism. It is largely based on examples drawn from United States and British experience, although where possible, material from a range of international sources is used, because tourism is essentially a world-wide phenomenon.

In order to provide a sound base of understanding tourism it is not sufficient to concentrate solely on business skills in the private sector or on planning and administration in the public sector. For this reason this book does not focus on such specific disciplines as business studies, law, geography, economics or management: such subject areas play a supporting role. The focus is on tourism. Its purpose is to highlight the interactions between the different sectors of the tourist industry and between components of the product consumed by tourists.

The remainder of this book focuses, therefore, on:

a) the study of tourism and its social, economic and environmental components;

b) providing an understanding of the operation of the private and public sectors and the interactions between them;

c) the behavioral aspects of tourism — tourists' motivations, perceptions and group characteristics.

ASSIGNMENTS

(i) Using visitor surveys, reports and annual statistics investigate the changes in the patterns of international and domestic tourism between 1974 and 1986 as they affect the United States.

(ii) You are employed by a national tourism office to produce a 750 word entry in a national tourism periodical. The task will, therefore, require you to consider the following:
(a) main resorts/visitor attractions?
(b) transport provision;
(c) amenity/entertainment;
(d) assessment of market;
(e) other factors, including climate.

You will be assessed according to the effectiveness of the 'copy' that you produce.

Chapter 2

The Development of the Tourist Industry

Learning Objectives: After reading this chapter and some of the references contained within it, you should understand how the industry has grown and developed; the form that the early tourist industry took; and the trends in travel and tourism in Britain and North America since 1945.

Introduction

Throughout the ages man has travelled in search of new places, new lands, new cultures and experiences. History offers many examples from Greek and Roman literature to Marco Polo, or Chaucer's pilgrims who were familiar with the famous shrines of Europe. For hundreds of years travel for the sake of pleasure was the prerogative of the rich because those who travelled needed an income to free their time for such purposes. For the majority of the population of Britain and Europe the feast days of the Church, i.e. holy-days, were their only break from work. Only those who were educated and prosperous and aware of foreign places engaged in such travel. It was only through trade or wars that most people visited distant places. Maps were crude or non-existent. Roads were bad, and risks abounded. Even in the late nineteenth century Robert Louis Stephenson commented on travelling in central France:

> 'A traveller of my sort was a thing hitherto unheard of in the district. I was looked on with contempt, like a man who should project a journey to the moon, yet with a respectful interest, like one setting forth for the inclement Pole.'

The Development of Mass Tourism

What changed this pattern? How did tourism, once the exclusive activity of the rich and well to-do, become an accepted part of life for the ordinary man and woman? To find the answer to these questions we must consider the requirements for travel and tourism. First, people must have the free time available and second, they must have the disposable income to spend. Thirdly, travel must be safe, reliable and relatively cheap. There must be attractions which travellers know of and which they wish to visit, and a range of amenities, especially accommodation, must be available. All of these conditions need to exist if mass tourism is to develop.

The Industrial Revolution from the mid-eighteenth century was the catalyst which brought all these conditions into being. Scientific inventions, new industrial processes, and new methods of production of manufactured goods changed society, first in Britain and then in America and Europe. An agricultural revolution formed part of this dynamic change improving the productivity of crops and animal husbandry and providing new wealth for industrial development. With the development of the steam engine and coal as a source of power, new manufacturing districts grew. The application of coal and coke to smelting iron, and later steel, accelerated this process. The reduction in the death rate through medical and public health improvements led to a steady growth in the population of Western Europe and North America.

The growth of Spas as Resort Towns

During the eighteenth century spa towns in England developed as places of resort for the rich and well to do, their seal of approval usually being a Royal visit. Conventional medicine vouched for the curative properties of their mineral waters which, though brackish and often foul-smelling, were drunk as well as bathed in. Bath is the best known of these with a reputation dating from Roman times.

The visits to Bath by King William in 1695 and Queen Anne in 1702 and 1703 set the seal on this as a fashionable place of resort. The town hired Beau Nash in 1705 to provide a range of entertainments during the 'season', although he also ensured that the city developed good roads, good accommodation for the visitor and set an example that many other towns were to copy. The medicinal reputation of the mineral waters was of prime importance for would-be spas and the distribution of mineral springs was therefore the earliest locational influence on these centres. Thus Scarborough developed as a spa town from 1627 (Lennard, 1931), and it was not until much later that its seaside location was to influence its long-term development as a resort.

The growth and spread of wealth among society encouraged more people to follow the fashion for taking mineral waters. By the mid-eighteenth century there were many spas, often of a purely local reputation, ranging from Bath at the height of fashion and the social scene, to Buxton, Leamington, Tunbridge Wells, Malvern and Gilsland. Epsom in fact came into being as a spa, and thereafter developed as a venue for horse racing with the Derby and the Oaks. By 1733 it was reported that the season at Scarborough had attracted almost one thousand of the nobility and the gentry, (Smollott, *Humphrey Clinker*). It was clear that by the mid-eighteenth century the now fashionable nature of this 'season' was an indication that the function of the larger spa towns was changing from that of a purely health resort to an important social centre where the leisured classes could spend their time.

During the second part of the eighteenth century there was a growth in small seaside 'watering places'. Sea bathing is depicted in an engraving of the South Bay, Scarborough (1735) and this print is the earliest record of bathing machines being used. In the seventeenth century sea bathing was recommended for gout and the medicinal value of sea water was given an added impetus by the publication of a *Dissertation concerning the Uses of Sea Water in Diseases of the Glands* by Dr Russel in 1753. The learned doctor also lived in Brighton and his advocacy of the virtues of sea water no doubt encouraged the growth of that resort. The arrival of the Prince of Wales in 1784 accelerated the growth of the town as a fashionable resort, just as royal visits to Bath had some eighty years earlier. In 1760 Brighton consisted of a large village with a population of 2,000. By 1820 it had over three thousand houses, a population of over 24,000 and more than 10,000 visitors a year. During the late-eighteenth century many other coastal towns realised the potential of their seaside location and Lewis' *Topographical Dictionary* of 1835 lists dozens of former hamlets and small fishing villages, from Bognor Regis to Rhyl, that were transformed as seaside watering places.

Travel was still restricted to coach or horseback and most of these resorts were one or two days' journey from the major towns and cities. They were still resorts for a very limited section of society. To most of the working population they were remote and unknown places.

The New World

In the New Colonial World travel was just as hazardous and difficult. Roads were nothing more than rutted tracks and long distance travel was by sea between coastal ports such as Boston, New York, Philadelphia, Baltimore, Williamsburg, Norfolk and Charleston. The aristocracy were centered in these seaport cities and most with roots to Western Europe were drawn to spas and coast locations to 'partake of the waters' just as their ancestors, relatives and friends in the Old World.

In the middle 1700s, only the aristocracy could afford expensive travel by sea for summer visits to Newport, Rhode Island. Newport provided the southern plantation owner the perfect cool seaside setting and rapidly became the social gathering place for visitors from the north as well as the south. Between 1767 and 1775 the Newport Mercury newspaper listed 700 summer visitors from southern colonies and even the West Indies (Dulles 1965). Newport was the 'in place', where new visitors, with the right letters of introduction, could establish a pattern in the social world. Newport was not visited for reasons of improving health, but rather as a place to see and be seen at card parties, dances, concerts and the theatre.

The Eastern mountains were also havens from the summer heat and humidity of the coastal plains. An early spa was located in the Blue Ridge Mountains of Virginia at Berkeley Springs with accommodation at a small tavern. Travel to Berkeley Springs was arduous, and once there summer temperatures were probably not much lower than those one would experience at a coastal location. Like their European ancestors, the colonialists sought out mineral springs for healing purposes. Bostonians travelled to nearby Lynn Springs. Saratoga Springs, in upstate New York, was yet to be developed as a full-fledged spa. New seaside resorts were continuing to attract visitors. Bathing machines are said to have appeared on Long Island in 1794.

The Age of Puritanism

After the Revolution, the social and economic structure of the new country began a gradual change. The urban population increased three fold between 1800 and 1850. Customs changed as society struggled to utilize seemingly endless resources in pursuit of new trade and growing industry. There was a renewed emphasis on work along with an almost prudish return to basic religious beliefs. During the first half of the 19th Century the Erie Canal was opened (1825) and the steam engine was refined for trains (1831) and ships. English travelers such as Trollope, Hall and Charles Dickens all observed that the dollar seemed to be the only pursuit of people in the United States. Americans were 'too absorbed in work's daily routine to recognize any other phase of life' (Dulles 1965). The wealthier classes as well as the urban laborers sought the traditional activities during periods of non-work. Principal amusements were centered around music, walking, conversation, riding, sailing, cards and shooting contests. Travel other than that necessary for commerce and industry was still the province of the new wealthy.

Pleasure travel increased in vogue between 1825 and 1850. Desire may have exceeded supply. As turnpikes, canals, and the steamboat and railroads improved access, new pleasuring sites quickly began to develop. Long Branch and Cape May, New Jersey, started growth as seaside resorts in the 1820s and the Mountain House in the Catskill Mountains offered primitive accommodation in 1824. Bar Harbor, Maine, started development in the 1840s. Saratoga Springs in New York gradually rivalled Newport as the most fashionable resort. Visitors did not come for health, rest or sport, but to solidify their position in the social world. One observer in 1838 stated that a visit to Saratoga provided the opportunity to sit at the same table with the first families of the country (Dulles 1965). New hotels at the spa such as the Congress House or United States Hotel (with beds for 2000), had wide verandahs, manicured gardens and lawns, in order for guests to sit or promenade and 'be seen'. The first half of the century was a time of probing for a self identity in work and leisure as the society of this new world evolved.

The growth of seaside resorts in Victorian England

The transport system was transformed by the invention of the railway and its spread throughout Britain between 1832 and 1870. For the first time, fast, cheap and readily accessible passenger transport was available to most of the country's population. Enterprising developers and railway companies promoted links between the growing industrial cities and the coastal resorts and, with improved accessibility, these prospered and rapidly grew in size.

On the 5th July 1841, Thomas Cook organized his first rail excursion for one shilling return and by the 1870s, all the railway companies ran regular cheap day excursions to the seaside. In 1871 the Bank Holiday Act provided four public holidays a year and after this date the extended family holiday at the seaside became more common.

For example, the London, Tilbury and Southend Railway was opened and the population of the resort grew from 4,000 to 20,000 in 1901. Its present day population is over 150,000 and it receives over 6 million visitors a year, many of them still day trippers from London. The same pattern occurred at Brighton, Southport, Blackpool and many other, now familiar, coastal resorts. For example, Brighton's population grew from 24,000 in 1820 to 99,000 in 1981 with the most rapid growth following the opening of the main London to Brighton line in 1841.

For the Victorian masses day excursions were the norm, rather than long holidays, although the diffusion of wealth and the growth of a middle class, anxious to escape for a time from the industrial towns and cities, introduced a wider spectrum of people to these resorts. This in turn led to a wider range of accommodation and amenities being offered.

Some resorts had originally developed piers to accommodate visitors arriving by paddle steamer, but the practice of taking the sea air for health and relaxation encouraged many resorts to build one if not more piers. The form and layout of most seaside resorts reflects both their development during the railway age and the strong attraction of the sea front (Figure 8). Most expanded parallel to

Figure 8: **Schematic Diagram of a 'Typical' Seaside Resort**

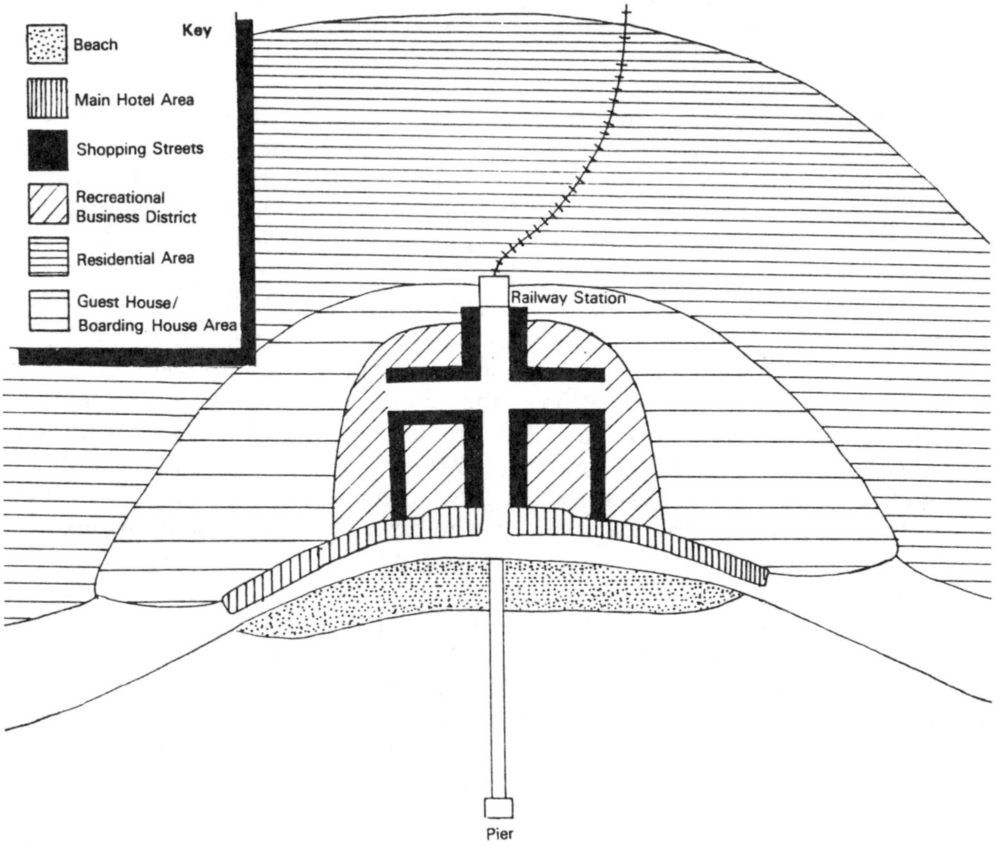

the sea front with relatively little development inland. The main beach or promenade took over and copied the earlier spa promenade, replacing the pump room as a focus of social life. Having arrived by train for a day visit or longer stay, the visitor found the resort was the self-contained provider of all his needs, from accommodation to entertainment. Most of the land and buildings associated with the tourism industry are located in a zone between the railway station and the sea front with the prime frontal locations usually occupied in almost unbroken succession by the larger hotels. This pattern still persists today.

Victorian Resorts in North America

Thirteen years after the Victorian Era began, the railroad mileage in the United States was approaching 5000, and steamboat excursions on the Hudson River were common, while on the Ohio and Mississippi the steamboat was providing ready access for western expansion. Looking to the East, the 'Great Western' made its first journey eastbound across the North Atlantic in January 1838, with 38 passengers (Lickorish and Kershaw 1958). By the end of the year, the number of Americans making the trip across the 'Herring Pond' was 6,245 and by 1860 the numbers travelling abroad to Europe had reached 26,400 (Lickorish and Kershaw 1958). Thomas Cook planned a trip to the United States at mid-century, but it was not until after the Civil War in 1865 that his son John came to North America on an exploratory planning trip. During the last half of the 19th Century, mass transport by steam engine provided the technological leap that spurred the development of resorts, an amusement industry, and a general acceptance of travel for pleasure.

With a major concentration of population along the northeast coast, plus cool summer temperatures, eastern resorts grew rapidly as the railroads expanded. Atlantic City, New Jersey, was connected by rail to Philadelphia in 1853, assuring its development as a seaside watering place for those of middle class. Southerners continued to visit Newport, Bar Harbor and Saratoga, believed to be 50,000 annually (Dulles 1965), until the slavery issue became too much of a schism. With new railroad access, the southern resorter turned to the Greenbrier at White Sulphur Springs, West Virginia, and even to a new resort in Clear Point, Alabama, at the Grand Hotel (1847). In some areas, the railroads were instrumental in the development and operation of the hotel resorts, a phenomenon that was common during the railway era. By 1860, on the eve of the Civil War, the railroad mileage had reached 30,000 (Lundberg 1974). In spite of the war, the Pullman railroad sleeping car was introduced in 1863, offering the comfort of overnight travel to the privileged and the wealthy, and even for Mrs. Lincoln to take the President's body back to Illinois from Washington D.C. in April 1865.

After the Civil War, the travel industry slowly began a steady period of growth. Mark Twain crossed the Atlantic and wrote of his experiences in *Innocents Abroad* in 1867. One writer has stated that Mark Twain's voyage on the 'Quaker City' to the Mediterranean and the Holy Land was the first conceived of as one for tourists. The cost of passage was $1,200 per adult (Lickorish & Kershaw 1955). The same source relates that there were two excursions from England to the United States in 1866 to visit Civil War battlefields in Virginia and Mammoth Cave in Kentucky.

Railroad mileage in the United States was more than 50,000 in 1870. The Union Pacific and Central Pacific Railroad completed the transcontinental connection in 1869. The dining car was introduced on the Chicago and Alton RR in 1868. The Santa Fe spurned dining cars, traffic was not great enough at that time on the Great Plains, and instead allowed Englishman Fred Harvey to open a restaurant adjacent to the railroad in Topeka, Kansas. Soon afterward, he opened a second, employing a recognized Chef from Chicago. For a reasonable price, he offered a tasteful cosmopolitan menu, served on Irish linen by a staff of proper young ladies, as the train watered and refuelled a few yards away. Harvey went on to build a dynasty of hotels and restaurants. His Harvey girls became a legend. As the railroads in the West were financing their expansion, and the nation's frontier, with land given to them from the public domain, railroads in the East were reaching new mountain and seaside resorts. By the 1880s railroads were almost half way toward the mileage apex of their development — Standard Time Zones were adopted in 1893; an innovation that became worldwide before the decade was over.

Similarly in Europe, once the railways linked the expanding industrial cities with the Mediterranean coast of France and Italy, the select resorts of the upper classes were newly discovered by the growing middle classes anxious to emulate aristocratic fashions. In 1865 the railway arrived at Nice and, two years later, at Menton (Burnet, 1963) leading, in the period from 1865 to 1914, to the appearance of a number of thriving resorts along the Riviera coast which transformed it into the premier holiday region of France.

Railways for the Masses

In the 1880s, there were more than 50 railroads in the United States and Canada *(American Journeys 1975)*. The railroad opened both nations to travel for the masses, even though speeds as reported by John Cook were not much in excess of fifteen and twenty miles an hour (*Cook's Tours* 1982). On his first visit to the United States, John Cook found the trains much to his satisfaction, especially sleeping cars (Pullmans) and the ice water dispensers in the carriages. Thomas Cook opened an office in New York City in 1871 and, with an enthusiastic but perhaps exploitative partner by the name of Jenkins, built a Cooks' Pavilion at the Centennial Exhibition in Philadelphia in 1876. By the 1880s and 1890s, Cook's was recognized in North America as a premiere tour operator, providing pleasure excursions for Americans to Europe and other parts of the world. Cook's system of cheques called Circular Notes was introduced in 1873. The notes were an early form of Traveller's Cheques that could be cashed in hotels and restaurants participating in the Cook system anywhere in the world. Cook's Notes predated the American Express Company's money orders which were not introduced until 1882.

The older established resorts did not languish, but grew with railroad expansion. Upstate New York, the Pocono Mountains of Pennsylvania, the White Mountains of New Hampshire, and the New England seashore, were all destinations for a populace that gradually accepted leisure travel and vacations as a part of their lifestyle, in spite of religious teachings that yielded slowly to this new view. In the Spring of 1890, the *New York Tribune* ran eight columns of summer hotel advertisements of New England resorts, appealing directly to the middle class (Dulles 1965). Gambling in the environs of the Saratoga resorts was quite a lure. Saratoga, like other resorts not only offered luxury accommodation, good dining, mineral waters or sea water, but other attractions and amusements on the premises or in the vicinity. Races, casinos, theatres and a variety of outdoor sporting activities, such as tennis, horseback racing, hiking and bicycling were now resort amenities. Today, few resorts in the United States function without a golf course, but it was not until 1888 that the St. Andrews Golf Club near New York was established and the sport was rapidly accepted. Its importance in a resort setting is frequently overlooked.

Early Seaside Resorts

Atlantic City appears to be the prime example of the early American seaside resort for the middle class. Its development has many attributes that are similar to seaside resorts in England. The pier was completed in 1881, and the Boardway or promenade was an early fixture, eventually six miles of wood and steel. There were some differences, such as the innovation of basketwork rolling chairs in 1905, that offered the visitor a very personalized promenade. Whereas rock candy was common to the British seaside, salt water taffy was its counterpart in America. The railroads provided the wealthy access to new eastern resorts, such as Wentworth-by-the-Sea in New Hampshire (1874), the Grand Hotel on Mackinac Island, Michigan (1887) and in the West, the Del Coronado Hotel in San Diego, California (1888). The Ponce de Leon in St. Augustine, Florida, was built in 1887. The resort hotels in Southern California and Florida suggest that, for those that could afford it, winter vacations in warmer climates were as essential as the summer resorts. The North American 'sun belt' was evolving (Figure 9 page 27).

The development of Florida as a winter resort was spearheaded by Henry Flagler and Henry Plant. Both men were millionaires and Presidents of railroad companies, with rights to extend their companies into Forida, Flagler on the east coast and Plant on the west side. The railroads used hotels to lure prospective clients to sunny Florida. Satisfied visitors would then purchase land (from land development companies operated by the railroads). As in the West, the Government gave the railroads land in order to finance development. Flagler systematically built luxury hotels in what are now recognized resort cities down Florida's east coast, at St. Augustine (Ponce de Leon and Alcazar Hotels), Ormond Beach, Palm Beach (Breakers 1890) and the Royal Palm in Miami (1897). Henry Plant built seven hotels on the west coast, the most impressive a large Moorish hotel in Tampa, fittingly named the Tampa Bay (Lundberg 1984).

The nation's railroads did not ignore the attractions of the expansive West. As the nation conquered the Western frontier, both the dangers and splendor of the mountains and deserts were part of the printed media hastened by the telegraph. The wildlife riches of the plains and mountains had been written about by the nation's explorers, and certainly the popular authors and painters of the day such as Whitman, Muir, Remington, Russell and even Theodore Roosevelt.

Photography was coming to fruition, with the first newspaper photography in 1880. Those that could afford the trek had, for a number of decades, travelled on hunting and fishing forays to the Rocky Mountains for sport. Initially, the grandeur of the national scenic gems such as Yellowstone, Grand Canyon and Yosemite, were seen only by the monied class. The railroads, constantly in pursuit of more passengers built spur lines to the Grand Canyon south slope, and to Mammoth Hot Springs at the northwest entrance to Yellowstone. Hotels soon followed, even before some of these areas became National Parks (Yellowstone 1872, Grand Canyon 1906, Yosemite 1890).

Luxury Hotels — The Resort

Some have mentioned that the resort is an American invention, the outgrowth of the luxury hotel. Certainly, in Europe, the rich originally used private accommodations when they travelled for business or pleasure. In a youthful, developing continent, North American society was forced to improvise as the frontier ex-

Figure 9:
EVOLUTION OF RESORT HOTELS AND AREAS IN THE UNITED STATES

ERAS	TECHNOLOGY-INSTITUTIONS	WESTERN U.S.	CENTRAL U.S.	EASTERN U.S.
ELEGANT "GRAND HOTELS" RAILROAD - STEAMSHIP - CARRIAGE PERIPHERAL RESORTS	1750s			1750s *Stafford Springs, Ct. *Berkeley Springs, VA (Pre-1750) Newport, R.I. *Homestead, VA (1766) (1892) *Saratoga Springs (1767)
	1800 Concord Coach			1800 Mountain House (Catskills 1824) Bar Harbor, ME. (1840's) Coney Is. House (1840's) New Jersey Shore (1852) Atlantic City (Real Estate Development)
	1850 Railroads		*Hot Springs, ARK. (1840's) Clear Point, ALA. (1847)	1850 *Greenbrier, W.VA. (1857) Balsam's N.H. (1873) Wentworth–By–The–Sea, N.H. (1874) Cape Cod Hotels, (1874) St. Augustine, FLA. (1885) Ponce De Leon Breakers, Royal Poinciana Palm Beach, FLA. 1st Golf Course, 1888 Mountain View House, N.H. (1890) Miami–Miami Beach, FLA. (1890's)
	1900 "Electricity" (1882) Amusement Parks	Del Coronado, CA. San Diego (1888)	Mackinac Is., MICH. (1887) French Lick, IND.	1900 Catskill Mt. Resorts (1900)
YEAR - ROUND RESORTS MASS TRAVEL	1920 National Parks Hotels Automobile Hard Surface Roads Highways-Uniform Hwy Signs Gambling legal Nevada (1931) Air Conditioning	Pebble Beach, CA. (1908) Halekulani (HI) (1909) Hawaii-Royal Hawaiian-Matson (1927) Biltmore - Wigwam, AZ. (1929) Ahwahnee - Yosemite Valley (1931) Sun Valley, ID. (1936) Camelback Inn, AZ. (1936) Harrah's Nevada (1938) Lake Tahoe	Pine Hurst, N.C. (1901) (Golf) Broadmoor, CO. (1918) Hershey, PA. (1933)	1920 Resort City–Coral Gables, Fla. (1920) Hotel Bldg Boom, Catskills Boca Raton, F.L.A. (1926) Cloister, GA (1928) Winter resorts – First snow train to N.H. (1931)
	1950's Theme Parks Jet Airliners (Direct Flights)	Palm Springs, CA.	–SUN BELT GROWTH–	1950's Fountain Bleau, Miami Beach, FLA. (1953) Sea Pines, S.C. (1957) 1st Condos
MODERN RESORT CONCEPT CONFERENCES	1960 Condominium Hotel Convention Hotels	Kahala Hilton (HI) (1964) Mauna Kea Beach - Hawaii (1965)		
	1970's Wide Body-Airliners Teleconference Facilities	Las Vegas Hilton (31,000 rooms)		1970's Gambling – Atlantic City Resort Hotel Complexes Disneyworld, Orlando, FLA. (1972)

*Examples of a spa

panded, so perhaps the self-contained luxury hotel was indeed a product of two nations attempting to outdo the old world and develop habits and customs that fit the society and environment. Class distinction was not rooted in North America, and the hotel catered to all classes of people with the only constraint being the ability to pay the fare. Lundberg (1984) states that tipping in hotels and restaurants was not common until after the arrival of several waves of immigrants, particularly in the latter decades of the 19th century. The American Plan for meals, where one charge covers all meals plus a room is an American innovation suitable in a setting where a luxury hotel-resort is isolated. The luxury and ambience of the American resort allowed the visitor the opportunity to live for a short time in the image of the well-to-do of the aristocracy of both the old and new worlds.

As the 20th Century dawned, leisure travel was an accepted lifestyle in North America, but Victorian morals were still firmly entrenched, particularly in rural areas. Americans were travellers, but the United States and Canada are large and a majority of citizens were not experienced international adventurers. Available time and cost can be tremendous travel inhibitors. Besides, there was much to experience on the North American Continent. Only 120,000 Americans travelled to Europe in 1900. Tourist travel to Europe is described by Lickorish and Kershaw (1958) as being closer to a pilgrimage than the more matter-of-fact inter-European tourism. They quote an American visitor to England by the name of Collier, in 1909, who said 'This is the England, I take it, that makes one feel his duty to be his religion, and the England that every American comes to as a shrine.'

The turn of the century brought with it the end of the Victorian reign in 1901, but what an exciting and socially changing period it had been. International Exhibitions in North America and abroad had awakened people to the wonders of the ever-advancing industrial revolution. Many inventions of this revolution had been, and would be in the future, adapted for leisure pursuits. The Columbian Exhibition in Chicago (1893) was a capstone to inspire more amusement parks with a variety of electrical rides. The short Sunday trip by electric trolley to picnic grounds and amusement parks near the urban area provided most people with a welcome leisure break. The fact that a man by the name of Duryea developed the first automobile in 1893 went unnoticed, but how this invention was going to change travel and leisure patterns in the new century!

Early 1900s — The Good Years

An era of recreational awakening in society began at the conclusion of World War I. Henry Ford put the Common Man on the road in the first two decades of this century as the Model T provided great flexibility over train travel. Train passenger travel continued to increase with a peak in railroad mileage in 1916. That same year the National Park System was established by Congress, the result of increased visitor pressure and the need for natural resource protection in parks that had been managed by the U.S. Army or the Forest Service. Congress appropriated funds to the U.S. Department of Agriculture to improve farm to market roads in 1916 but improved hard surface roads were not available until the late-1920s when Macadamize and asphalt surfaces became more common. Along with improved roads came a national highway numbering system, highway maps, and in a few states, offices to promote leisure travel.

The post World War I economic boom stimulated the desire for leisure travel. The commercial bus industry developed rapidly. The railroad did not provide access to every community and the bus could. More than 7,000 bus routes were available in the mid 1920s and during the next fifteen years bus passengers increased by more than 200% while railroad passengers declined by almost 20 percent. Many components of the travel industry of today were initiated, refined and promoted during the inter-war years. The tourist court, later highway motel, appeared in the mid-1920s. Florida and Southern California experienced real estate booms. Henry Ford began the development of Greenfield Village and the restoration of Williamsburg was envisioned. Williamsburg along with Sturbridge Village in Massachusetts were two of the first large scale developments incorporating living history as a part of their appeal. Highway travel to reach the mountains, lakes, and cultural/historical attractions included the visual attraction of the ubiquitous billboard, an American promotional feature that fortunately has not been copied in most other countries.

The stock market crash of 1929 had worldwide implications and, for at least a decade, somewhat limited the discretionary travel income of most of the population. At the zenith of the economic boom in 1929, 517,000 U.S. travelers went overseas and spent $269 million. By 1937 overseas travelers had reduced to 435,000 and expenditures overseas dropped to $148 million (U.S. Department of Commerce). During the Depression, New Deal political actions of the Roosevelt Administration provided jobs for the unemployed. The Civilian Conservation Corps (CCC) and the Works Project Administration (WPA) helped to renew and expand outdoor recreation resources such as state parks. Prior to World War II the work week was mandated at 40 hours by the Fair Labor Standards Act of 1938. A similar act occurred the same year in England. The Holidays with Pay Act assured the British workers of a holiday with pay. In both countries these governmental acts gave a new stimulus to domestic tourism and initiated significant social change as more time was available for nonwork activities. But for the wealthy leisure travel, particularly to Europe, continued on the luxury liners of the day. During the 1930s most of the great transoceanic ships were constructed such as the Queen Mary and Queen Elizabeth, by the Cunard Line, and the Frenchline's Normandie. Even though Lindbergh had spanned the Atlantic in 1927, aerodynamic technology, engine development and international political agreements, in the case of crossing the Atlantic, inhibited long distance air travel. The Douglas Commercial Transport (DC-3) had evolved by 1935 and, for the first time, an aircraft of sufficient speed and passenger carrying capacity was available for domestic airline development. Pan American World Airways was crossing the Pacific to Hong Kong by 1939 using the Boeing 314, a specially designed flying boat, but this mode of travel was extremely expensive. By 1940 an agreement was concluded with the United Kingdom and both countries operated flying boats across the Atlantic. Transoceanic travel intensified during World War II as the urgency of the war hastened technological development of the airplane, and particularly the jet engined airplane which would bring low cost intercontinental transportation to the masses within a few decades.

Mass Recreation (1946 – 1958)

An era of recreational awakening in society began at the conclusion of World War I but was slowed and altered during the depression of the 1930s.

After World War II and until 1958 the era of mass recreation resumed a phenomenal growth. Postwar prosperity and population growth led to an upsurge of traveling by the middle class. Servicemen returning from tours of duty desired to spend their vacation time from newly found civilian jobs touring their own country, as well as foreign lands. Postwar women, given a sense of independence by working outside the home during the War, were eager to travel as well. This postwar change set into motion an egalitarian travel industry that was further affected by the numerous economic, social, and technological changes during the 1950s.

In 1950 only 676,000 U.S. citizens out of a population of 151 million chose to go abroad for their vacations, spending $321 million in the process. The West Indies and Central America attracted almost one half of these tourists while the grand tour to Europe and the Mediterranean was the destination for another 302,000. Sixty percent of the tourists went by air rather than sea to both destinations. Another $701 million was spent by U.S. visitors to Canada and Mexico in 1950 *(Statistical Abstract of the United States, 1961)*.

At home, these were the years of a rapidly-developing crisis in outdoor recreation described by Marion Clawson (1959). The initiation of 'Mission 66' by the National Park Service and 'Operation Outdoors' by the U.S. Forest Service recognized the recreation land use 'crisis' and were honest efforts to provide outdoor recreation opportunities for a highly mobile populace. The Outdoor Recreation Resources Review Commission was established in 1958. This was the first major governmental research program focusing on recreation and leisure. This was also the period when the geographer Edward Ullman (1954) described 'Amenities as Factors in Regional Growth' and implied the development of the future Sunbelt. During this first era a new entertainment attraction, Disneyland, opened in southern California's ideal climate. The theme park was an innovation that diffused very rapidly.

Several factors brought this era to a close although the total impact at that time could not be recognized. The jet engine commercial aircraft and the Federal Aid Highway Act (Interstate Highways) hastened the demise of the nation's railroad passenger service and, at the same time, ushered in the second era of Mass Mobility and Transience from 1958 to 1974.

Mass Mobility and Transience (1958 – 1974)

As society moved into this new era of mass mobility, social reform movements gained momentum. The civil rights movements reached a zenith and minorities began to insist on services and amenities once denied them. A vocal youth movement in the 1960s sparked a desire to do things their way. The 'Me generation' changed traditional mores regarding work, sexual attitudes, marriage, and work ethics. The Equal Rights Amendment focused on the unequal treatment of women and minorities in society. Traditional ways were gradually bent and reshaped by all of these social movements as the desire for new lifestyles emerged. The society had truly reached a period of travel democratization, the flowering of mass travel (De Santis 1978). Travel for pleasure was included in these changes.

By 1970, 5¼ million U.S. citizens took vacations abroad. Europe and the Mediterranean (55 percent) had superseded the West Indies and Central America (32 percent) as popular destinations. Only 2% of these travelers went by ship. New Boeing 707s and Douglas DC–8s had ushered in the jet age of mass travel. The low cost and the rapidity of jet airline travel is further emphasized by the fact that overseas travelers spent more money at these European destinations than in Canada and Mexico. In 1970 U.S. travelers spent $1.7 billion in the neighbor nations and $2 billion overseas *(Statistical Abstract of the United States, 1971)*. In Europe, the United Kingdom, France, Italy and Germany were the popular destinations of U.S. travelers. These same countries were popular that year with 5.75 million Britons; however, almost one-third of them went on package holidays to Spain, lured by the sun, sea and sand of the Costa Del Sol, Costa Blanca, and Costa Brava.

This was an era of prosperity, high employment, 3-day week ends with the Uniform Monday Holiday Act, recreation vehicles, new theme parks, private campgrounds, hotel/motel growth, and credit cards. By the beginning of the 1970s basic population changes and family changes were more evident. Population growth began to slow, more and more women left the home for the work force and extra family income. The number of older Americans began to increase and with earlier retirements, retirement communities began to take shape.

Table 4:
CHANGES IN U.S. MARKET COMPOSITION--TOP 12 COUNTRIES
1977 – 1982 – 1986

RESIDENCE	SHARE OF TOTAL ARRIVALS		
	1977	1982	1986
CANADA	64.9%	47.6%	43.2%
MEXICO	10.9	11.9	21.9*
JAPAN	4.0	6.6	6.6
U.K.	2.9	5.9	4.5
GERMANY	2.0	3.0	2.6
VENEZUELA	1.0	2.5	0.5
FRANCE	1.2	1.9	1.7
AUSTRALIA	0.8	1.2	0.9
BRAZIL	0.3	1.1	1.0
ITALY	0.7	1.1	1.0
COLOMBIA	0.5	1.0	0.6
BAHAMAS	0.5	0.9	1.0

*In 1986 the U.S. Travel and Tourism Administration began using the World Tourism Organization definition of a tourist, a stay of one night or longer. Prior to 1986 Mexican visitors were counted only if their stay was 3 nights or more.

Seasonal travel migrations could be recognized by the Southern states as the older population frequented traditional States such as Florida and California but also began visiting the non-traditional ones such as Texas as well. This was a nation on the move as a result of new lifestyles, economic prosperity, and very inexpensive transportation costs. The euphoria of this era was shaken by world events that caused the Organization of Petroleum Exporting Countries (OPEC) to raise the price of petroleum. This was catastrophic for a nation dependent upon low priced energy, particularly for fueling the family status symbol, the motor vehicle. The travel industry was still not viewed as economically important compared to other traditional industry sectors.

Post Mobility Adjustment (1974 to Present)

With the first energy crisis in 1973, the United States moved into a more austere inflationary era, one of Post-Mobility Adjustment. The nation is still in the throes of this era. For some it has been a time of belt tightening and a desire to return to a simple, almost nostalgic lifestyle, but for many inflation and zero-economic growth have seemed to spark a 'do it now' attitude because tomorrow may be too late. Leisure travel is considered a right and individual awareness, self-actualization and self-improvement are manifested by high risk recreation activities, physical fitness pursuits, and individual customized travel, all financed by instant credit. Some things, however, have changed. People are doing 'do it yourself' repairs and construction (some even consider this leisure). More of the public lakes, parks, and museums charge user fees. A vocal public has discovered it has political influence at the local and state level and can indeed shape some public policy regarding leisure and travel services. Attitudes and behavior changed even more after the second energy crisis in 1979. People accepted smaller automobiles with better fuel economy because the automobile is a symbol of affluence, individuality, mobility and self image.

U.S. citizens continued foreign travel during this era (Figure 10) Travel to Canada was substantial. However, visits did decline from 13 million to 11 million between 1974 and 1980. Visitors to Mexico increased modestly during this period as a result of the devaluation of the peso in 1976 (Table 4, page 31). In 1976 the U.S. Bicentennial Celebration tended to keep U.S. citizens at home and drew more visitors from Canada and overseas. The second energy crisis in 1979 - 1980 and a weakened dollar encouraged travel to the United States in 1981 and for the first time the United States did not have a travel gap but a surplus of foreign visitors. This was short lived. As the nation recovered from an economic recession, and the dollar gained strength overseas, the travel gap widened between 1982 and 1986. There was a small decline in overseas travel in 1986 influenced by a fear of terrorism and a sharp drop in the price of domestic motor fuel which encouraged vacation travel at home.

This era might also be labelled the Era of Leisure Travel Awareness. At the national level there are a Recreation Coalition and a Tourism Industry Government Affairs Council in Congress and some states have legislative tourism caucuses. Tourism has become economically important due to improvement in data collection and sophistication in measuring its impact. It generates jobs in the service employment sector and contributes billions of dollars in federal, state, and local taxes. Travel is now considered a right, not just for the privileged few.

Figure 10:
TRENDS IN INTERNATIONAL TRAVELERS
TO AND FROM THE UNITED STATES

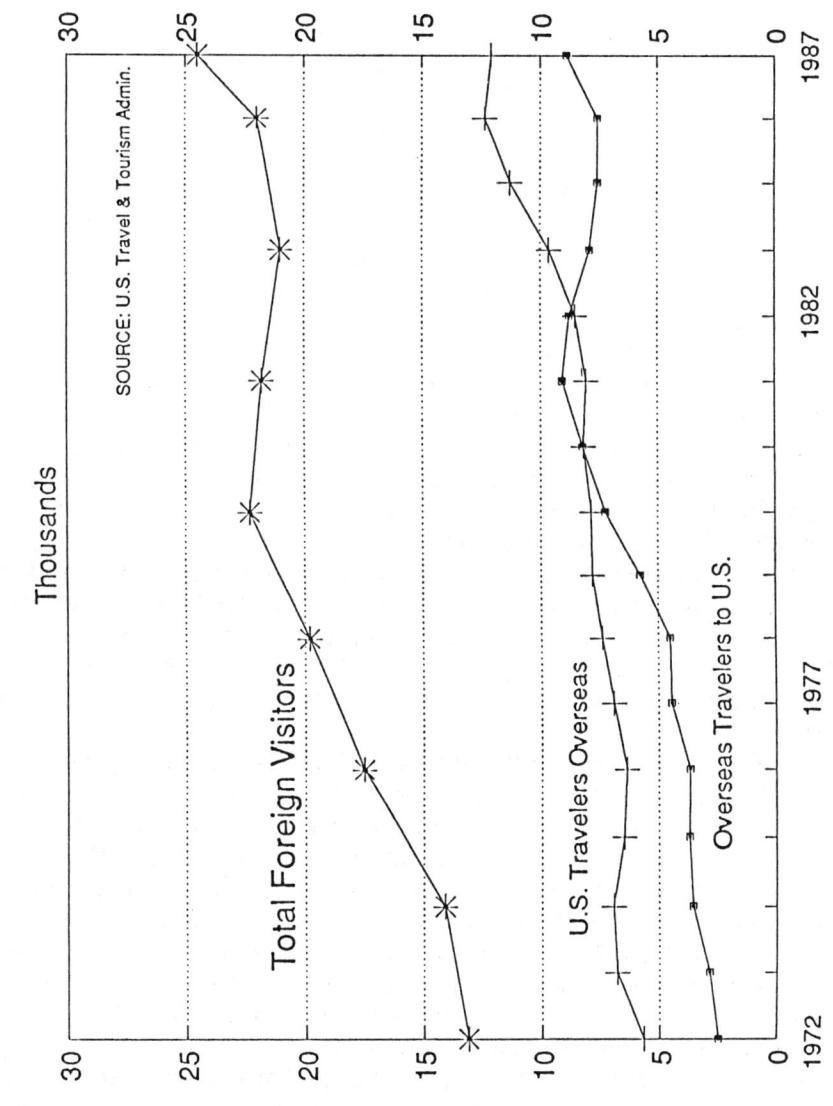

Thousands

SOURCE: U.S. Travel & Tourism Admin.

Total Foreign Visitors

U.S. Travelers Overseas

Overseas Travelers to U.S.

Post – 1945 British Tourism

Since World War II the tourism industry in Britain has experienced many of the same technological, social, and economic changes as the United States. The number of people spending a holiday away from home continued to grow as the population of Britain grew and more of the workforce had holidays with pay. There was little change in the pattern of tourist destinations. More than two thirds of all main holidays were taken at the seaside. Holiday camps were replacing the traditional resort as a basis for a self-contained 'package' catering for all the visitors' needs. Public transport was still popular in 1951 and only 25 per cent traveled by car. The Festival of Britain in 1951 and the Coronation of Elizabeth the Second in 1953 gave an impetus to the development of new tourist facilities. The Government introduced a grant scheme to provide financial help (albeit limited) to hotels catering for overseas visitors and in the 1956 *Distribution of Industry Act,* which gave the Treasury powers to make loans or grants in areas of high unemployment, hotels were included for the first time. During this period the jet engined Comet airliner was introduced by BOAC (now British Airways).

The number of visitors to Britain from overseas also grew rapidly from 203,000 in 1946 to 1.7 million in 1960. Initially 69 percent of these foreign visitors arrived by sea and 31 percent by air. But the dramatic growth in air travel during the 1960s reversed these figures. From the development of holidays with pay in the 1930s to the growth of overseas visitors during the 1950s and 1960s the domestic tourist industry came of age. Within the space of thirty years there emerged a major industry employing hundreds of thousands of people and producing many millions of pounds for the national economy.

Until the late 1950s the bulk of the British took their main holiday in the UK, often at a seaside resort, and usually during July and August. There had been little change in the nature of the holiday destination for over 100 years. In 1951 only 1½ million out of a total population of 50 million Britons chose to go abroad for their holidays, (British Travel Association, 1970) spending $168 million in the process.

By 1970 5¾ million Britons took their holidays abroad, spending $1.1 billion. Over 25 percent of these holidaymakers were aged between 16 and 24. In 1950 France was the most popular holiday destination attracting 40 percent of Britons taking foreign holidays. The most dramatic change during this period was the tremendous growth in the popularity of Spain. Of the 5.75 million Britons taking foreign holidays in 1970, nearly one-third went to Spain.

What brought about this dramatic growth in foreign holidays? The immediate post war years were a period when there were many surplus aircraft and highly trained aircrews who wished to continue flying in civilian life.

Technological improvements in aircraft and engine design during the 1950s helped to reduce the relative cost of air travel. The cost of travel to a foreign country is a key element in its attractiveness as a holiday destination, together with the level of accommodation and general living costs that exist there. Between 1950 and 1968 the cost of a high season return from London to New York almost halved in price and almost every route operated showed a marked reduction in the cost of air travel during this 18-year period.

To have the means to travel is not enough. There need to be enough air services between the tourist generating countries (such as Britain) and the tourist receiving countries (such as Spain or Italy) to meet the peak season travel demands. Two trends emerged during this period. First average aircraft seating capacity almost doubled (Table 17) for intra-European flights and almost trebled for transatlantic routes. Second, in Britain, private airline companies were allowed by the Government to develop and to set up in competition with the State airlines. By the early 1960s the potential airline traveler to Spain or Greece, for example, could travel as an independent passenger on a scheduled or chartered flight as part of an inclusive group tour, or as an inclusive tour passenger on a scheduled flight in the mid and late 1950s.

It was the development of chartered flights which transformed the pattern of annual holidays for millions of British tourists. Foreign travel, for so long the prerogative of the rich, became easily accessible to the general population. In the early 1950s tour operators began to market package tours to the Continent linking up with private airlines such as Laker Airways and, by the early 1960s, Spain and the Mediterranean were being promoted and developed as holiday destinations for millions of Britons. The tour operators, for the first time, put together a foreign holiday 'package' covering travel, accommodation, meals and sometimes other items at an inclusive price. By chartering aircraft and filling every seat, the operator could keep travel costs down and, by making block bookings in particular hotels, could also provide accommodation at competitive prices. During the 1960s extensive tracts of the Costa Brava and Costa Blanca in Spain, and in the 1970s the Languedoc-Rousillon coast, were developed to meet this tourist boom. Today there are many kinds of holiday package and as many different holiday destinations. The sun, sea and sand package of the summer months is replaced by the sun, snow and skiing package over the Christmas — winter period.

Throughout the 1960s to the 1980s, individual income levels continued to grow and levels of car ownership in Britain grew from 2 million in 1950 to 17.7 million in 1981. By 1980, 39 percent of overseas travel to Western Europe used the Channel ferries — much of this traffic being private cars. The escalation in petrol prices following the 1973 Arab-Israeli conflict caused a temporary downturn in this trend, but by the early 1980s the number of Britons taking their cars on Continental holidays was again increasing. The development of motorway links to the Channel ports in Britain and similar improvements on the autoroutes in France, Belgium and Holland brought many more European resorts within driving distance from Britain, and this too — together with the easing of EEC frontier controls — made foreign travel much easier and attractive.

Even the recession from the late 1970s has failed to halt the demand for foreign holidays. In 1982, despite massive growth in unemployment, 8 percent more Britons traveled abroad and spent 20 percent more. (TAC *Anatomy of UK Tourism*).

In Britain, the Government took the first steps to a national policy for tourism with the Development of Tourism Act in 1969. It established a British Tourist Authority, English, Scottish and Wales Tourist Boards, with powers to provide loans and grants for hotel development schemes; to encourage the provision and improvement of tourist amenities and facilities; and to promote Britain as a tourist destination for overseas visitors. By the 1970s, the Government recognized the growing importance of the tourist industry both as an employer of labor and as a major contributor to the national economy.

Other trends in tourism are beginning to emerge as new vacation innovations are attempted in both countries. Time-sharing, Club Med, Club 18 to 30, adventure vacations, cruises, Amtrak's auto-train, hot air balloon, winery tours, trips to China, India, Turkey, all highlight the importance of travel in our lives and the inventiveness of the industry to develop and market new leisure travel experiences.

ASSIGNMENT

1. On the basis of tourist data showing trends in domestic and international tourism 1950 to 1980, provide a summary of the main changes which have taken place during this period, and outline the underlying causes of these changes.

2. Identify and compare as many of the social, technological, and tourism development and management contributions that British and American cultures have made to the present day world tourism scene. Which of the contributions, schemes, policies, etc. have been innovations that have diffused and been adopted in other societies? Suggestions: package tours, national parks, holiday camps, theme parks, etc.

Chapter 3

The Tourism Product — attractions

Learning Objectives: After reading this chapter your should understand the nature of and the linkages between the different sectors of the tourism industry and the tourism product, the attractions.

Introduction

The demand for tourism, which has grown steadily over the past 40 years, is a demand for a bundle of goods and services and these are provided by both the private and public sectors of the national economy. The private sector provides much of the accommodation and visitor attractions, the public sector provides much of the existing infrastructure especially the transport facilities; parks, forests, and reservoirs. Within the tourist industry there is a great degree of interdependence between the private and public sectors and the structure of the industry clearly reflects this characteristic.

The travel industry in the United States employs more than 5 million and earns over $260 billion a year. It is big business and will continue to grow. The industry is geared to two ends. First, (domestic travel) meeting the needs of U.S. citizens taking a vacation within the United States and meeting the needs of incoming visitors to this country; and secondly, serving U.S. citizens seeking foreign vacations (outgoing tourism) (Figure 11). **The tourist industry in Britain directly employs over one million people, and earns over $10 billion a year from spending by overseas visitors.**

The Tourism Product

This chapter highlights one of the major sectors of the tourism industry, the product or attractions. The tourist product is the resort or historic town, the beaches, scenery, mountains, historic sites, theme parks, museums and other similar tourist attractions. It is also the stock of accommodation that caters for the needs of the tourist. The difference between the tourist industry and other industries is that the tourist goods and services, unlike other goods and services, are not transported to their users but, instead, the consumers are transported to where the tourist product exists, and production and consumption take place there. The industry therefore consists of five main sectors. These sectors include:

1. **The attractions,** products supplied and supported by both public and private institutions such as National Parks, theme parks and museums;

2. **The retail travel sector,** travel agencies, tour companies and travel suppliers;

3. **The passenger transport sector,** airlines, airports, highways, automobile rental, railroads, bus services and water transport;

4. **Lodging and food services;**

Figure 11:
TOP 20 STATES RANKED BY TOTAL NUMBER OF VISITORS
1986

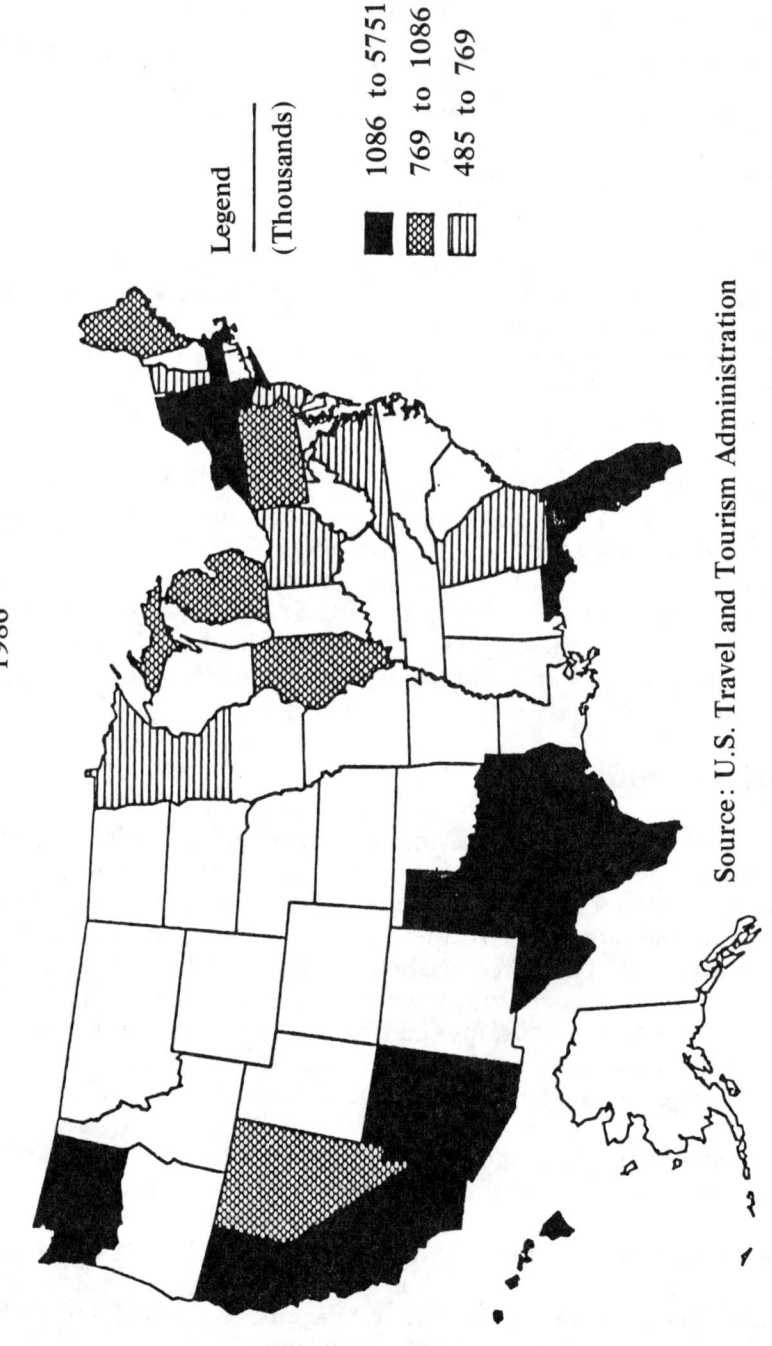

Legend
(Thousands)
■ 1086 to 5751
▦ 769 to 1086
▥ 485 to 769

Source: U.S. Travel and Tourism Administration

5. **Public and private institutions** that plan, develop, promote, and regulate some aspect of the travel and tourism industry.

These sectors are not mutually exclusive and have, in practice, linkages and interfaces with other sectors. It could be easily argued that automobile rental is a part of the retail sector but we have included it here under transportation. The next few chapters discuss each of the five sectors, using a number of approaches useful in describing this industry (McIntosh and Goeldner, 1986). This chapter and the three that follow, will focus on products, institutions, management activities and economics. Later chapters utilize institutional, sociological, economic, and geographic methods to describe public contributions, tourism impact and basic marketing. This industry must be studied using the interdisciplinary methods that these various approaches exemplify.

The firms involved in the sectors listed above range in size from multinational corporations to small, private, family owned and operated businesses. Some enterprises, such as tourist attractions and transport facilities, are in the public or quasi-public sector, while others that were recently in the public sector have now been privatized, such as British Airways and the British Airports Authority. All facets of the travel and tourism industries undergo constant change.

One way to visualize the broad scope that travel and tourism embrace is to become familiar with the Standard Industrial Classifications of the various sectors. Governmental Census in the United States, Canada and the United Nations periodicially publish statistical data for a variety of geographical entities that can be useful in analyzing and understanding the magnitude of travel and tourism. The main classifications for tourism are listed in **Table 5**.

The Attractions Sector

Attractions are the reason that tourism exists. As Gunn writes, 'attractions provide the energizing power' of the travel/tourism system (Gunn, 1988). An attraction, as anticipated and mentally visualized by a potential traveler, provides the motivation and magnetism for moving from one point to another. The success of the attraction depends upon the manner in which a visitor to that attraction measures the benefits and satisfactions of the visit. The attraction is tangible but a measure of its value to a visitor is intangible. The success of a private attraction can be measured in terms of visitor numbers and money spent at the attraction. However, to maintain visitor numbers the attraction, or supplier, must ultimately measure the psychological and social factors that have influenced the visitor's decision to select one destination over another. The psychological or internal factors influencing travel behavior include perception, learning, personality, motives, and attitudes (Jarvis and Mayo, 1981). Social or external factors to the individual decision-maker include family influences, reference groups, social classes, and culture-subculture. As various types and classifications of tourist/travel attractions are discussed in the chapter, the reader may react positively and negatively, depending upon past travel experiences, and may wish to reflect if the reaction is based upon certain psychological or social factors or a combination of both.

Table 5:

Standard Industrial Classifications Related to Travel and Tourism

	STATISTICS CANADA (1980)		APPROXIMATE EQUIVALENTS	
			UNITED STATES (1972)	UNITED NATIONS (1971)

Primary Classifications—all or some establishments primarily concerned with tourism

Accommodation	9111–4	Hotels, motels, tourist courts, tourist homes	7011/21	6320*
	9131	Camping grounds and travel trailer parks	7033	6320*
	9141/9	Outfitters, other recreation camps	7032	6320*
Transportation	4511/2	Air	4511/2	7131
	4572	Interurban and rural transit	4131	7112*
	4574	Charter and sightseeing bus services	4142/4119*	7116*
	4531	Railway transport	4011	7111
	9921	Automobile and truck rental	7512	7116*
	4541/2/9	Water transport	441-5	7121-3
Travel Trade	9961-2	Travel agencies, tour wholesalers & operators	4722*	7191*
Government Departments	8172/8272/ 8372	Resource conservation and industrial development	9512	9100*

Secondary Classifications—some establishments derive much of business from tourism

Food Service	9211-13	Restaurants, take-outs	5812	6310*
	9221	Taverns, bars, nightclubs	5813	6310*
Retail Trade	6331	Gasoline service stations	5541	6200*
	6322	Boat, etc. dealers	5551	6200*
	6321	Motor home and travel trailer dealers	5561	6200*
Recreation	9651	Golf courses	7992	9490*
	9653	Skiing facilities	7999*	9490*
	9654	Boat rentals and marinas	4469	9490*
Culture/ Entertainment	8551	Museums and archives	8411	9420*
	9696	Botanical and zoological gardens	8421	9420*
	9631/9	Theatre and entertainment	7922/9	9414
	9641	Professional sports clubs	7941	9490*
	9643/4	Race tracks	7948	9490*
	9692	Amusement parks	7996	9490*

Tertiary Classifications—some establishments have significant tourism business

	4575	Limousines and taxis	4111*/21	7113*
	7122	Credit card companies	6153*	8102*
	7741	Advertising agencies	7311	8325
	9723	Self-service laundries/dry cleaners	7215	9520*
	6351	Garages (general repairs)	7358	9531
	6571	Camera and photographic supply stores	5946	6200*
	6582	Gift, novelty, and souvenir stores	5947	6200*

**Industry classification more general than in Canadia SIC.

Source: J.R. Brent Ritchie & Charles R. Goeldner. Travel, Tourism and Hospitality Research. New York: John Wiley and Sons, 1987, pp. 58-59. Reproduced with the permission of authors and publisher.

A Scheme for Classifying Attractions

Attractions can be classified on a continuum from those highly dependent upon a natural resource to those that are based on cultural resources. In the middle of this continuum is a gray area in which a combination of factors both natural and cultural are present but neither is dominant (**Figure 12**).

In this middle area, man himself is the dominant actor as he or she interacts with a beautiful vista, appreciates a play or concert, or suns on the beach. This middle ground on the continuum is the social and recreational arena. How, where, and when human beings relate to the natural and cultural resources are dependent upon location, accessibility, population density, business development and the timing, planned or unplanned, of events that we find interesting. The attractions continuum is illustrated in Figure 13 and is adapted from the generic classification originally proposed by Gearing, Swart and Var (1976).

As Gunn (1988) states, attractions change over time due to physical deterioration and as a result of changing markets. It is theorized that attractions are deemed to follow a cycle of rise and fall (Plog, 1974). The first visitors to a new attraction or resort destination are allocentric. The allocentric is described as a curious, active person who prefers non-tourist areas, minimal development, different cultures and experiences that may be challenging. Opposite to the allocentric is the psychocentric person. This person prefers a familiar atmosphere, hotels, restaurants, shops, and is not prone to seek adventure. The psychocentric individual takes a guided tour, has a low activity level and may not trust a foreigner or even a new environment. As the new destination develops and more people 'discover' it, its attraction to the allocentric visitor declines. The midcentric, and then the psychocentric traveler embraces the destination; group travel begins and a cycle of mass tourism growth is initiated. The attraction appeals to a broad market and may quickly reach a peak in the growth cycle. By this time it is theorized that the allocentric has moved on to new and novel destinations and the cycle may begin to decline. Today the allocentric wants to go to China, Butan, or developing tourist areas in east Africa.

To be successful, attractions and the supporting infrastructure should be well planned and clustered together. Clustering of attractions is efficient for the supplier and certainly for the visitor who has a number of choices. Attractions will be discussed in the following order: natural attractions, cultural, social, and recreation attractions and then in a more specific context: cities, theme parks and resorts.

The infrastructure and services classification in the schematic will be covered in later chapters. In every classification the human elements, social, and recreational, are considered dominant and are used to highlight an attraction/human interface as well as the complex nature of the attractions sector.

Cultural-Social-Entertainment Attractions

The cultural resources include the people of the host country who must be congenial and tolerant of the visitor. A cultural landscape, different from the vacationer's home country, is a part of the overall appeal to the traveler. Different religions, architecture, museums, art galleries, manner of dress, fairs, exhibits,

Figure 12:

Kinds of Attractions	Dependency Upon Natural Resources	Dependency Upon Other Than Natural and Cultural Resources	Dependency Upon Cultural Resources
Touring Circuit:			
Roadside scenic areas	●	○	○
Outstanding natural areas	●	○	○
Camping areas	○	●	○
Water touring areas	●	☆	☆
Homes: friends/relatives	☆	●	☆
Unusual institutions	○	●	○
Shrines, cultural places	☆	★	●
Food, entertainment	☆	●	○
Historic bldgs, sites	☆	○	●
Ethnic areas	☆	★	★
Shopping areas	☆	●	☆
Crafts, lore places	☆	★	●
Longer-stay:			
Resorts	●	★	☆
Camping areas	●	★	○
Hunting, water sports	●	☆	○
Organization camps	●	☆	○
Vacation home complexes	●	○	○
Festival, event places	○	●	●
Convention, meeting places	☆	●	☆
Gaming centers	☆	●	○
Sports arenas, complexes	○	●	○
Trade centers	○	●	★
Service, tech. centers	○	●	○
Theme parks	☆	●	○

● Highly Dependent   ★ Dependent   ☆ Somewhat Dependent   ○ Low or No Dependency

Resource Dependency of Attractions. The relationships among kinds of touring circuit and longer-stay developments and three categories of resources—natural, cultural, nonnatural.

Reproduced from <u>Tourism Planning</u> by C. A. Gunn with permission of the Author and Pulbisher, Taylor and Francis.

Figure 13: CLASSIFYING ATTRACTIONS

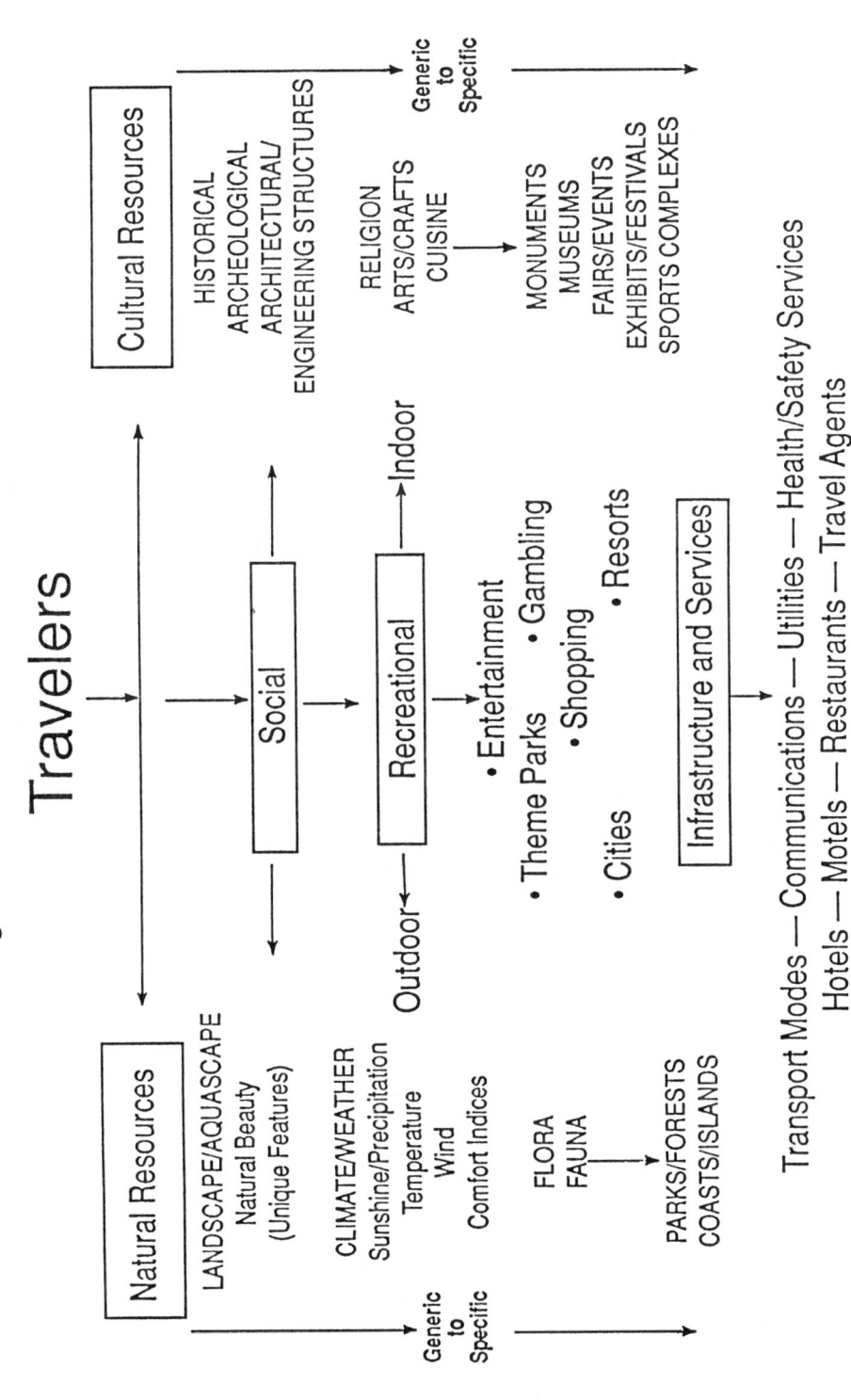

Travelers

Natural Resources

LANDSCAPE/AQUASCAPE
Natural Beauty
(Unique Features)

CLIMATE/WEATHER
Sunshine/Precipitation
Temperature
Wind
Comfort Indices

FLORA
FAUNA → PARKS/FORESTS
COASTS/ISLANDS

Generic to Specific

Social

Recreational

Outdoor / Indoor

- Entertainment
- Theme Parks • Gambling
  • Shopping
- Cities • Resorts

Cultural Resources

HISTORICAL
ARCHEOLOGICAL
ARCHITECTURAL/
ENGINEERING STRUCTURES

RELIGION
ARTS/CRAFTS
CUISINE
→ MONUMENTS
MUSEUMS
FAIRS/EVENTS
EXHIBITS/FESTIVALS
SPORTS COMPLEXES

Generic to Specific

Infrastructure and Services

Transport Modes — Communications — Utilities — Health/Safety Services
Hotels — Motels — Restaurants — Travel Agents

(Adapted from Gearing, Swart, and Var, 1976).

and handicrafts in combination add to the charm of a vacation destination and offer many avenues for exploration and individual insight. Ancient ruins, castles, homes, forts and battlefields are attractions that provide perspectives on the past. Reconstruction of settlements provides tangible evidence and reality to a historical attraction. Examples in the United States are Plymouth Plantation, Colonial Williamsburg, Lincoln's New Salem, Mystic Seaport and Mount Vernon. One cannot visit England without an awareness of the Roman and Norman occupations, lineage of the Royal Family, and the country's historic association with naval power. A foreigner visiting the United States and Canada cannot escape the heritage of revolutionary independence, settlement of the frontier, gangsters, endless distances and Mickey Mouse.

Recreational activities frequently are added bonuses to a tourist destination. A resort hotel must have a golf course, swimming pool and perhaps a beach, tennis courts and even access to a mountain stream for fishing. The sporting specialist may travel long distances to participate in the activity at a renowned location. To play golf at St. Andrews, to fish for salmon in Alaska or Scotland, to surf in Hawaii, to ski at Snow Mass, may provide the ultimate aspiration for the amateur sportsman. Simple outdoor activities at a destination include horseback riding, walking and bicycling. For some, a stroll in a well landscaped park in the center of the city or in the solitude of a forest may be a never to be forgotten vacation experience. Spectator sports also constitute attractions in themselves. Examples are the Super Bowl, World Football championships, the Grand National and the Kentucky Derby, World Series of Baseball, and the Olympic Games. Night clubs, discotheques, theaters and casinos are popular night-time experiences at a vacation destination.

Entertainment in our age of mass communication has been a factor in creating tourist attractions. What we see on the silver screen or television creates images of places, events and the desire to visit the filming locations. To a foreigner the United States is cowboys and indians, gangsters in Chicago, and Disneyland. People from Texas are the Ewings; cruise ships are all Love Boats. In Dallas, Texas, the leading attraction is television's Southfork Ranch which has gained as much notoriety as Elvis Presley's Graceland Mansion in Memphis. Forty percent of visitors to Southfork are from foreign nations. In Tucson, Arizona, the permanent western movie set, Old Tucson, is a popular attraction as are the Universal Studio tours in Hollywood. Movie production locations are authentic for the industry they serve; however, the settings themselves may be contrived. For the vacationer interested in a pleasurable experience, it makes little difference if the scene is illusory. Being there is enough. The tourist himself, depending upon age, travel experience, values, attitudes and priorities, accepts or rejects different types of attractions as settings for an experience.

Natural Attractions

Natural attractions include mountains, forested areas, lakes, rivers, and deserts. For people living in northern latitudes, lush tropical vegetation and warm temperatures provide the lure to travel south in the winter. Weather and climate are determinants of activities, snow for skiing or warm water for swimming. In addition, climate dictates seasonal operations for many tourist attractions. The sun, sea, and sand mentality of many vacationers accounts for the success of resorts in the Caribbean, Mediterranean and the South Pacific such as the Great Barrier Reef of Australia. Surface water temperature at various world beaches in July range from a high of 86° at Galveston, Texas and Miami, Florida, to lows of 63° in Brighton, England and 59° at Bar Harbor, Maine *(The Big Picture, 1985)*. All of these areas are major resorting spots where visitors partake of different social and recreational activities that are dictated to a large degree by the physical land and water environments (**Figure 14**).

Table 6:

RECREATION VISITOR DAYS IN LEADING NATIONAL PARKS AREAS
(Millions)
1987

Blue Ridge Parkway	VA – NC	13.5
Yellowstone National Park	WY	7.4
Yosemite National Park	CA	6.9
Lake Mead National Recreation Area	NV	6.4
Great Smoky Mountains National Park	TN – NC	5.9
Glen Canyon National Recreation Area	AZ – UT	5.3
Gateway National Recreation Area	NY – NJ	4.3
Grand Canyon National Park	AZ	4.2
Golden Gate National Recreation Area	CA	3.8
Sequoia National Park	CA	3.1
		60.8

Source: U.S. National Park Service, 1988

Major natural attractions are areas set aside by governments for preservation and conservation. Most developed countries have national areas of this type of a unique character in which the resource is protected. In the United States, Canada, and Britain, National Parks are primary vacation destination areas. The United States has preserved within the National Park system stretches of ocean and lake front as **National Seashores and National Lakeshores (Figure 15). In England and Wales the Heritage Coast is the Comparable type of resource (Figure 16).**

The U.S. National Park Service operates 341 areas under 23 types of classifications, ranging from large National Parks to the White House. In all, the Service controls a gross acreage of 79 million and, in 1987, hosted 287 million recreation visits. A visit is any person except National Park Service (NPS) personnel who enters lands administered by the park service. Only 19% of all visits are to the 49 National Parks while 19.5% of visits are to National Recreation Areas that have been established since the 1970s in the vicinity of large cities such as New York City and San Francisco (Table 6). National Sea and Lake Shores received 8%, historic parks and sites 13%, and National Parkways, Monuments, Battlefields, Military Parks, Memorials and the White House, 45% of all visits in the system in 1987.

Figure 14:

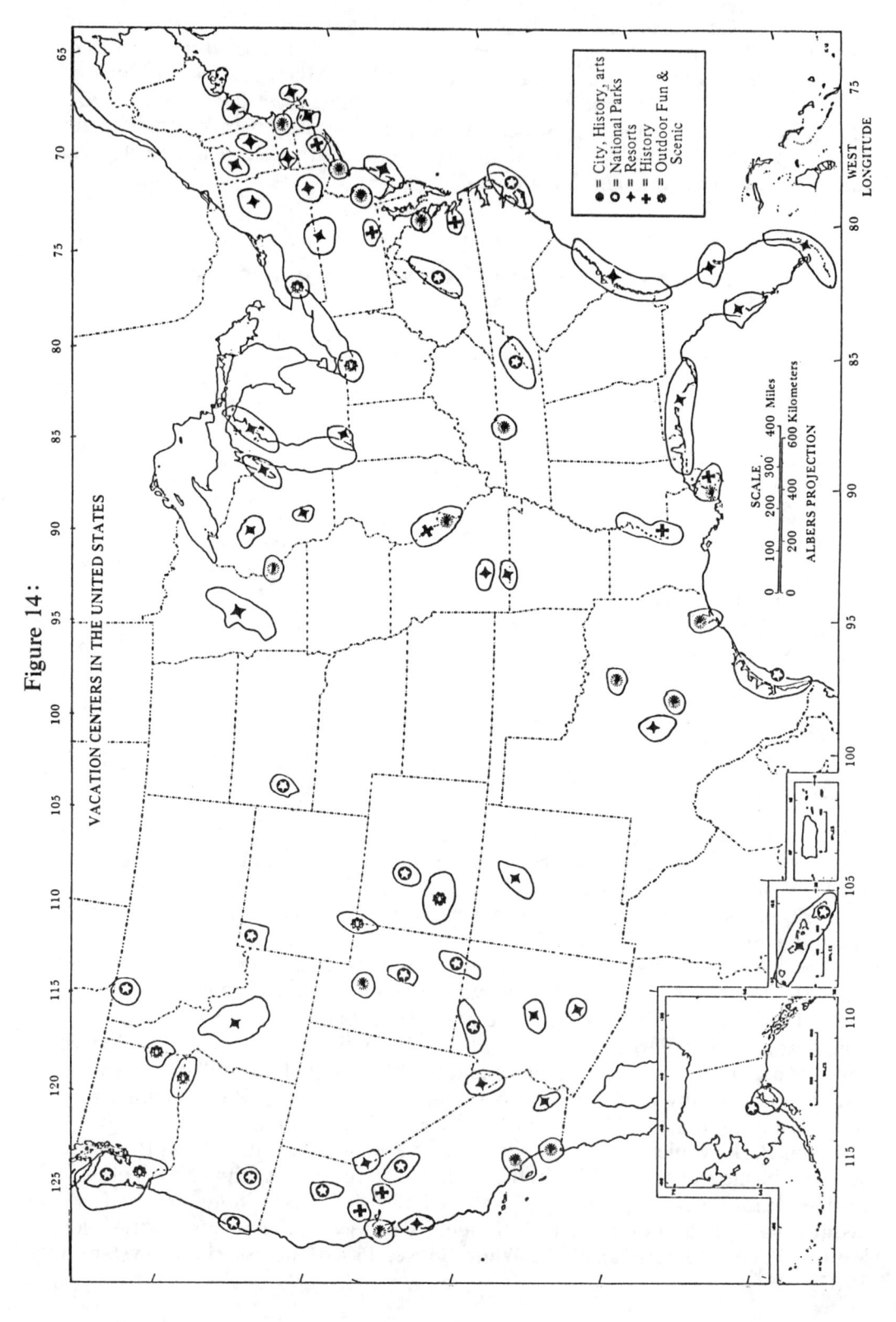

VACATION CENTERS IN THE UNITED STATES

Figure 15:
NATIONAL PARKS, NATIONAL SEASHORES, AND NATIONAL LAKESHORES
IN THE UNITED STATES

★ NATIONAL PARKS
● NATIONAL SEASHORES AND LAKESHORES

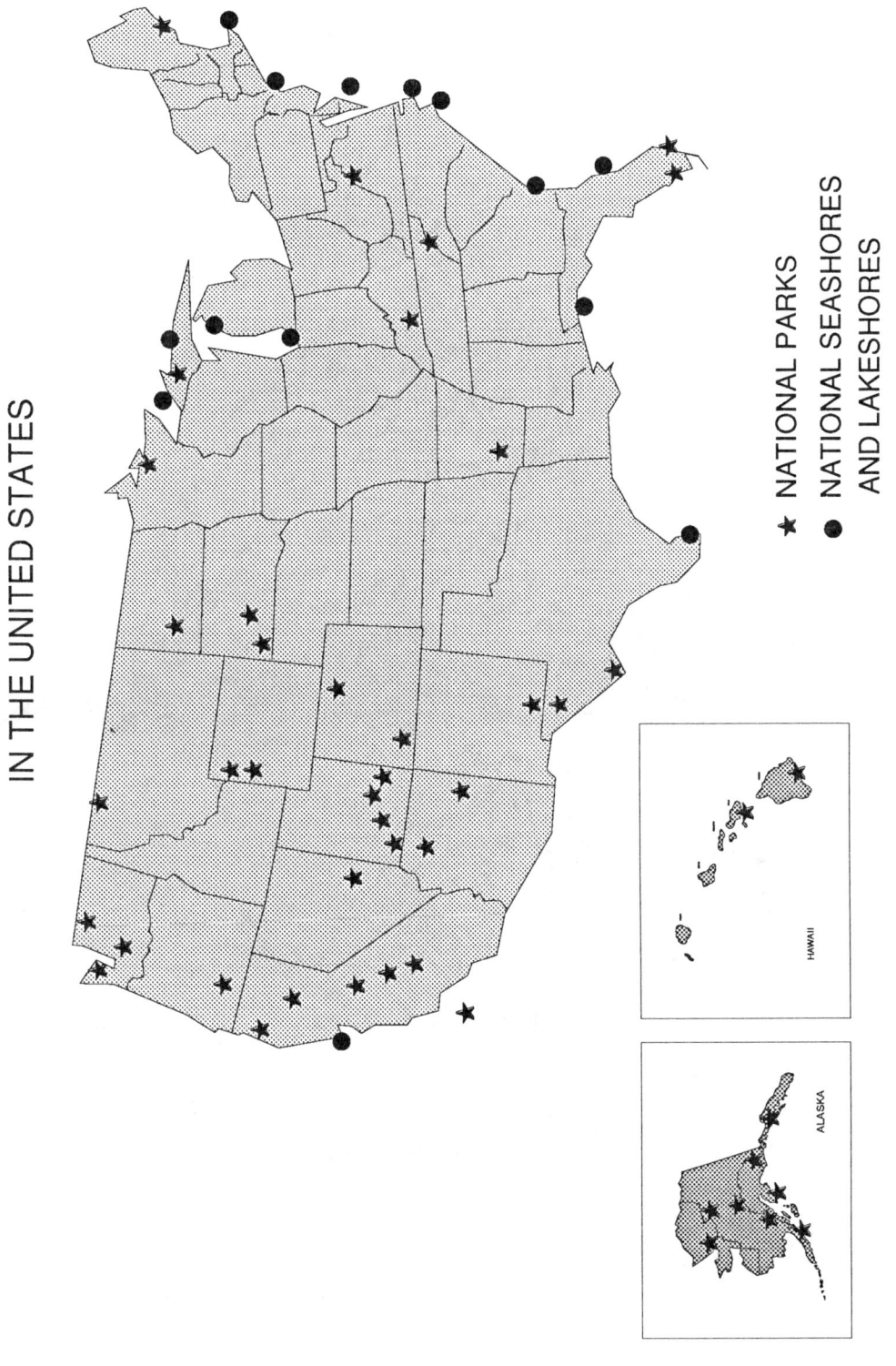

Figure 16: **National Parks, AONB's and Stretches of Heritage Coast in England & Wales**

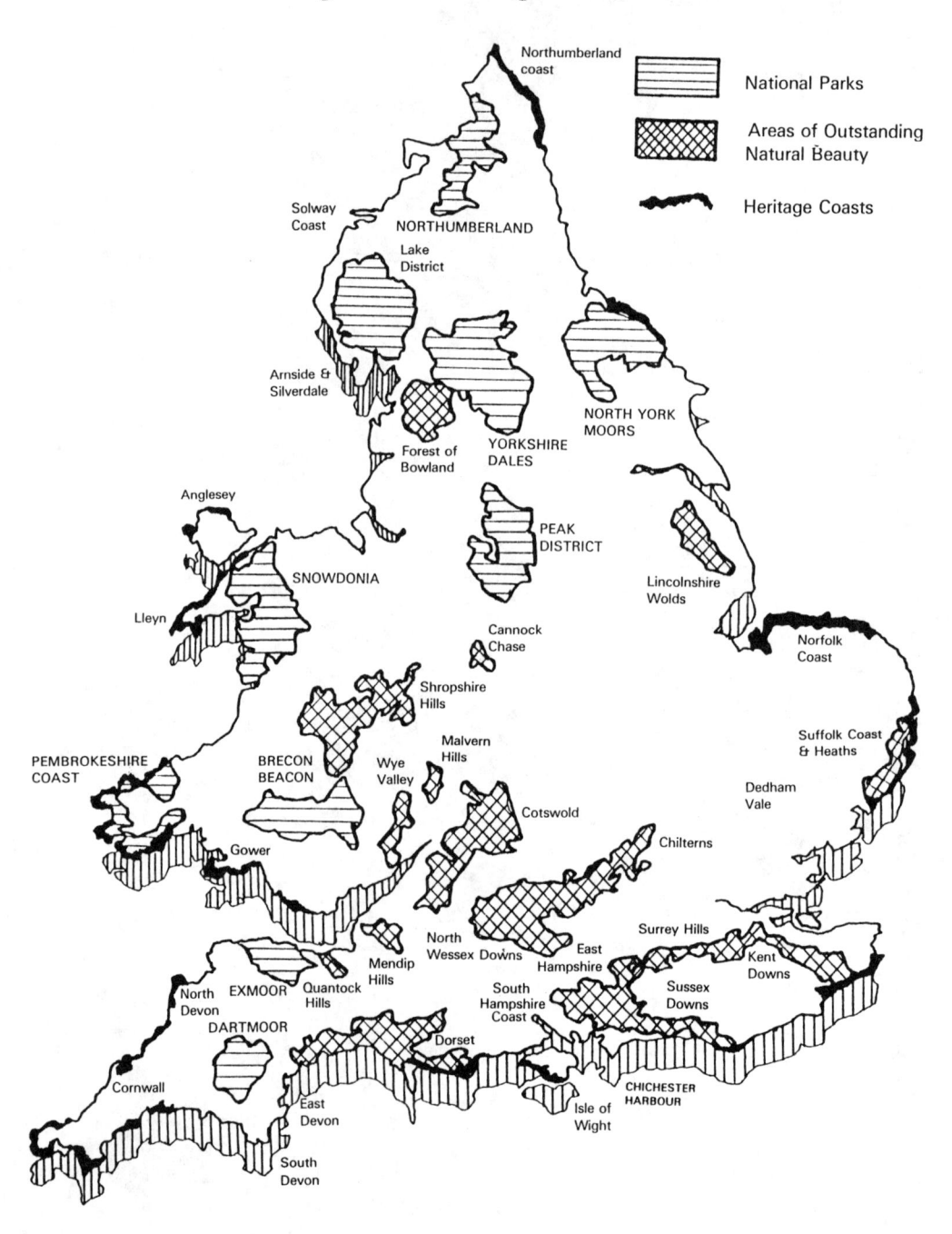

According to a nationwide survey, the average U.S. citizen visits a National Park about three times annually. Most of the park system acreage is in the western one-half of the country (Figure 15). But a number of properties such as historic sites, memorials and monuments, are in the East and are classified as urban parks because they are located within the suburban or central city area of a Metropolitan Statistical Area.

In some parks, their success as attractions is spoiling their grandeur and ecological balance. The 750,000 acre Yosemite National Park is just a 4½ hours drive from San Francisco. The average daily visitation in the summer is 14,000. Most of these visitors concentrate in the seven square miles of the Yosemite valley where Yosemite Village is located. The Village consists of luxury hotels and tent cabins, pizza parlors, and even a jail. Between 1983 and 1987, park visitation increased 30%. With continued crowding in popular parks like Yosemite, one may have to make a reservation to visit a National Park in the future.

Since their creation in the late 1940s, the 10 National Parks of England and Wales (Figure 16) have attracted growing numbers of tourists — although they often contained long-established resorts such as Keswick (Lake District), Buxton (Peak District), or Tenby (Pembrokeshire). More recently, some of the National Parks have seen the growth of timesharing developments — an issue discussed in more detail in Chapter 13.

State Park systems in the United States also operate parks that are major attractions for the tourist. In 1982, the State Park systems hosted 553 million day visitors and the U.S. Forest Service recorded 233 million visitor days in the nation's forests.

The City as an Attraction

Like most of the world's developed industrial nations, the population of the United States is predominately urban dwelling. It is not surprising then that cities are the primary destination of one-third of all domestic vacationers. Many cities are using tourism as a catalyst to revitalize inner city and river and harbor areas. Baltimore's Harborplace is an excellent example. Most of the inner city developments such as Underground Atlanta and Dallas' West End Historic District can be historically themed. These attractions are complexes that include a variety of tastes from shopping malls to the arts, with festivals and events staged regularly to attract visitors.

The standby city attractions still remain. In New York City, the three top attractions are the Empire State Building (although not now the world's tallest structure), the Statue of Liberty, and the Museum of Modern Art. In Washington, D.C., the National Gallery of Art had more than 8 million visitors in 1987. The Smithsonian Institution operates 14 museums and galleries and hosted 7.3 million at the National Air and Space Museum in 1987. The White House had more than one million visitors in 1987, all hoping for a glimpse of the President. Besides the arts, the theater and the zoo, cities host professional and amateur athletic events. To attend a baseball game in the legendary Yankee Stadium or in Chicago's Wrigley Field, with its ivy covered walls, is an event. Cities are popular because they offer the tourist a critical mass of leisure needs, accommodations, shopping, food services, mass transportation, cultural and historical structures and events, plus night time stimulus. For foreign and domestic visitors, shopping is a major interest and accounts for significant expenditures. In the United Kingdom, 38% of all tourism spending is estimated to be for shopping *(Travel Industry World Yearbook, 1987)*. These are the reasons to go to the city and reason enough to stay for more than a day or so. Some isolated tourist/resort areas have declined because a critical mass of tourist components was not developed.

Theme Parks and New Malls

The suburbs of cities contain the amusement parks just as they did at the turn of the century. There are some differences. These suburbs are newer and farther from the city center than those eighty years ago, and the larger amusement parks, now called theme parks and shopping malls, are big business enterprises. The International Association of Amusement Parks and Attractions estimate that in 1987, 600 amusement parks in the United States had 235 million paid visitors. These visitors spent $4 billion. Many funseekers are repeat visitors. The themed park, labelled after Walt Disney's 1955 Disneyland in California, because it was divided by various structural and landscaped themes such as Tomorrowland, Fantasyland, etc., is today a high technology operation that has attracted to its environs a host of supporting facilities and services. The amusement-park association believes that 28 of the 40 largest metropolitan areas have at least one park within a radius of 100 miles (*Newsweek,* June 27, 1988). The parks attracting the most visitors are Walt Disney World and Epcot Center (Experimental Prototype Community of Tomorrow) in Florida, 22 million; Disneyland in California, 12 million and Sea World of Florida, 4 million.

These parks are as successful as man's imagination and the fullness of his pocketbook. Disneyland originally cost $17 million in 1955. It was situated on 73 acres. Disney World required an estimated investment of $400 million and the purchase of 27,520 acres. The Disney Corporation learned their lesson in California. Disney World was developed from swampland with not only a theme park, but what amounts to a variety of resort settings which include hotels, shopping malls, sport facilities, and convention centers. Examples of the investment and variety of facilities developed include a Contemporary Resort, Polynesian Resort, Disney Inn, Disney Village Resort, Disney Caribbean Beach Resort, Grand Floridian Beach Resort and Disney's Beach and Yacht Club Resort, all within the vicinity of the Epcot or the Magic Kingdom. These themed resort hotel complexes contain more than 6,000 rooms with more hotel construction planned. Disney, however, does not have a monopoly on accommodations. In the Orlando area there were more than 59,000 rooms in 1987 *(Travel Industry World Yearbook, 1988)*. The concept of a critical mass to attract and keep the leisure traveler on Disney property for the duration of their stay has been an unquestioned success. Indeed Disney theme parks are known worldwide. Tokyo Disneyland opened in 1983 and a Disneyland is now under construction near Paris, France.

Theme parks are very expensive to build and, with few exceptions, most parks in operation were built prior to 1977. Water parks, with a good location have been successful ventures in recent years but are limited by seasonality since few are enclosed. Water parks, like theme parks, have experienced increasing costs for liability insurance and some marginal ventures have closed as a result.

The future may hold promise for theme park development in conjunction with the shopping mall. The West Edmonton Mall in Edmonton, Alberta, is the likely prototype for such structures. This megamall contains 5.2 million square feet and cost $750 million to construct. It receives 100,000 people a day *(Travel Industry World Yearbook, 1987)*. It encloses a skating rink, marine theater, roller coaster, lake and swimming pool, video arcade, petting zoo, 13 fountains, 20 theaters, 135 eating places and 828 stores. On some business days, 40% of mall visitors are from the United States. The success of this venture will cause it to be emulated elsewhere.

The Resorts

If the tourist product is the resort or historic town, or an amalgam of natural or man-made attractions, it follows that the industry which services this product will be concentrated in quite specific locations which are associated with it. From the large, brash seaside resorts such as Blackpool or Brighton in England, or Atlantic City or Miami Beach in the United States, they all have one feature in common — a large part of their economy is bound up with hosting for and entertaining visitors.

Resorts in general are peripheral (Figure 17) — both in North America and Western Europe — and most have coastal location. The popularity of seaside holidays in Britain has long established the pre-eminence of coastal towns as centers of the tourist industry. In Western Europe (including Britain), over 90% of resorts have a coastal location. Added to these are two other types of resort — the capital cities such as London, Paris, Rome, Washington D..C., or Ottawa whose position as centers of government, business and culture make them major attractions in their own right, and secondly European towns with historic cultural associations such as Stratford, York, Heidlberg, or Oxford.

The traditional resort town shows a pattern of land use that is often centered on the 'resort' function of the town. Thus the traditional seaside resort shows a pattern of land use, shape and layout that is repeated world-wide. Buildings with a tourism function, and the associated infrastructure of the resort, are often concentrated in a relatively narrow sector of the town, such as along the coastal/beach-front strip — particularly opposite the main pier/amusement park or casino — with a gradual decline in tourist activity away from the main foci of interest. Most seaside resorts expanded parallel to the sea-front with relatively little development inland.

The townscape of most resorts reflects their history of rapid development with a great influx of capital investment in the form of hotels, entertainment complexes, amusement parks, promenades and piers — all of which are so familiar to us today. As Gunn has stated: 'Probably no other land form has been as compelling for tourism as the waterfront, especially the coastal zone' *(Vacationscape-- Designing Tourist Regions, 1988)*. However, Gunn states that the linear coast requires special designs. He has classified the coast into four zones each with unique needs. The 'near-shore' zone *(Neretic)* is just off the beach and is the water activity zone for sailing, surfing and fishing. It contains sandbars and, in tropical zones, coral reefs. The *beach* itself supports water oriented activities for swimming, beach games, socializing and 'people watching.' The *Shoreland* behind the beach is a place of commercial lodging and park development and must have both

Figure 17:

RESORT HOTEL CENTERS OF THE UNITED STATES

(BY NUMBER OF ROOMS: 1985–1986)

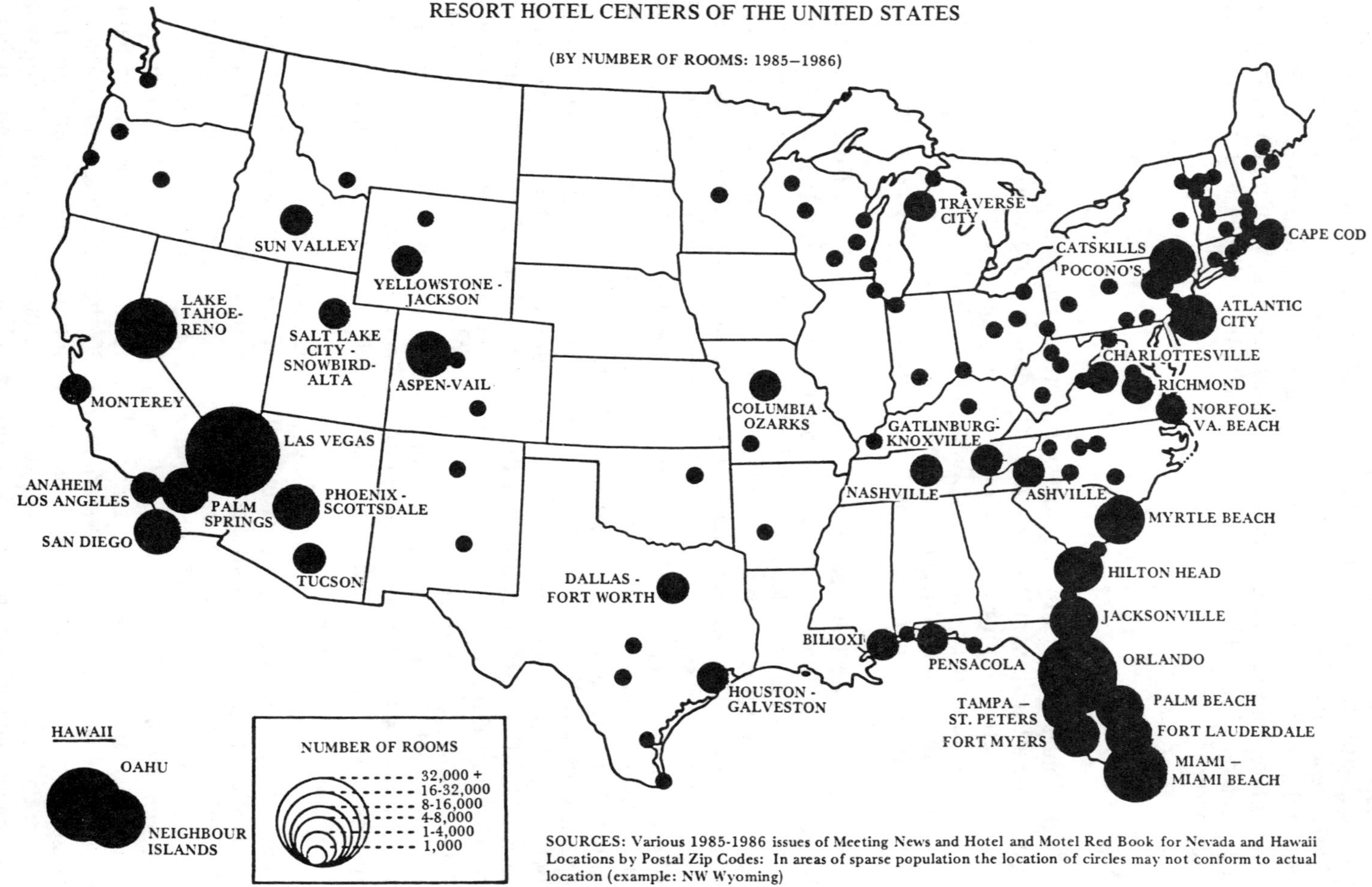

SOURCES: Various 1985-1986 issues of Meeting News and Hotel and Motel Red Book for Nevada and Hawaii Locations by Postal Zip Codes: In areas of sparse population the location of circles may not conform to actual location (example: NW Wyoming)

visual and physical access to the beach. The coastal backland *(Vicinage)* provides the setting for more resort-hotel and private home or cottage developments. These zones are shown in Figure 18. Also illustrated are Gunn's other unique drawings of past and potential waterfront scenarios. Examples of all these scenarios can be found in most countries where coastal resorts are located.

In Britain, most resorts were well-established by the late nineteenth century. For most tourists up to the 1960s the most popular form of travel was by rail, and having arrived by train, the visitor found the resort a self-contained provider of all his needs, from accommodation to entertainment, because he was not mobile and spent most of his vacation within the resort. This was reflected in the layout of the seaside resorts, with the railway station, the main shopping and tourist streets leading to or along the sea-front, which usually had a promenade and pier. Along this sea-front area were grouped the hotels and boarding houses, shops and entertainment areas.

Although this range of land uses persists, the types of tourists and the patterns of tourism are quite different from those who contributed to the original growth and wealth of resorts. Today's tourist, if they are from overseas, will be visiting several resorts, perhaps staying a short time in each, and will be highly mobile. Most domestic vacationers arrive by car and more often tend to use resorts for short break vacations in spring or autumn as a supplement to an annual vacation abroad. They have quite different wants and objectives compared with their predecessors. They are much more mobile, much more curious about the surrounding area, and more affluent and discriminating. Seaside resorts have had to adapt to this new kind of tourist, and to more fierce competition from abroad or other alternative forms of tourist destination.

Resort hotels within and outside the country are major attractions for U.S. tourists. The gambling meccas, Las Vegas and Atlantic City, have an appeal not only for the gambler but as centers of lavish stage shows and outdoor sporting activities. According to the publication *Tourism's Top Twenty,* in 1986 two of the top four resort hotels in terms of annual sales were: the Las Vegas Hilton and Atlantic City's Resorts International Hotel. The Las Vegas Hilton has 3,174 rooms, 12 restaurants, 22 shops, 6 tennis courts, an 18-hole golf course, a health club and 220,000 square feet of convention space. The remaining two resort hotels of the top four were the Boca Raton Hotel and Club, in Florida, and the Opryland Hotel in Nashville, Tennessee. Nashville is the center of country music with the Grand Ole Opry and Opryland Theme Park. The city hosts about 7 million tourists a year *(Travel Industry World Yearbook, 1988)* most on package tours.

The islands of the Caribbean provide North Americans with their own Mediterranean Sea for an escape to a warmer climate. The Caribbean and Gulf of Mexico regions have a longer warm season than Mediterranean locations and are a winter and summer haven for tourists. The Bahamas nearest to the mainland, and the Territory of Puerto Rico, receive the most travelers from the United States (Table 7). Other sun, sea and sand resorts for U.S. tourists are the Gulf of Mexico and Pacific Coastal resorts of Cancun, Acapulco, Puerto Vallarta, and Mazatlan. European vacationers have the Canary Islands and Bermuda as temperate ocean resort retreats to the West, while North Americans have the Hawaiian Islands. The tourist industry is worth about $6 billion to the Hawaiian economy. In 1987, 20 million passengers embarked or disembarked at the Honolulu International Airport. The island of Oahu has more than 37,000 hotel rooms and condo units

Figure 18: COASTAL ZONE SENARIOS

Urban Waterfronts

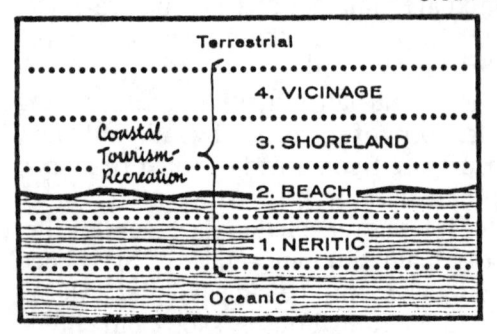

6-17. *Littoral coastal zones.* Four coastal zones with differing tourism design potential.

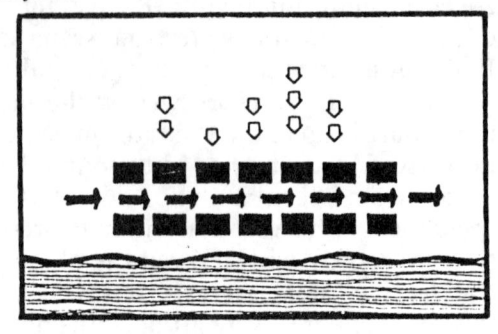

6-18 *Traditional coastal development.* In the past, highways too close to the shoreline have restricted use of this valuable asset to only a few people, blocking views and access from the backlands.

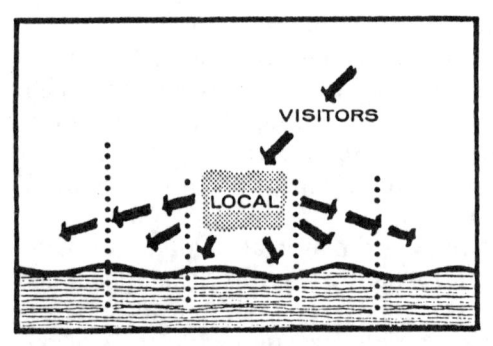

6-19. *Coastal zone protection.* By keeping access highways back and allowing access to segments, one can greatly increase the destination's potential while protecting the environment.

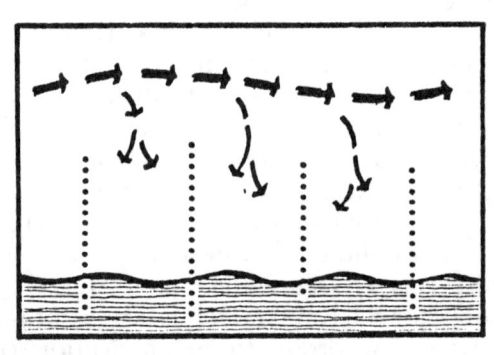

6-20. *Typical approach to coastal attractions.* Residents and visitors most often approach coasts through coastal cities.

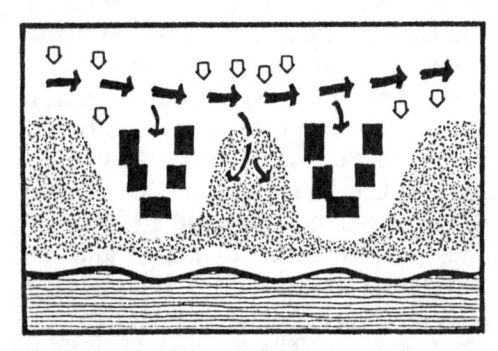

6-21. *Building envelopes.* Groups of structures separated by open space offer an environmentally sensitive solution and protect access and vistas to waterfronts.

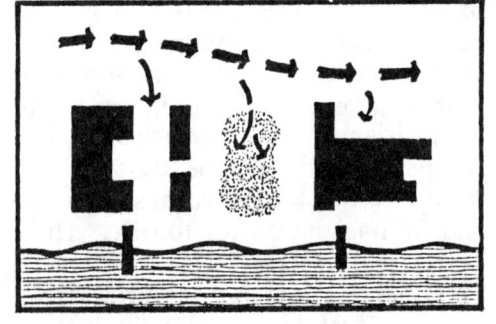

6-22. *Waterfront industrial tourism.* The water's edge holds fascination for visitors, especially if they are given public park access.

Reproduced from <u>Vacationscape Designing Tourist Regions</u> by C. A. Gunn with the permission of the Author and Publisher, Van Nostrand Reinhold.

for vacation rental and, in 1986, Honolulu's average hotel occupancy percentage was 86.8% *(Travel Weekly, 1988)*. Four million annual visitors stay an average of seven days.

Attractions whether natural, climatic, or cultural, are the energizing factor in leisure travel. When attractions are clustered with support services, and are accessible, they will usually succeed. Examples of other types of attractions are living history museums, ethnic and religious complexes, industrial plant tours, breweries, wineries, aquariums, sealife parks, World's Fairs and other types of festivals.

Table 7:
Caribbean Destinations of U.S. Visitors — 1987

COUNTY OR TERRITORY	NUMBER (in thousands)
Bahamas	1,300
Puerto Rico	1,300
Jamaica	545
U.S. Virgin Islands	505
Dominican Republic	300
St. Martin/SINT Maarten	280
Barbados	175
Cayman Islands	170
Aruba	161
British Virgin Islands	116

Source: Caribbean Tourism Research and Development Center

One of the overriding issues facing many traditional resorts is that of adapting the resort amenities and infrastructure to meet the changing needs of tourists in the 1980s and beyond. Resorts need to identify development opportunities, they need to consider ways and means of increasing their share of the tourist market, of attracting commercial investment and of promoting the resort development package.

A key element in their development strategy is the provision of all-weather leisure attractions in the form of indoor resort complexes, such as the multi-million pound Sandcastle development opened in Blackpool (England) in 1986.

ASSIGNMENTS:

1) Select a city or region and inventory the tourism and travel products that are available. Classify these products using a generic approach. Have these attractions in the area selected reached their full potential for development?

2) Using the U.S. Census of Services data for the two most recent surveys, look at the changing nature of tourism and travel employment. What sectors of the industry have shown the greatest change? From your reading, can you account for these changes?

Chapter 4
International Tourism : An Overview

Learning Objectives: After reading this chapter and the source material referred to, and tackling one of the assignments, you should understand the nature, scope and distribution of international tourism, the factors that influence its development and its importance in the world economy.

Introduction

Tourism is the largest industry in the world, and by any definition the most international activity. International Tourism, that is travel for holiday or pleasure from one country to another, is not a new phenomenon and can be traced back to Greek and Roman times. As Chapter 2 indicated, international tourism grew rapidly through the nineteenth and early twentieth centuries, but in terms of sheer volume of tourists travelling abroad, it is a relatively recent phenomenon. Mass tourism is a post World War II development. This chapter seeks to give a brief account of recent trends in international tourism and its impact on the world's economy and analyzes the factors that have affected, and are likely to affect, the future expansion of international tourism.

Data Sources on International Tourism

The most comprehensive set of statistics on international tourism are published by the Organization for Economic Cooperation and Development, based in Paris. This organization, which was established in 1960, represents most of the advanced industrial nations of the world and includes among its members all the European countries, the United States, Japan, New Zealand and Australia. The OECD publishes an annual report on *Tourism Policy and International Tourism in OECD Member Countries* and this contains a wide range of detailed returns on tourist flows and expenditures for all the OECD member states. The first half of this annual report includes a country by country update on government policy and action relating to tourism. Although this OECD data provides much valuable information on international tourist flows, it must be used carefully. Each member state makes a count of all foreign visitors as they enter the country and this is recorded under 'arrivals'. If, for example, an English tourist is en route overland for Austria, he could be recorded as an 'arrival' in France, Germany and Switzerland before he reaches his main tourist destination, so it is important to treat 'arrivals' statistics with caution. Moreover, no checks are made on the purpose of the visit, and few countries collect detailed information on the international travel patterns of their own population.

Since 1966, the World Tourism Organization has produced an *Annual*

Economic Review of World Tourism. However, although this includes information on Africa, Asia and Oceania not contained in the OECD report, it does not have the sheer volume of detailed statistical data and is much more of an annual overview of trends in the main regions of the world.

A further useful source is a US publication, the *Travel Industry World Yearbook : The Big Picture.* This publication, which appears annually, provides a very comprehensive overview of trends in World Tourism drawing on a wide range of national and international tourist statistics. Although biased towards the USA market, it brings together a valuable set of data on travel trends, economic and political influences and forecasts on the future prospects for world tourism.

The Economist Intelligence Unit publishes *International Tourism Quarterly,* renamed *International Tourism Reports* in 1986, which provides detailed country and regional profiles of tourism. EIU also publishes *Travel and Tourism Analyst* on a monthly basis, an invaluable source of data on international tourism developments.

One of the problems faced when dealing with international travel and tourism statistics is that there are great differences between international organizations and individual countries in the coverage and systems of data collection. The four main international organizations dealing with the collection of travel and tourism data are the United National Statistical Office (UNSO), the World Tourism Organization (WTO), the International Civil Aviation Organization (ICAO) and the International Air Transport Association (IATA). These four bodies use six different classifications for world tourism regions. The Department of Trade and Industry in the UK, groups tourism origin and destination countries into four regions, while the US Travel and Tourism Administration uses nine regions worldwide. This variation in systems of regionalization means that data on tourist flows within and between regions must be treated with caution.

Tourist Generating Countries

Although Tourism is now a world-wide phenomenon, the main tourist generating countries are concentrated in North America and Western Europe. Two countries in particular, West Germany and the United States, account for about 40 per cent of tourist arrivals, and Europe and North America account for 83 per cent of the entire movement of international tourist arrivals. (WTO 1986). This pattern has remained fairly constant for the past 20 years, although Japan is now becoming more important as a tourist generating country. Table 8 on page 59 which is based on WTO and OECD statistics, emphasizes the predominance of the United States and Europe on the world scene.

The main tourist generating countries have five common characteristics. Their domestic populations have the disposable income to spend on foreign holidays; they have a level of awareness of foreign countries, through literature, the media and promotional campaigns; the infrastructure exists to package, sell and organize foreign travel; they have the free time to take holidays and, lastly, the geographical characteristics of these regions provide a variety of destinations that are in close proximity and accessible.

Table 8:
**International Tourist Arrivals
(Millions) 1965 — 1987**

Region	1965	1975	1985	1987
Africa	2,083	3,500	9,819	10,000
Middle East	2,835	3,000	7,115	7,500
Europe	85,993	151,500	227,645	234,500
Latin America & Caribbean	3,759)	47,000	58,609	66,000
North America	19,394)			
Asia & Australasia	1,829	8,000	29,524	37,000
	115,893	213,000	332,712	355,000

Source: World Tourism Organization

Table 9:
**International Tourist Receipts
(Millions $) 1965 — 1987**

Region	1965	1975	1985	1987
Africa	296	3,000	2,000	3,500
Middle East	296	420	1,500	4,500
Europe	7,249	17,600	64,000	90,000
Latin America & Caribbean	1,365)	6,400	18,500	31,500
North America	1,903)			
Asia & Australasia	523	4,480	6,500	20,500
	11,632	31,900	92,500	150,000

Source: World Tourism Organization

General Trends in International Tourism

In 1987, total international trips, including travel for holidays and leisure as well as for business and other special reasons, were estimated at $355 million (WTO 1986) and total receipt from internation travel were $92.5 million. The demand for internation tourism (Figure 19) has increased steadily since 1960 and the total number of arrivals has grown more than four times over the past 27 years. However, although demand has grown dramatically, most of thishas remained concentrated in Europe and North America (Figure 20). Despite this, the developing countries have increased their share of tourist arrivals every year. Some regions such as parts of North Africa, East Asia, and the Pacific have shown above average growth in their share of tourist arrivals.

In the Americas, over 7 million more tourists arrived between 1985 and 1987, but Central and South America and the Caribbean showed a greater overall growth in international arrivals. Most of the tourist traffic is generated by the USA and Canada, who accounted, for example, for 90% of arrivals in the Carib-

Figure 19:

International Tourism Demand

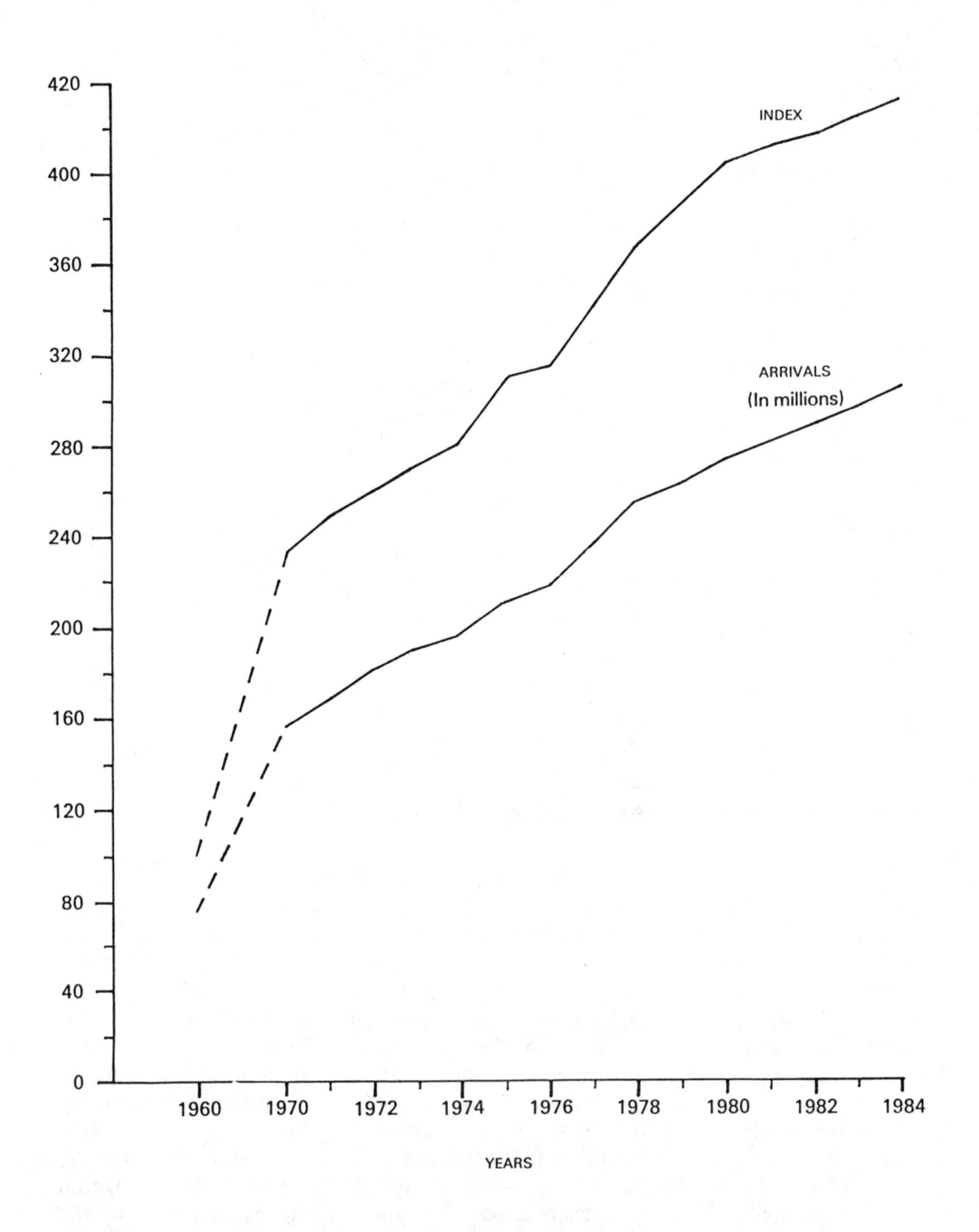

YEARS

Figure 20: **The Growth of International Tourist Expenditures in EEC Compared with North America and Total OECD Countries, 1972—1981 (1972=100)**

········· EEC as a percentage of Total Europe
— — — EEC as a percentage of North America
——— EEC as a percentage of Total OECD

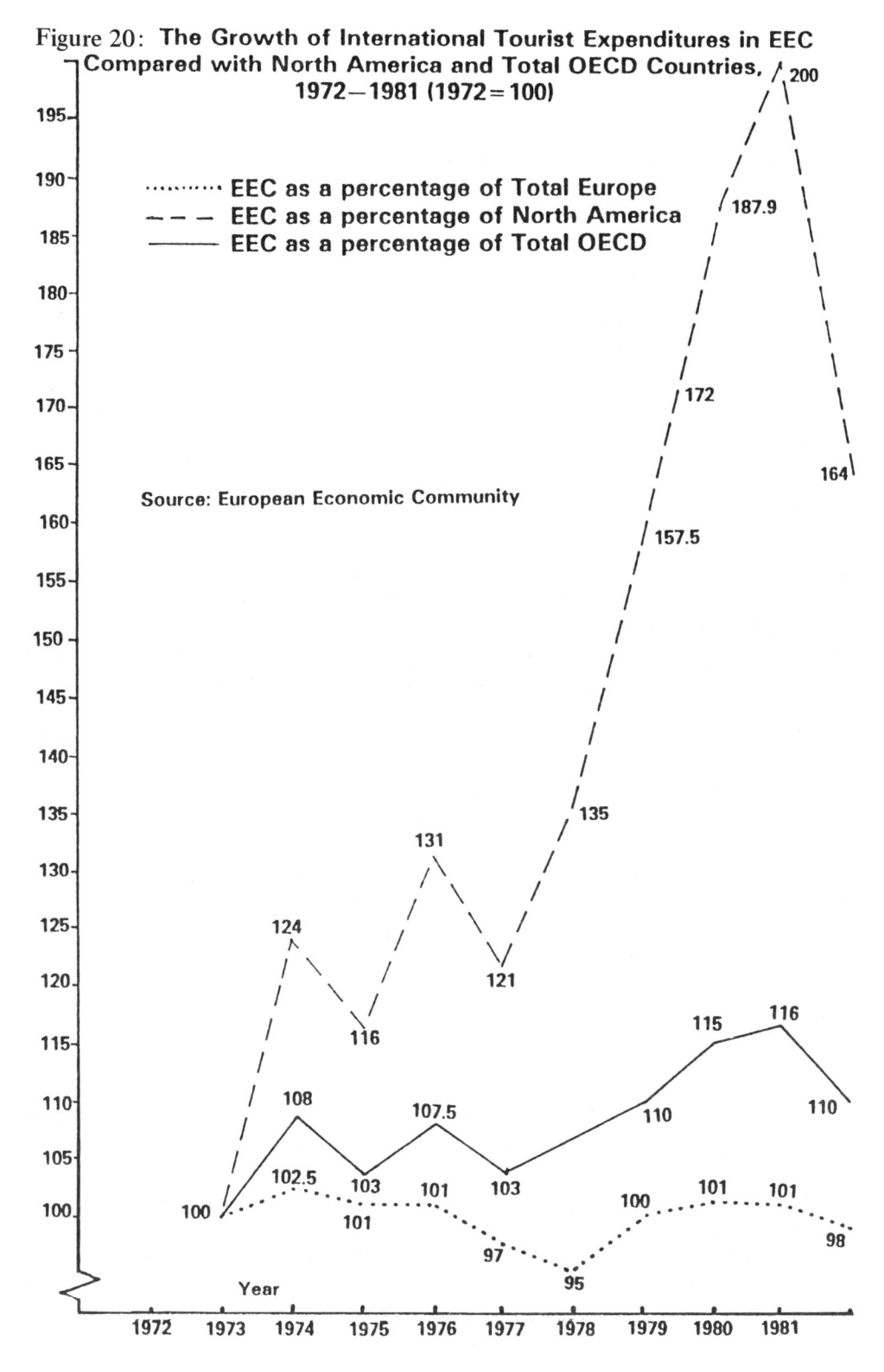

Source: European Economic Community

bean (WTO 1986). Because of the sheer size of the USA and Canada, and the vast distances involved in traveling to other countries, most of their domestic populations prefer to take holidays within their own countries. Similarly, in Central and South America over 75% of arrivals are from within Latin America.

In the early 1980s, Europe alone took up 70% of international tourist arrivals. The strength of Europe both as a generator and receiver of tourists is due to the following factors:

(i) More than half of the population takes a period of paid holidays and leisure every year;

(ii) European incomes are higher than incomes in many regions of the world and there is a comparable system of paid leave, flexible frontier controls, protection of tourists and a government commitment to tourism development;

(iii) There is a large and well established tourist industry and infrastructure;

(iv) There is a wealth of natural, cultural and historical attractions;

(v) The geography of Europe means that distances between countries are relatively small: there is a comprehensive road, rail and air network which makes travel quick and easy; and Europeans are highly mobile.

Within Europe, in the period between 1967 and 1987, there has been a redistribution of tourist demand with Britain, Spain and Greece sharing the greatest growth income from international tourism. Between 1967 and 1981, the number of overseas visitors to Britain increased by 500% and to Greece by over 160%. For the same period, Europe as a whole almost doubled its share of international tourism, taking $58,000 million in 1984 (WTO 1986). Eighty per cent of international travel in Europe is a result of intra-European travel. This is particularly the case in the main European tourist destinations, where intra-regional arrivals accounted for 91 per cent of international arrivals to Italy and 95 per cent to Spain. In 1987, Spain received over 51 million visitors with a revenue of over $10 million.

In Africa, the recovery in travel to the Mediterranean coast of North Africa largely accounts for the growth in international tourism to the continent in the 1980s. This part of Northern Africa, with its proximity to the main tourist generating countries of Europe and a long established tourism tradition, accounts for over 60 per cent of international arrivals in Africa. The other main tourist region is West Africa, particularly Kenya and Zimbabwe which receive over 17 per cent of international arrivals (WTO 1986).

The growth of international tourism in Africa was encouraged by increased promotion and the development of inclusive tours designed to attract tourists from Europe and North America. Between 1977 and 1983, tourism receipts in Africa increased by over 9 per cent per year, with Southern Africa achieving the fastest growth with over 20 per cent per year (WTO 1987).

In East Asia and the Pacific, there were over 26.5 million tourist arrivals in 1984 (WTO 1986). The main tourist destinations within the region are Singapore, Hong Kong, Fiji and Samoa. Table 10 on page 63 brings out the importance of tourism to the economies of these areas. Asia is the second most popular long-haul market for Europeans after the United States. In 1984, about 3.2 million Europeans traveled to Asia compared with 1.6 million to sub-Saharan Africa and 1 million to

Table 10:
International Tourist Receipts as a proportion of national income for selected destinations

Place	International Tourist Receipts as a proportion of national income
	Per Cent
Singapore	16.0
Fiji	13.0
Samoa	12.5
Hong Kong	5.5

(By comparison UK = 1.2 per cent)

(Source: WTO Economic Review of World Tourism 1986)

---

the Caribbean. Although there was growth in business travel from Europe to Hong Kong and Japan in the first half of the 1980s, there has only been a slight increase in leisure travel to this region. The weakening of the dollar — to which a number of Asian currencies are linked — will have an impact, and should encourage the growth of long haul trips in the late 1980s.

In Japan, the domestic tourist industry is having to deal with the long term increase in the value of the yen against other international currencies, and arrivals figures in 1986 showed a continuing drop in the number of inland tourists. In contrast, the Japanese outbound market is very strong with over 6.5 million Japanese taking overseas holidays in 1987.

The economic significance of international tourism is best measured by comparing receipts with Gross Domestic Product (GDP) and expenditures with Private Final Consumption (PFC). Unfortunately, it is not possible to make detailed comparisons on a world scale because of the deficiencies in world economic data, and in this case the only detailed data exist for the OECD member states.

Table 11 indicates the relative share of tourist activity in total economic activity for 1981. It shows that total receipts accounted for the greatest direct contri-

Table 11:
The Share of Tourist Activity in Total Economic Activity, 1981

	Receipts as a % GDP			Expenditures as a % of PFC		
	Internal	Domestic	Total	Internal	Domestic	Total
Belgium & Luxembourg	1.6	1.7	3.3	4.2	2.7	6.9
Denmark	2.1	1.1	3.2	3.9	1.9	5.8
France	1.2	4.0	5.2	1.5	6.1	7.6
Germany	0.9	3.7	4.6	4.3	6.2	10.5
Greece	4.9	0.2	5.1	0.9	0.2	1.1
Ireland	3.1	0.8	3.9	5.2	1.3	6.5
Italy	2.1	1.8	3.9	0.7	2.8	3.5
Netherlands	1.2	2.1	3.3	4.7	3.7	8.4
UK	1.2	1.7	2.9	2.1	2.7	4.8
EUR-10	1.4	2.8	4.2	2.6	4.5	7.1

Sources: OECD, Tourism Policy and International Tourism, Paris, 1982, and Commission of the European Communities, European Economy, November 1981.

bution to economic activity in France and Greece, where they came to over 5 per cent of GDP, and Germany and the United Kingdom (over 4 per cent of GDP).

Total tourist expenditures as a component of Private Final Consumption were most important in West Germany where they accounted for 10.5 per cent of PFC, and France (7.6%). This percentage was least significant in Greece (only 1% of PFC).

The contribution of tourism to economic activity is significantly greater than the estimates based on direct visitor spending would suggest. Tourist spending in a region also makes an indirect contribution to the economy, as receipts are re-spent within the country or region, thereby generating further income as the effects of the initial spending continue to filter through the economy. This issue is discussed in greater detail in Chapter 11 which considers the income 'multiplier effect' as this process is known.

Factors Affecting the Development of International Tourism

The growth and development of international tourism can be influenced by direct government intervention in the management of tourist resources, especially in those countries where the tourist sector is an important element in the national development plan. However, the private sector usually has a crucial part to play in the development of tourist facilities.

The first stage is to develop an effective plan to market a locality for international tourists. In order to do this several basic questions must be asked, such as:

'What is the existing market for tourism from abroad?'
'What tourist products and services do we have?'
'What are the prospects for growth?'
'What will attract potential visitors to the country?'
'What are the strengths and weaknesses of our tourist product?'
'What alternative destinations are there for international tourists?'
'Can our existing infrastructure cope with an increase in tourist numbers?'

In order to provide answers to these questions, the public or private tourist organization will have to carry out detailed research. This may be desk research or field research, and both of these methods are examined in more detail in Chapter 10.

At a material level, development of international tourism can be encouraged by promoting a range of natural and created tourist facilities. For those countries with tourism potential, where international tourism has not yet developed, the first task is to produce a detailed survey of existing tourist attractions whether they are natural (scenery, climate, wildlife), cultural (museums and galleries, theaters, historic buildings or sites), or entertainments. The process of planning and development of tourism is discussed in more detail in Chapter 9.

There are three general factors that will influence the development of international tourism, particularly in the developing regions of the world. These are:

(i)   a growth in lower cost long-distance travel;

(ii) provision of suitable accommodation and tourist facilities in the destination countries and a properly trained workforce to service them;

(iii) a stable political and financial climate.

The introduction of larger aircraft, such as the Boeing 747, has already had a dramatic impact on long-haul flights. The deregulation of airline fares, and the introduction of new types of aircraft with lower unit costs, should enable lower fares to be introduced. The growth of inclusive tour packages should help to reduce the overall cost of international travel together with creative pricing policies for the off-peak season. Boeing forecasts, in its *Current Market Outlooks,* that annual increases in air travel in the 1990s will be greater than the total size of the market in 1960. One impetus to increased air travel will be the development of more fuel-efficient engines and lighter airframes which will offer much greater operating range for aircraft. Improvements in aircraft technology will also enable aircraft to fly to long-haul destinations on two engines where three or four would have been necessary before.

During the 1990s, the new generation Boeing 747 – 400 is expected to dominate the long-haul tourism market. Already, non-stop flights are available to Hong Kong from the UK, and there will be an upward growth in non-stop flights between Europe and the Far East and the United States and Australasia. If the demand for international tourism continues as predicted, the Boeing company plan to launch a further aircraft, the 747 – 500 model, in the mid 1990s with a range of over 8,500 miles and over 500 seats.

The most dramatic growth in air travel is expected to be in Asia where its market share of world traffic is expected to increase from 25.8% in 1982 to 33.3% in 1992. (ICAO).

Having made it easier to travel from Europe to say the Seychelles or Sri Lanka, it is important that the tourist destination has the infrastructure and trained staff to handle tourists en masse. Any new tourist facilities will be competing with much nearer and more familiar tourist attractions and will have to offer amenities and facilities that are of a high standard and at a competitive price. In breaking into a new market, it is essential that the new tourist destination does not simply replicate facilities found all over Europe. The aim should be to develop distinctive facilities that relate to and enhance the atmosphere of the country

At the same time there is a need to develop and train a workforce for the newly-emerging tourist industry. The quality of service that international tourists receive is at least as important, if not more so, than the standard of tourist facilities. This training will need to take account of:

— New techniques and technology, including computerized reservation and booking systems and modern production techniques particularly for food service and preparation.

— Restructuring employment in the tourism enterprize so as to increase the level of services. This is particularly important in developing countries where local unemployment levels may be high.

— Adapting training to improve the level and quality of personal service provided. Although more international tourists are opting for an informal, independent form of travel, the idea of personal service is becoming increasingly valued. Moreover, the search for greater cultural content in holidays, and the development of special interest tourism, provide increasing opportunities for careers in these tourist activities.

The importance of a stable political and financial climate is crucial for the future development of international tourism. Three quite different examples help to emphasize this point. In April 1986, President Reagan approved a bombing raid on Libya using aircraft based in Britain. One immediate repercussion was a fear of terrorist reprisals, leading to a dramatic decline in Americans travelling to Europe. In Britain, in May 1986, there were 40 per cent fewer Americans than in the same month in 1985. Overall in 1986, Britain lost about $435 million in tourist revenue because of the sharp fall in American tourists. The picture was worse in Europe where US tourists were down 60 per cent in Greece and France, and 50 per cent down in Italy. In Northern Ireland, after 18 years of civil strife and bombings, the international tourist industry, which once was thriving, has all but collapsed. In Sri Lanka, once a fast-growing tourist destination, civil war has had similar impact on the tourist traffic, where the number of visitors between 1981 and 1984 fell by over 54,000. However, the current outlook is more promising.

A stable financial climate is important for two particular reasons. First, the private sector needs to have confidence in the stability of the national economy before it will invest in tourism development projects, and often loans and other financial concessions will be necessary for the development of tourist facilities in the early stages. Secondly, exchange rates can play a major part in international travel, particularly to and from the United States. When the value of the US dollar is high compared to other (European) currencies this acts as a greater incentive for Americans to travel abroad. Conversely, a high value dollar will cause a sharp decline in the inflow of overseas visitors to the United States.

ASSIGNMENTS

1. Using data on international tourist arrivals for 1965 and 1985 produce 2 maps to show the main tourist flows and identify:

    (a) the main tourist generating countries;
    (b) the main destinations;
    (c) the main links and routes between them.

    Give a brief account of the changes that have taken place in this period and suggest reasons for these.

2. Identify what you think will be the major international tourist destinations in the 1990s and justify the choices that you have made.

Chapter 5

The Retail Travel Sector

Learning Objectives: After reading this chapter you should have an introduction to the retail travel business and an understanding of:

— the range of services offered by the retail travel agent;
— the place of the retail travel sector in the tourist industry;
— the procedures involved in setting up and managing a travel agency;
— the relationship between travel agents and tour operators;
— job opportunities, total manpower needs, and the future of this sector of the tourist industry.

Introduction

The retail travel sector — in the form of the High or Main Street travel agent — is the one activity most clearly recognized by the general public to represent the tourist industry. Travel agents have been in existence for over 100 years, with Thomas Cook pioneering the business. Although Thomas Cook began as a tour operator, the rapid growth in his business led to him opening an office in London and acting as a sales agent for several steamship lines and railway companies. By the end of the nineteenth century, travel agencies had developed in the United States, including American Express which, as an offshoot of the Wells Fargo Company, borrowed Cook's idea of traveller's cheques in 1891.

However, it was not until the 1950s and 1960s that the number of travel agencies increased dramatically. This was due largely to two factors:

(i) The large-scale growth of the commercial airlines. By the end of the 1930s, there were over 50 commercial airlines worldwide flying over 200 million miles, serving over 400,000 passengers. (Lickorish & Kershaw 1958). These commercial airlines soon discovered the benefits of allowing travel agents to promote their services and were willing to pay commissions for this.

(ii) The post-war growth in package tours beginning with the early charter flights and foreign holiday packages, put together by enterprising tour operators who then used the retail travel agencies to sell this product. Now the bulk of British retail travel agents' business is package holidays.

In Britain there are now about 7,000 retail travel agents, 5,000 of whom are members of the Association of British Travel Agents (ABTA) and 2,000 who are non-members. In the United States, there are about 30,000 retail travel agents (Figure 21). In 1987, the U.S. Bureau of Labor Statistics released data stating that the travel agency industry will experience the second fastest growth rate in

Figure 21: TRAVEL AGENCIES 1986

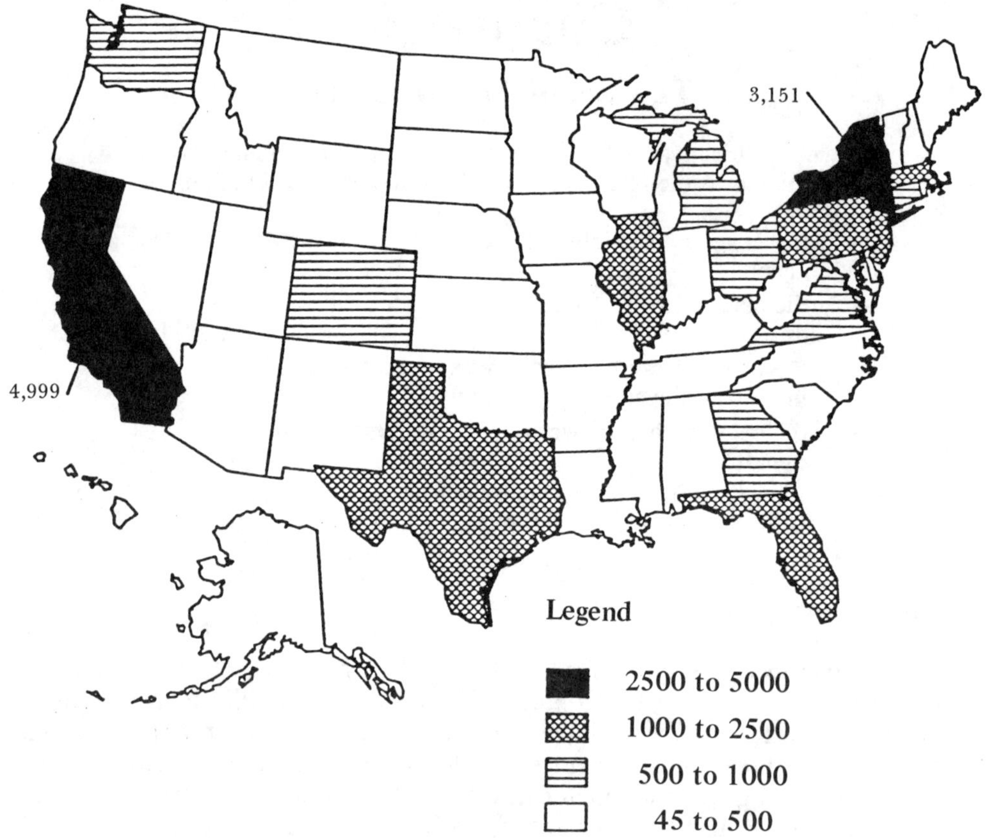

3,151

4,999

Legend

- ■ 2500 to 5000
- ▨ 1000 to 2500
- ☰ 500 to 1000
- ☐ 45 to 500

Source: Airlines Reporting Corporation, *Travel Weekly* Jan 26, 1987

the nation until the year 2,000. A growth rate of 5.9% is projected. Only the computer equipment industry has a higher projected rate at 7.4%. Since travel agencies are dependent upon computers the two fastest growing industries are dependent upon each other. There are now 170,000 full time employees in the passenger transportation arrangement industry and, by the year 2,000, the lowest projection is that there will be 217,000 employees.

Services Offered by the Travel Agent

Most tourists are unaware that the travel agent is acting on behalf of a third party. The travel agent is a retailer and, with the exception of a few agents who are also tour operators (for example Thomas Cook), the agent does not put together the tours or package holidays but only promotes or sells them on behalf of the tour operator. Most small towns and every city will have a number of travel agents in their main shopping district, and although there are a number of large national chains, many agencies are small in size, perhaps employing 4 or 5 staff.

What is the role and function of the travel agent?

The travel agent generally offers the following range of services:

— selling prepared package tours, preparing individual itineraries, personally escorted tours and group tours;
— arranging transport; selling airline tickets, rail, coach, and cruise trips and arranging car rental abroad;
— arranging hotels, motels, sightseeing trips, music festivals, transfers of passengers between terminals and hotels;
— handling and advising on many details involved in travel, especially foreign travel, such as travel and luggage insurance, medical insurance, travellers cheques, visa requirements and so on;
— providing information and advice on airline rail and coach schedules and fares; hotel rates; whether rooms have baths; whether their rates include local taxes. All of this information can take days of the intending tourists' time or weeks of endless phone calls and letters;
— arranging reservations for special interest activities such as business travel, sporting vacations, religious pilgrimages and so on;
— in the case of legitimate complaints from customers, writing to the principal (tour operator or airline) to try and get a refund or a written statement or apology for any mishaps that may have occurred;
— interpreting and advising clients of the many complex discounted fares offered by the airlines and to warn clients of 'overbooking'.

The travel agent then represents all the package tour companies, all the airlines and all the coach and rail operators who use his services. A good travel agent will be able to advise the potential traveler on a wide range of matters concerning his journey, accommodation and final destination (holiday resort). Agents must therefore have a good knowledge of the product, and should know what they are selling. They are giving professional advice and, if they have not been to an area or resort they are selling, they can pick up information from trade journals, promotional material and current information from colleagues who know the area. In other words, the good agent should know where to go for current information on reliable tour operators and tourist destinations. Many small travel agencies may rely on tour operators' brochures and thus offer a limited range of advice to their customers based on these brochures alone. However, there are a wide range of travel and accommodation directories available (mainly for Britain and the United States) and these provide a wealth of ancillary information on travel and accommodation which can be used to provide fast and accurate data.

Establishing a Travel Agency

The capital cost of setting up a retail travel agency is much less than for almost any other kind of retail business, because the agent requires relatively little in the form of stock. He is buying or leasing office space, viewdata systems with access to airlines and tour operators booking and information services, telephones and office equipment. The stock — in the form of brochures, tickets and related material, is supplied, sometimes at a cost, by the tour operator (wholesaler) or carrier (airline rail or cruise company). In opening a travel agency the most critical step is finding the right location. This is related to several factors such as:

— identifying the market for your product and the type of clientele you wish to attract. The location must be in a neighborhood that will service clients who will wish to take foreign or domestic package vacations, cruises, special interest vacations etc;
— the location of competitors. Although the American Society of Travel Agents (ASTA) does not object to new members on the grounds of a nearby competitor, the tour operators and transport operators may be less inclined to give agency agreements or licenses;
— accessibility. Much of the U.S. travel agent's business is conducted on one of the major airlines' computer systems. The agency must be visible and easily accessible to its customers. A ground-floor office in the main shopping and business district, with ample nearby parking is the ideal location.
— ample investment capital. Most airlines, for example, will not give commission on the sale of tickets until the agency receives appointment as an official agent for the International Air Transport Association (IATA) and (in the United States) the Airlines Reporting Corporation. Approval or licenses can take some time to obtain, and an agency should have at least 2 years operating capital available as it may take some time to make a profit from its operations.

Travel Agency Appointments and Commissions

The travel agency obtains the bulk of its income from commissions on the sale of its products and, to collect commissions must be officially appointed as an agent for the airline and transport companies and the tour operators (wholesalers). In the United States, in order to be appointed as an official travel agent, the firm must meet certain requirements set by 'conferences' representing the domestic and international airlines, shipping companies and railways. Each group has its own regulating board or 'conference'. The main conferences are the Airlines Reporting Corporation representing U.S. domestic airlines, and the International Air Transport Association (IATA), now called the International Airlines Travel Agent Network, for international airline tickets. In addition, appointments are required for cruises with the Cruise Lines International Association and from the National Railroad Passenger Corporation for Amtrak. (Figure 22).

Appointment by the Airlines Reporting Corporation is the most important prerequisite for a travel agency in the United States and, once obtained, most of the other agency appointments are relatively straightforward. To obtain an ARC appointment the travel agency must be open for business; be operated under the direction of a qualified manager; have a good credit rating and (to protect the financial interests of the public and the airlines) have its operations investigated and approved by a bonding company who will guarantee responsibility for the agency's commitments up to $15,000; have sufficient funding to operate for one year without commission from the principal; and be actively involved in the production of travel.

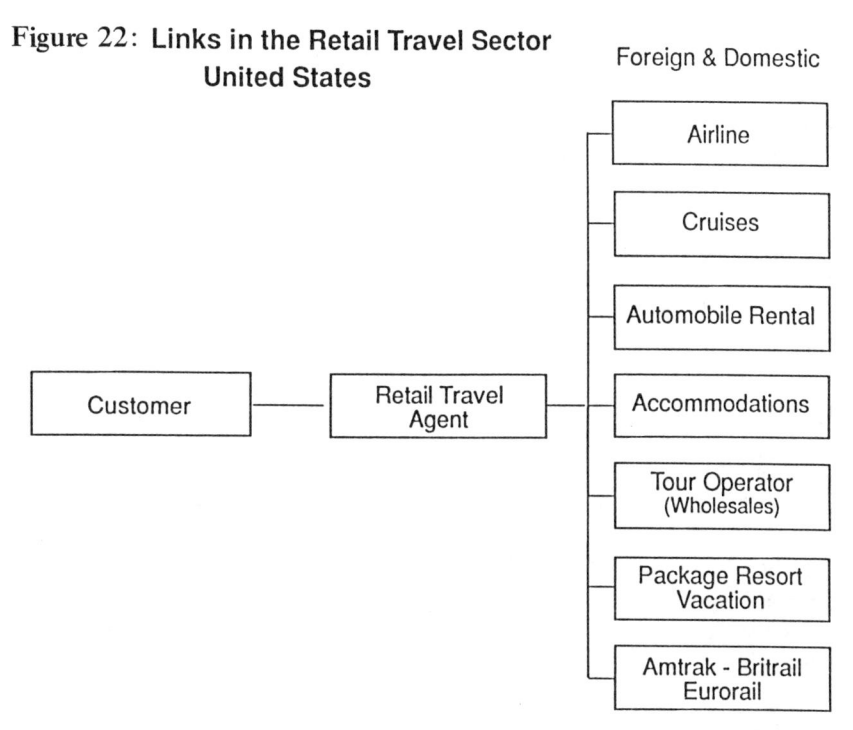

**Figure 22: Links in the Retail Travel Sector
United States**

```
                                              Foreign & Domestic
                                              ┌─ Airline
                                              ├─ Cruises
                                              ├─ Automobile Rental
Customer ── Retail Travel Agent ──────────────┼─ Accommodations
                                              ├─ Tour Operator (Wholesales)
                                              ├─ Package Resort Vacation
                                              └─ Amtrak - Britrail Eurorail
```

To obtain commission on airline ticket sales, a travel agency must obtain a license from IATA. Since any retail agency obtains much of its income from commissions on the sale of airline tickets it is usually necessary to obtain an IATA appointment. IATA insists on similar requirements for retail travel agents as those sought by the Airlines Reporting Corporation and, in addition, requires that at least one employee have one year or more experience in international ticketing and reservations. Proof that the travel agency is actively promoting international air travel is also needed.

In Britain, to obtain commission on package tour vacations offered by the main tour operators, travel agents should be members of the Association of British Travel Agents (ABTA). Prospective members of ABTA must provide evidence of financial stability and deposit a bond (of $13,500 if they are a sole trader or $6,300 if a company) in favor of ABTA as financial protection to the Association. ABTA travel agents have the sole right to sell inclusive package tours of ABTA tour operators and they do not sell package tours arranged by non-ABTA companies

**Figure 23: Links in the Retail Travel Sector
Britain**

```
                        ┌──── Tour Operator (Direct Sales) ────┬─ Accommodations
Customer ── Retail Travel Agent ─┤                              ├─ Carriers
                                 └── Tour Operator (Wholesales)─┴─ Ancillary Services
```

operators and they do not sell package tours arranged by non-ABTA companies (Figure 23). This is because ABTA has a retailer fund, paid for by members, which reimburses members of the public who have lost money following an ABTA member becoming bankrupt. This ABTA booking arrangement has been in existence since 1965 and is known in the trade as *Operation Stabiliser*.

Unlike the United States there are about 2,000 non ABTA members that offer discounts on regular charter flights to the main vacation destinations. These maverick agencies are called 'bucket shops' and are not tolerated in the United States. With the growth in air traffic in the 1970s, and the increasing competition between the major carriers, many of the airlines have established a practice in Britain of selling off unsold seats at large discounts through non-appointed travel agents. The spread and success of these 'bucket shops' is unwelcome competition for the IATA appointed travel agencies who, under the terms of their agreement, are not allowed to sell heavily discounted tickets. At the present time the ABTA/IATA agents are seeking agreement to be allowed to sell their tickets on the same basis.

Other travel services, such as car rental companies and hotels do not need individual agency appointments but will pay commissions for any reservations or bookings made by a travel agency that has been appointed as an official agent by the major travel and tourism organizations.

Commissions

Once the retail travel agent has been appointed to represent IATA, ARC or ABTA, the agency immediately becomes eligible to receive commissions on the sale of any travel tickets or tour operators' packages that are members of these associations. The amount of money the travel agency earns from these sales varies according to the supplier and the kind of service provided. (This issue is discussed in detail in the next section of this chapter.) In general terms, companies operating in the same sector of the tourist industry tend to offer the same rates of commission for specific similar services. The *rates* of commission tend to be set by the particular association. For example, IATA sets the rates for the international airline industry — at present this is generally about 8 to 10 per cent. In terms of domestic airline fares, deregulation in Britain and the United States has meant that airlines are free to establish their own rates of commission, although most have kept to deregulation levels. The cruise lines at present pay 10 per cent commission and often pay higher commission for group bookings. Most tour operators generally pay 10 per cent commission and, depending on the individual operator, this percentage may increase with group booking or marked increase in sales during the year.

In Britain, the brand leaders among the tour operators now concentrate their business on the more productive retail outlets. The most recent spur to improving efficiency and productivity among retailers is the introduction of credit card discount schemes for holidaymakers booking with Barclaycard and the TSB Trust Card (*TTG* January 1987).

A survey of travel agents' remuneration, carried out by Thornton Baker Associates on behalf of ABTA (1984), found that all the UK agents surveyed experienced a decline in profits between 1980 and 1983 (*Thornton Baker* 1984). However, those agents who concentrated on business travel showed the smallest decline, while the smaller agents, who generally tend to be less profitable, experienced the most severe decline in profits from 15% to 10%. It is clear that the larger agencies (i.e. with an income of over $900,000) are in a better position to introduce economies of scale in their operations than the smaller agents.

Sales of inclusive tours grew by 28% overall during this period, although prices showed little change and commissions showed a marginal increase from 9.1% to 9.4%. Despite this growth in volume of sales, operating costs rose by over 30% in the same period, leading to an overall decline in profits. Two conclusions from this survey were that there was some scope for fundamental improvements in the efficiency of retail travel agents, and that the existing volume of business could be carried out through a smaller number of businesses (Table 12).

Table 12: **Travel Agency Turnover as a Percentage of Total Turnover 1980 – 83**

SOURCE	1980 %	1983 %
Inclusive Tours	52.3	54.5
Air Tickets	33.0	31.1
Rail Tickets	2.7	2.6
Ferry Tickets	2.4	2.3
Insurance	0.8	1.0
Car Hire	0.3	0.3
Other	8.5	8.2
TOTAL	100.0	100.0

Source: *Thornton-Baker ABTA Survey* 1984

Given that travel agents' income is largely made up of commissions paid by tour operators and other sources, calculated by reference to the value of business transacted, it is useful to look at the sources of turnover, as a percentage of total turnover, as an indicator of the average mix of business. These are set out in Table 8 below. The average mix of business changed very little, although inclusive tours increased in overall importance.

In the United States, airline deregulation and the growth in the usage of computer reservation systems have had a considerable impact on retail travel agents over the past 10 years. Although there are now about 30,000 travel agents in the USA, just 7% of them account for 28% of agency sales, and the picture has been one of fewer agents doing more business. In many cases, declining profits have led to amalgamation and many agents have formed or joined chains that are able to offer good national coverage and the kinds of discounts on air tickets, hotel rooms and car hire that come with volume of business.

Business Travel

The business sector is often the most profitable element of retail travel and it is a fast-growing sector of the travel market, as Figure 24 clearly shows. The UK

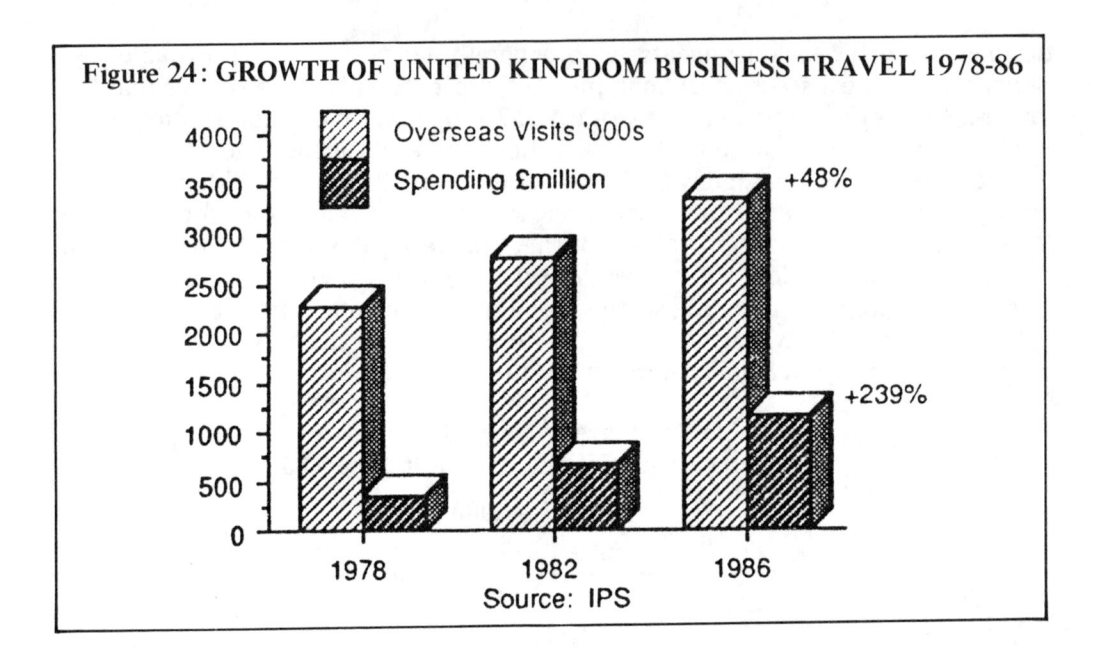

Figure 24: GROWTH OF UNITED KINGDOM BUSINESS TRAVEL 1978-86

- Overseas Visits '000s
- Spending £million

+48%
+239%

1978, 1982, 1986
Source: IPS

market for all business travel is now worth over $30 billion a year, and the volume and spending on this sector has more than doubled since 1978. The travel and tourism industry has responded to the growth in this sector of the market by providing special incentives for business travelers, with hotels, airlines and car hire companies stressing first class service and competitive price packages.

In the United States, business travel is now the third largest area of corporate expenditure, after salaries and data processing. (*ABC International* 1988). The worldwide boom in business, and the growth of conference and exhibition centers, have all contributed to the expansion in this sector. Globally, business travel is estimated to be in excess of $150 billion. A recent study of over 17,500 passengers on international scheduled airline flights found that 85% of them were flying on business.

The larger, well-established multiple retail travel chains are the market leaders in UK business travel. For example, Thomas Cook has 6,000 business clients managed through about 80 specialist travel centers. Hogg Robinson travel handles more than $300 million worth of business each year for 1,700 companies. In the United States, Hogg Robinson is a member of Woodside Management Systems which is one of the largest consortia of travel agents in the US market. Pickfords Business Travel (which recently took over Lunn Poly's Business Travel) is the third largest company dealing in this sector.

One measure of the growth in the market segment has been the growing interest in it by the financial services sector, with firms from American Express to Access and Visa and many others offering a wide range of travel support products from accessories and valet service to worldwide insurance and money supply.

If retail travel agents are to capture a share of this important market, they need to be able to offer an efficient and cost-effective service for the corporate client. This involves five main stages in business travel planning:

1. Setting out the guidelines by which executives travel and the ways in which travel arrangements are made.

2. Seeking out the most effective value for money travel arrangements and those hotels or car hire companies that offer the best corporate rates.

3. The trip itself. It is important to be able to change the travel itinerary at short notice and to have an efficient system for settling expenses.

4. There is a need to guarantee corporate clients that company money is being used efficiently and properly, that corporate travel policy is followed and that the system is easy to administer. An effective travel expense system must be able to list specific costs incurred, explain the reasons for these and identify hidden costs that might go unnoticed. Expense reporting, payment, overdue claims and reconciliation are all included here.

5. Finally there is the review and analysis phase of corporate travel, which provides the opportunity to review existing company procedures and the development of more cost effective systems both for the retail travel agent and the company who are the client.

The growing use of personal computers in High and Main Street travel agents will make this whole process more feasible by enabling them to establish databases on business travel and to improve their existing accounting and administration. In Chapter 13, this is discussed in more detail in the section dealing with the application of information technology to the travel and tourism industry.

Travel Agency Operations

It is clear from the evidence above that only a limited number of retail travel agents are highly profitable. Although it is relatively easy to set up in business as a retail travel agent, it is much more difficult to achieve a worthwhile level of profitability even after 2 years of trading. Most travel agencies kept inadequate financial information on revenue and expenditure, generally because the accounts were prepared, not for the agency manager, but for the major carriers. There is a need therefore to establish a system of financial planning which provides a cash flow analysis/projection of the agencies' actual and estimated income and expenses on a weekly, monthly, seasonal and annual basis. With this kind of information the agency owner/manager can identify how the business is performing or likely to perform and can identify weaknesses in the operation and goals to be achieved in terms of improved sales performance, new target markets and so on.

Given that the travel agent is offering a *service* and *selling* a product it is *time* that is the most valuable component in his operation. An analysis of sales performance over the year can help identify the 'quiet' periods in the operation of the business when files can be updated, mailing lists reviewed, familiarization visits organized and business plans for the coming year updated. Having done this, an agency needs also to analyze the operation of the office and the book-keeping and reservations systems.

Booking an airline ticket may take 20 minutes or several hours depending on the knowledge of the client and the experience of the travel agency staff. Access to computerized information and centralized booking systems can greatly speed up this process.

In the last decade, airlines' sophisticated computer reservations systems have been developed that travel agencies pay a fee to the airline to utilize. Examples are Saber (American Airlines), PARS (TWA), Apollo (United) System One (Continental) and Datas II (Delta). Travel agents in Britain do not have computer reservation systems as sophisticated as those in the United States. Their systems are focused on package tours with a smaller percentage of airline sales. Their systems are currently being challenged by some American systems. British Airways, KLM, Alitalia, and Swissair are developing Galileo which markets Apollo, while on the Continent, Lufthansa and Air France are developing Amadeus *(Travel Weekly,* Sept. 25, 1988). In the United States, travel agency and airline satellite printers comprise 3 percent of airline ticket sales and this innovation will probably increase.

When small travel agents are declared bankrupt three contributing factors generally exist:

(i) poor financial planning, due to inadequate records or failure to use available financial information;

(ii) poor market analysis and management of sales;

(iii) failure to offset general administration costs by additional revenues.

Good financial control can help identify where things are going wrong or going well in the business. There is a need therefore to produce a budget showing expenditure and income from commissions on a regular basis and link this to an accounting system which shows deviations from the planned budget. If the budget does not balance there are two possible courses of action; increase sales without increasing the overhead; or increase income by reducing the overhead. This process can be helped by analyzing the nature of the firm's business over the past year and dropping those areas or clients that are not providing value for money.

In the United States, Canada and Britain, two-thirds of travel agencies are independent and one-fifth have branch locations. There are a few large travel agencies. American Express and Ask Mr. Foster both had 1987 airline sales volume in excess of one billion dollars. American Express has 600 locations while Ask Mr. Foster has 409 locations *(Business Travel News,* 1988).

A majority of travel agency owners and their agents are female and most agencies have from three to six sales agents. *Travel Weekly* periodically surveys travel agents in order to provide benchline data on agency business.

The American Society of Travel Agents (ASTA) also conducts surveys of agency members. In 1985, about 10 percent of travel agencies had sales exceeding $10 million while 66 percent had sales of less than $2 million *(Travel Industry World Yearbook, 1987).* According to the Yearbook, the estimated percentage of total airline volume booked by travel agents is 67 percent domestic and 80 percent international. Ninety-two percent of cruises are booked by travel agents, 18 percent of domestic hotel reservations and 79 percent of international hotel bookings. Forty percent of rental cars, primarily at airport locations, are booked by travel agents. Package tour sales in the United States as well as in Europe are highly dependent upon travel agency bookings. It is estimated that tour operators receive 90 percent of their sales from travel agents. But in the United States, unlike Europe, 70 percent of all sales are for domestic rather than international travel. A majority of an agent's income is derived from the sale of airline tickets. The average travel agency business mix is 51 percent for leisure travel, 40 percent business and 9 percent group travel (*Travel Weekly,* July 31, 1987).

One-half of a travel agency's operating costs (53%) are for personnel payrolls and employee benefits. Rent takes 7 percent, advertising and promotion 5 percent, automation 5 percent, dues, subscriptions and supplies 4 percent and communication 4 percent. Approximately 20 percent is consumed by postage costs, insurance, professional fees, depreciation and bad debts (ASTA 1984 Expense Analysis Survey).

Travel agents are very dependent on repeat business. A 1986 survey by *Better Homes and Gardens* magazine of family travel patterns asked consumers why they use travel agents. The responses indicate that the public places a great deal of trust in the professional competence of a travel agent. The five reasons mentioned were: to save money and find the best value on travel; to make bookings on major trips; to recommend transportation/airline; to recommend travel offerings and to recommend a hotel (ASTA STAT., Feb., 1988). For travel agents committed to professional competence the Institute of Certified Travel Agents in the United States, and the British Commonwealth Institute of Travel Agents, offer educational programs that culminate in a professional certification. In the United States, an agent can become a Certified Travel Counselor (CTC) by successfully passing examinations covering four categories; business management, marketing, sales, and international travel and tourism. In addition, a counselor must write an original research paper and have five years' experience in the industry. These programs have done much to improve the individual travel agent's stature and professional image with the public.

Tour Operators

Tour operators plan, price, package and market an inclusive foreign holiday. They are the 'manufacturing' element of the tourist industry. Most tour operators are wholesalers in that they produce a package holiday and negotiate with retail travel agents who then sell this product. Some tour operators, such as Thomas Cook and American Express, are both wholesalers and retailers.

There are three types of tour operator:

1. *Direct sell* tour operators who by-pass the travel agent and sell directly to the public. They will put together package holidays and advertise and sell to their own clientele. The operator may be a small agency or a multi-branch organization that markets thousands of tours.
2. *Wholesale* operators do not deal directly with the public and put together and operate tours exclusively through travel agents. They do not accept direct bookings and have no direct contact with the public.
3. *General Tour Contractors.* These are tour operators who do not package and promote their own tours. Instead, reservations are forwarded to local contractors or to wholesalers. Organizations such as British Airways, who brought the direct-sell operator Martin Rooks, special affinity groups organizing travel to North America or Australasia, and non-profit organizations all come into this category.

Organizing Tour Operations

The tour operator must be planning the inclusive holiday package at least one to two years before the first departure date and tours for some events, such as the World Cup, the Olympics, or the Passion Play at Oberammergau have to be planned years in advance. The first 5 to 6 months will be spent in putting a saleable package together, that is chartering aircraft, arranging transfers to coaches or ferries, booking hotel rooms, meals and arranging sightseeing tours. The next 4 to 5 months will be spent laying out and printing promotional material. The tour operator then spends 4 to 6 months checking up on new places and tourist developments and hotel operations. Tour testing is an important element in designing package tours and most operators will sample more than once before the package is made available to the public, to iron out any snags in the tour arrangements.

The three main elements of a tour package are the cost of the transport, the hotel accommodation and the ancillary services. Some companies have *integrated operations* where the tour operator has acquired or established its own airline. In Britain, for example, Horizon Holidays has established Orion Airways, Intasun (part of the International Leisure Group) has developed Air Europe, Martin Rooks, whose parent company is British Airways, use the British Airways subsidiary British Air Tours, and the International Thomson Organization has Britannia Airways.

Tour companies in the United States have not established their own airlines to the extent that tour companies have done so in Britain. U.S. companies are inclined to use chartered aircraft from scheduled and non-scheduled carriers or block scheduled airline seats well in advance of the trip.

Mass Market Tour Operations

One of the most competitive parts of the vacation package tour business is inclusive air tours. In Britain, the market is now dominated by three main operators: International Thomson Organization, International Leisure Group and Horizon Holidays. Thomson had a 44 per cent share, International Leisure 19 per cent and Horizon 11 per cent (*Times Business* 12.1.87) in 1987. The three operators accounted for 70 per cent of the market. The economies of scale available to the larger operators give them such a cost advantage that it becomes harder and harder for the smaller companies to compete unless they specialize, and the high cost of entry into the business means that a competitor, once squeezed out, is less likely to be replaced. The growth of these three companies underlines the importance of size to profitability in the tour operations business. Many of the normal risks can then be reduced or removed. Forward buying can provide a hedge against currency changes and companies can impose fuel surcharges of up to $18 if fuel prices increase.

The hotel accommodation forms the second main part of the holiday package and here the tour operator buys bed space or guarantees a specific number of rooms to the hotel management. By 'guaranteeing' rooms, the operator must pay for them whether they are sold or not. Location of the property is another prime factor as are the grade and type of hotel. Problems occur from time to time when hotels oversell their bedspace in the expectation that some bookings will be cancelled, and then are unable to cope with the influx of tourists who expect accommodation.

High volumes of business also reduce overheads per holiday and increase an operator's ability to buy aircraft seats or hotel beds at competitive prices. The smaller tour operators may be squeezed out as they lose their market share and competitive edge in bidding for hotel bedspaces and aircraft seats.

In addition, most, if not all, tour operators employ tour escorts or representatives who are key elements in a successful tour operation. These are professionals who should be fluent in the local language, have an extensive knowledge of the area, and sufficient experience to deal with the logistics of transferring tourists and luggage to their hotels. They must deal with a myriad number of complaints and have a good public relations sense.

With the growth of consumer spending in foreign locations during the 1980s, the competition for the mass market has been fierce. In 1986, 10 million Britons took package holidays. In the United States it is estimated that 11 million people take week-long tours each year. More than 500 companies, belonging to the National Tour Association, offer these tours. Most companies are small as the tour industry is not dominated by a few large operators as is the case in Britain.

ASSIGNMENTS

1. Using your local copy of *Yellow Pages* identify the location and type of travel agencies listed. Select 10 in one large town, identify their location and plot this on a street plan. What locational characteristics do they show? How many are:
    (a) General travel agents?
    (b) Specialized travel agents?
    (c) Branches of larger chains?
    (d) Independent retailers?
    (e) Members of ASTA/IATA?

2. You are the manager of a small retail travel agency located in the main central shopping area. Next door is a camera shop, and across the road is a sports shop. Design a joint advertising campaign that will link all of these businesses to the travel agency and increase your turnover in package tour sales.

Chapter 6

The Passenger Transport Sector

Learning Objectives: After reading this chapter you should understand:

— the importance to the tourist industry of air, sea, rail and road transport
— the effects of regulation and deregulation of transport
— the impact on tourist resorts/tourist regions following the growth in car ownership since the 1950s
— the role of public and private transport in Britain and the United States
— the levels of tourism-related employment in the passenger transport sector.

Introduction

As Chapters 2 and 4 demonstrate, the growth of mass tourism is closely linked with improvements in the means of transport. These improvements enabled the main carriers to transport people in much greater numbers than before, and to lower the unit cost of this travel, making the opportunity to travel available to a much greater proportion of the public. In addition, the speed of travel has increased considerably over the past 30 years so that trains travelling at 125 miles an hour, and passenger aircraft at 500 miles an hour, are commonplace. This has had the effect of shortening journey times and of bringing more distant destinations within the reach of the average traveler. Journey time and also reduced unit cost, due to greater utilization of vehicles and accessibility, are key factors to be considered when a tour operator puts an inclusive tour together, and the inclusion in mass market brochures of regions such as the Gambia or the Seychelles is a result of reducing journey times from Europe to these more distant destinations. It has also meant that more countries have to cope with the impact of mass tourism on the environment. The issues that this raises are discussed in detail in Chapter 12.

More than a century ago, road transport was largely horse-drawn and still slow and subject to frequent stops to rest the horses. It was the growth of rail and sea transport during the second half of the nineteenth century that had a significant influence on the types of tourism and tourist resort that developed. Rail and sea routes were developed to transport freight, but their presence and shorter journey times attracted passengers, especially in the hinterland of major cities where railways provided a quick and reliable means of journey to work.

Rail Transport

Chapter 2 described the growth of seaside resorts following the invention of the railway and the development of rail links between resorts and main centres of population. By the end of the nineteenth century, most tourists arrived by rail and the land use pattern of resorts reflects their development during the railway age, even though today rail travel is much less important for mass tourism.

Rail travel in Britain was organized on a regional basis until the railways were nationalized to form British Rail in 1947. If we concentrate on the passenger carrying role, BR divide their railway business into three sectors:

(1) Inter-City
(ii) London and the South East
(iii) Provincial services

The inter-city network covers six main routes (Fig 25 on page 83) radiating outward from London, and it is this network and the provincial services that are mainly used by tourists. The London and South East network is mainly commuter traffic although it does handle day trippers to Brighton, Southend and the North Kent resorts.

Although the railways monopolized the mass travel market during the nineteenth century they suffered from competition from coach and car transport during the twentieth century, and more recently, lost traffic to the airlines, particularly in the United States. This was in part due to their failure to recognize the importance of the mass travel market, possibly conditioned by the priority given to the freight and parcels services. The increasing competition from road freight operations and a decline in revenue during the 1950s, led to a drastic overhaul of British Rail's operations in the early 1960s. The Beeching Report *The Reshaping of British Railways* led to a drastic reduction in the overall size and geographic extent of the rail network, particularly serving rural areas many of which are tourist destinations.

Unlike in Britain, railroads in the United States are used primarily for freight transport. Passenger travel on railroads declined steadily after World War II and most rail companies threatened to stop passenger traffic altogether in the late 1960s. At this point, the U.S. Congress passed the Rail Passenger Service Act of 1970. This Act established the National Railroad Passenger Corporation commonly known as Amtrak. This quasi-public corporation, with monetary subsidy from the government, was charged with providing modern and efficient intercity passenger service at a profit developing successful marketing programs for proposed updated equipment that had customer appeal. The Corporation has been partially successful after a very slow start. By the 1980s, the passenger rail system had reached 500 communities, had 24,000 miles of track and a ridership of 20 million. It has been most successful in the Northeast corridor, running trains between Washington, D.C., Philadelphia, and New York City. Modern light-weight and comfortable rail passenger cars have been purchased and it is currently marketing package rail tours. Amtrak cannot compete with air travel if cost is the sole factor. Discount air fares and time savings make air travel much more attractive. However, for the small proportion of people who are afraid to fly, Amtrak provides a preferred alternative. Compared to Western Europe and Japan, railroad passenger travel to leisure destinations in North America is relatively unimportant (Figure 26). Via Rail, formed in 1977, is Canada's Amtrak equivalent. Tourists who have experienced a trip through the Canadian Rocky Mountains on Via Rail are impressed with the service and the magnificent scenery.

Figure 25: **The Main BR Inter-City Rail Network**

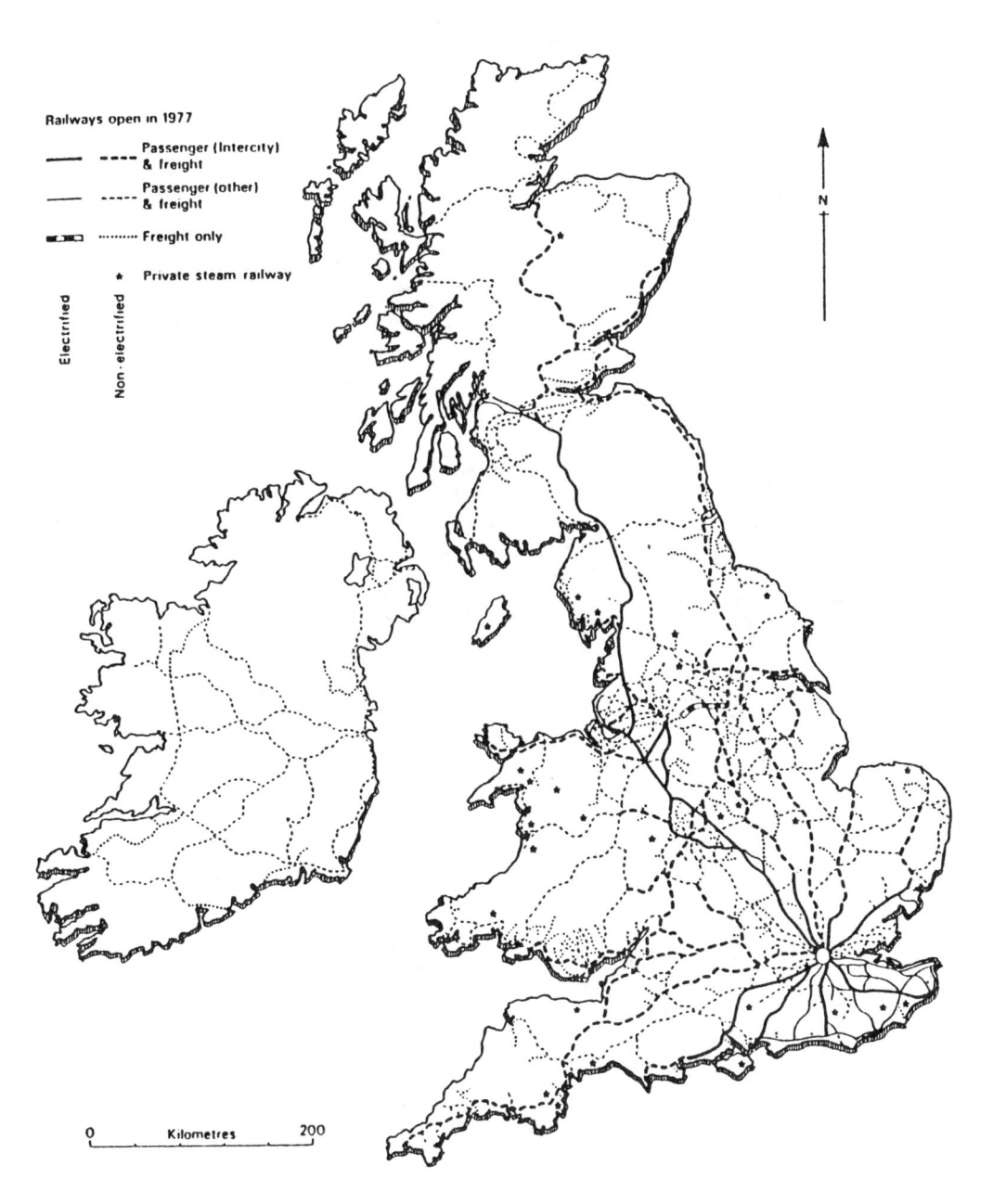

Railways open in 1977

——— – – – Passenger (Intercity) & freight
——— – – – Passenger (other) & freight
▬▬▬ .... Freight only
Electrified / Non-electrified

∗ Private steam railway

0 — Kilometres — 200

The present railway network.

Figure 26:

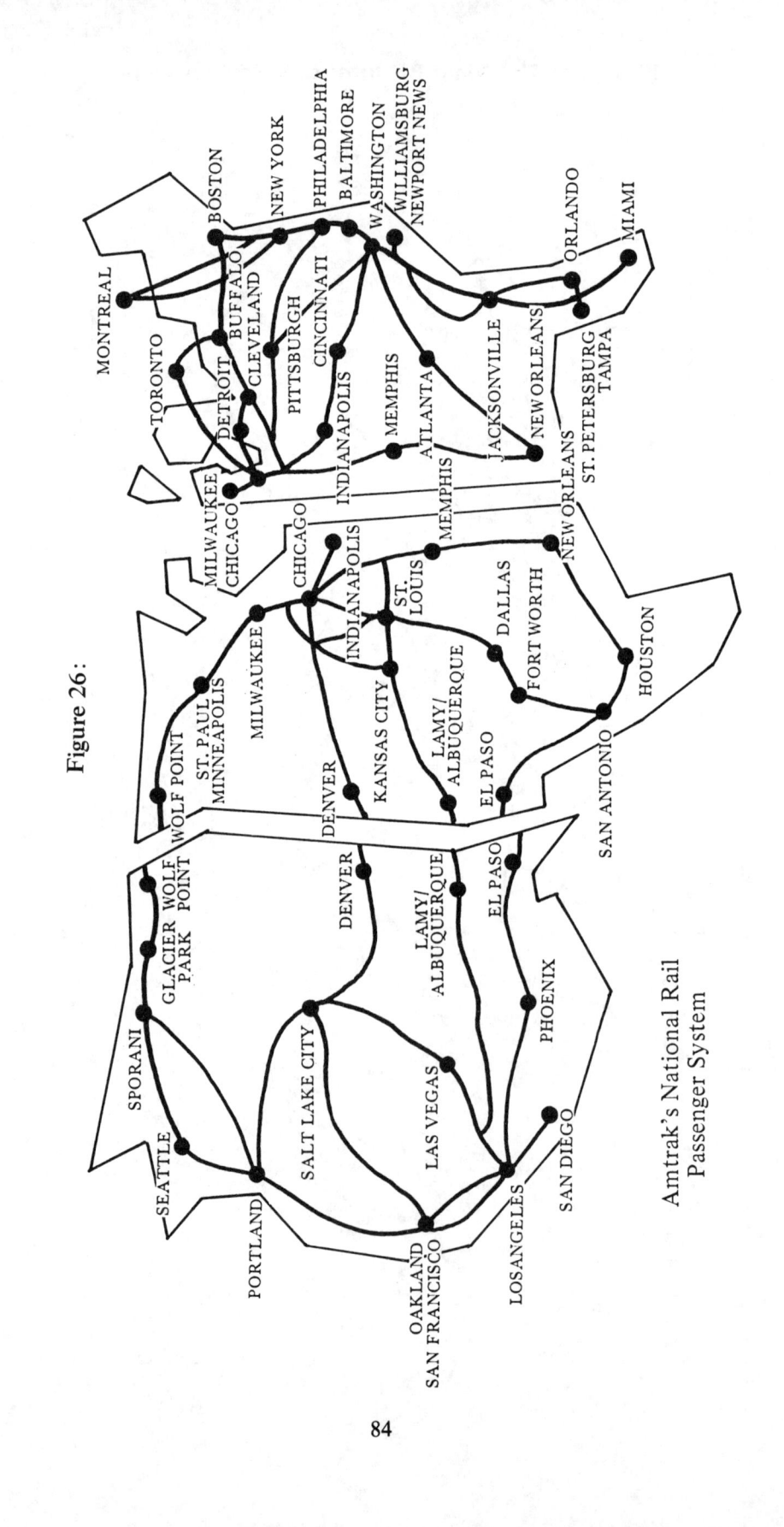

Amtrak's National Rail Passenger System

In 1988, a special daylight run from Vancouver to Banff or Jasper was introduced and seat occupancy was well above 60% (*Travel Weekly,* July 21, 1988). Some railroads are tourist attractions offering short duration one-half day to day long excursions. Examples are Ontario's Algoma Central Railway and Colorado's Durango to Silverton Railroad. Similar trains in Britain are the Watercress Line in Hampshire and the Nene Valley Railway near Peterborough. On the European Continent, a restored Orient Express attracts many upscale passengers for deluxe tours of a week or more.

Road Transport: (1) The Private Car

The growth in private car ownership with most families having access to at least one car, is a relatively recent phenomenon. But it has had a dramatic impact on the types of holiday that people take as well as on the environment of the resorts and holiday regions.

Figure 27 on page 86 highlights the growth in automobile usage between 1945 and 1985. Since the War, the proportion of families taking vacations by automobile has consistently been above 75% of all modes of vacation travel. The deregulation of the airlines in 1978 brought reduced airfares and the automobile percentage had declined (Table 2 page 10). However, fly-drive packages have increased the use of rental cars at a vacation destination. There were 130 million cars in the United States in 1984 or 1.8 people per car; the United Kingdom with 16 million cars has 3.4 people per car; France 2.6 and China 10,220. As the number of car owning households increases, and as more households acquire a second car, the private car will continue to dominate the domestic tourist scene in Britain, the United States and most European countries. In the peak summer period, a considerable proportion of the road traffic travelling to the south of France or through Germany and Switzerland to Italy, is generated by tourists in private cars.

Assuming a reasonable road system, the private car provides an unrivalled degree of mobility for the tourist and a degree of convenience not offered by any other form of transport. It enables the tourist to travel from his home to his destination with all his family and luggage with the minimum amount of transfer and without having a rigid timetable. Once at the resort, the car enables the tourist to gain access to the surrounding region.

In addition, use of the private car for holiday travel is perceived by the tourist as being cheaper than other modes of travel. Although it is expensive to acquire a car, once bought the cost of journeys is relatively small, particularly if several passengers are carried, and most drivers just calculate the cost of oil and gasoline when considering using the car for holiday travel.

The American Automobile Association predicted that, in the summer of 1988, a family of four automobile travelers would spend on the average $192 per day. Meals would cost $90, lodging $80 and gasoline and oil $22.

According to the Recreation Vehicle Association, one in ten Americans owns a recreation vehicle and 25 million people experience recreation vehicle travel. A recent survey found that R.V. owners on vacation travel almost 6,000 miles over a period of 23 days each year and spend $60 per day, even when they stay in some of the nation's 16,000 public and privately managed campgrounds.

The growth in car ownership has also led to a growing preference for touring

Figure 27:

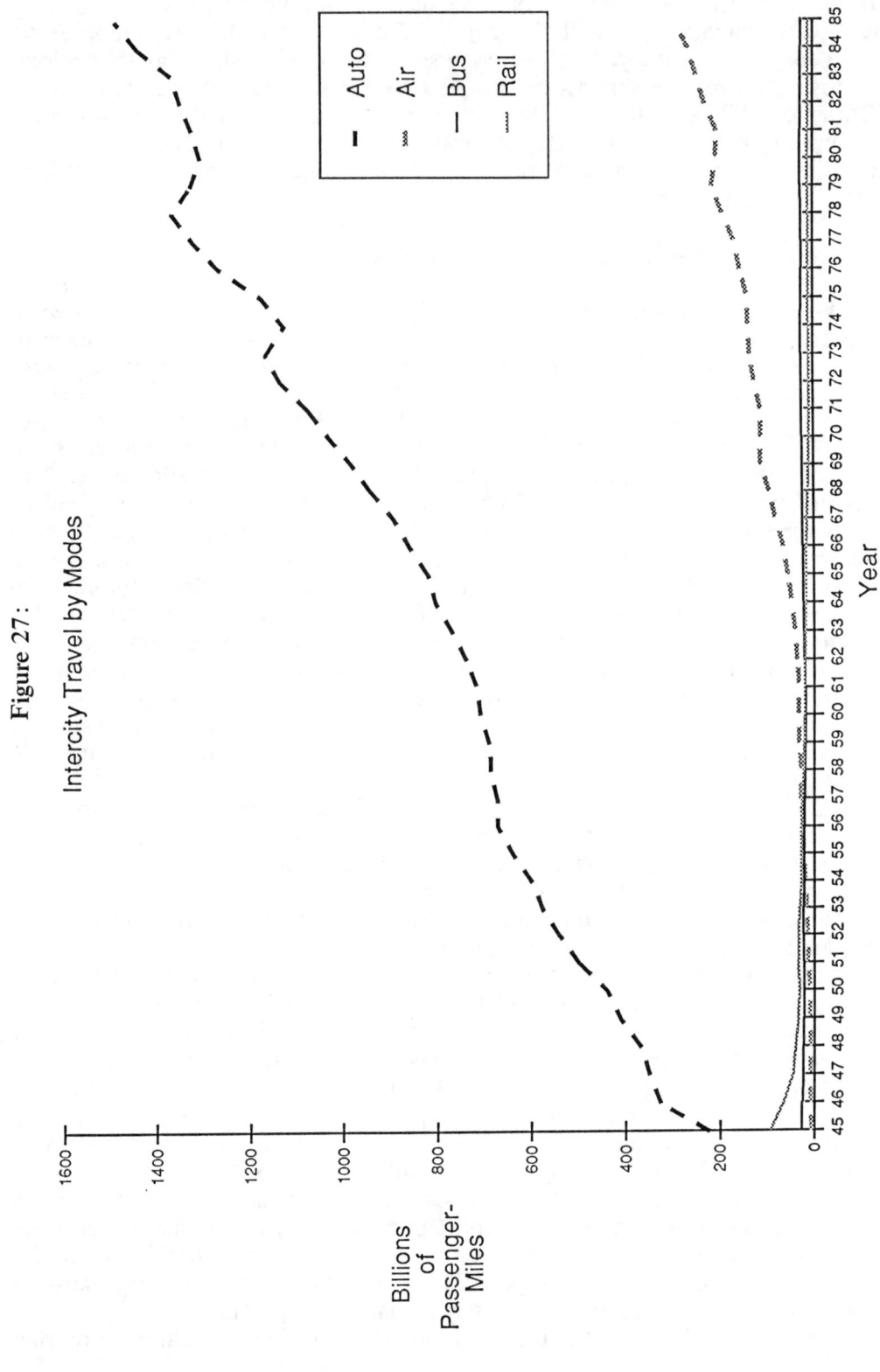

Intercity Travel by Modes

holidays where resorts are now seen as a base from which to visit a much wider hinterland. Resorts have to face competition from a wide range of attractions in the surrounding region, and indeed many now market these attractions as part of the overall 'appeal' of the resort.

In Western Europe, and the United States and Canada, there has been a corresponding growth in the ownership of touring caravans and campers. This trend has affected the tourist resorts and holiday regions in two ways. First, the traditional forms of holiday accommodation have lost some of their market share as caravanning and camping have increased. Secondly, the proliferation of caravans and tents has spread from the fringes of the traditional seaside resort into the formerly less accessible parts of the tourist regions, creating significant planning problems. This issue is discussed in more detail in Chapter 12.

The number of cars operated by rental car businesses in the United States has increased at a more rapid rate than private car ownership during the last decade. Even though rentals are primarily for business purposes, the leisure rental of automobiles is increasing. Most of the 7,000 rental locations are at airports and the Big Four car rental companies, Hertz, Avis, Budget, and National maintain fierce competition. In 1986 there were ¾ of a million rental cars available for hire in the United States. The larger firms are international and provide rental services at tourist destinations worldwide.

Congestion and disrepair on major highways and expressways is increasing in all developed countries. Highways are more congested on weekends and during the summer months and such congestion, in spite of good highway information, beautification and sign controls, detracts from the slogan that 'getting there is half the fun'. It has long been recognized that the pleasure traveler often selects his route according to the resource amenities and surrounding attractions to be seen en route. The average pleasure traveler may spend seven to eight hours a day on the road. Our highways do portray the beautiful and the not so beautiful landscapes of our nation.

Table 13:
**Hours of Recreation Per Year Provided
By National Parks and Roads and Streets**

Item Compared	National Parks	Roads and Streets
Hours of Recreation	896 Million	2,740 Million
Acres of Land	30 Million	22 Million
Recreation Provided by one acre	30 Hours	124 Hours

Source: U.S. Dept. of Transportation, *Social and Economic Effects of Highways,* 1976.

The allocation of land for highways has been a relatively efficient use of land, even for recreational purposes. The Interstate Highway System in the United States is used to illustrate the efficiency of space utilization. The System occupies less than 2% of all highway mileage. There are 700,000 miles of highways, roads and streets in the nation that occupy 22 million acres of land. Ten percent of all land uses for roads are for the Interstate System, but this System carries 20% of all vehicle traffic. More important is the fact that all highway space provides recreational as well as transportation benefits. Some claim that our highways provide more hours of recreation per acre than do the National Parks and do so with more efficient use of space.

The rationale for these figures of 124 hours of recreation for one acre of land devoted to roads and streets is based on the estimate that a third or more of all driving is for pleasure (Table 13). One may not agree with the logic of these figures but it certainly can be accepted that pleasure driving on weekends or vacation is, at times, enjoyable and without our extensive road network this type of recreation would not be possible.

Road Transport: (2) Coach Transport

Like the airline industry, intercity transport by bus was slowed in its development by technology and the lack of good all-weather highways. Most early 1920s buses were operated as commuter lines in and around cities. Greyhound Company, originated in Minnesota by Earl Wickman, was established in 1920. It was not until 1928 that a New York City to Los Angeles bus service was established. Intercity bus service has improved in terms of speed of travel and in comfort to the passenger. In 1947, buses were second to the railroads in total passenger miles but, by 1955, the bus was third behind rail and air and by 1976, bus travel passenger miles were higher than the railroads and have remained so into the 1980s. The ridership on intercity buses has declined, while passengers carried on coach tours and bus charters has increased.

Coach transport has several functions. It can provide:

a) Express services between major cities and major tourist resorts;
b) Group travel for special interest groups, associations and so on;
c) Transfers between airport or ferry terminals and hotels;
d) Tours and Excursions.

The advantage of coach travel is that, like the private car, it is very flexible, accessible particularly in rural areas, and is relatively cheap. The bus is more than three times as efficient as the automobile and six times as fuel efficient as the airlines. Besides being the most fuel efficient, bus travel is the most safe of all transport modes. Studies have shown that passengers are more than 30 times safer in an intercity bus than in a private automobile and six times safer than on a scheduled airline (*Travel Holiday,* 1981). By leaving the driving to someone else, bus passengers now have air-suspended rides, air conditioning and heating with onboard lavatories. In Britain, National Express Rapide Coaches have attendants and offer food and beverage service.

President Reagan signed the Bus Regulatory Reform Act in 1982. This Bill deregulated the coach industry. Since then, about 1,700 new bus companies have received Interstate Commerce Commission operating authority and there are now 3,000 operating bus companies in the United States (Travel Industry World Yearbook 1988). Many of these new companies, just like their counterparts in Britain, are small and very aggressive in seeking passengers. Competition has created a strong downward pressure on prices for charters and tours. Aggressive marketing and pricing, and increasing insurance costs, resulted in business failures by 45 to 50 of the older previously well established companies. The average fare paid by a charter or tour passenger dropped from $10.57 in 1982 to $8.80 in 1984. As fares went down, ridership went up. There was an increase of 4 million passengers on charters and tours in 1984 (US Travel Data Center). However, since deregulation, profitability has declined steadily in the face of cuts in fares. In Britain, as in the United States, this will affect the larger carriers more since they have a higher cost structure and overheads.

The fastest growing segment of the bus industry is the tour and charter business. Tours and excursions come under two categories. The first are local, based on individual resorts and providing a variety of day and half day excursions to tourist attractions in the surrounding hinterland. The second type are long-distance tours usually of 8 to 14 days duration, for example, through New England or the Western national parks. These are packaged to include guides, overnight stops and local tours from the main resorts on the itinerary. These tours appeal to the elderly and retired in that they offer a local pick-up service, a courier to deal with any day-to-day problems, and the transport of heavy luggage right to the hotel. Often a spirit of 'camaraderie' builds between the coach passengers, driver and guide, and the companies in this field find that they have a high level of repeat business.

The National Tour Association and the American Bus Association, in 1984, established joint agreement to provide membership benefits between the associations in order to further cooperation in developing bus tours. The ABA has, for the last few years, published a list of the top 100 celebrations, fairs and events that take place both in the United States and Canada. The prestigious list has resulted in more coach tours and visitor increases at these events. Examples include Cheyenne Frontier Days (Wyo.), Macy's Thanksgiving Day Parade (NYC) and the Saskatchewan Air Show in Canada.

The National Tour Association estimated, in 1986, that the total impact of motorcoach tours in North America was $9 billion from 40 million tour passengers. The best example of bus travel to a vacation destination is exemplified by the contrast of travel modes at the two major gambling locations in the United States. Arrivals to Las Vegas, an isolated desert spa at least a day's highway travel from cities in the region are: car, 48%; air, 40%; and bus, 12%. In contrast, arrivals in Atlantic City, New Jersey, a few hours drive from New York City and Philadelphia are: car, 54%; air, 1%; and bus 45%

The British deregulated the motor coach industry with the 1980 Transport Act. This ended the licensing regulations affecting express coach routes and tours and excursions of over 30 miles. This led to a short-lived price war on several express routes between a consortium of private coach companies (British Coachways) and the publicly owned National Bus Company. Up to 1986, the market was still dominated by the National Bus Company, which was administered through a network of 70 regional groups, employing over 70,000 people, with a fleet of 17,000 vehicles. One important effect of the 1980 Act was that the coach companies with more competitive fares and improved quality of vehicles with videos, toilets etc., won a greater share of the travel market mainly at the expense of British Rail.

The 1985 Transport Act had, as one of its main objectives, privatizing the National Bus Company and, by wholesale deregulation, to open up the market to private operators on any route. A program is now under way to sell off the 70 regional groups and many may be subject to management buy-outs.

The 1980 deregulation of express services is generally thought to have produced faster, cheaper and more luxurious coaches and it was these results, among other experiments, that prompted the move to complete deregulation in 1985. The coach travel related to tourism will tend to gain from competition especially on the main routes between the major towns and cities and irregular services such as excursions or transfers. The larger independent operators will continue to dominate the express and touring market, but there will be more scope for smaller firms with their lower overheads to compete for excursion traffic and feeder routes. It is almost certain that, while deregulation will make coach operations more competitive, some of the independent operators will go bankrupt — particularly those who are least experienced in this business. Coach companies wishing to develop their tourist trade will increasingly rely on entrepreneurial senior managers to develop and maintain their market share.

Maritime Transport

This can be divided into three categories, two of which are strictly maritime:

(i) Cruises and ocean-going ships
(ii) Ferries
(iii) Services on Lakes, inland waters and canals.

The main shipping lines who organize cruises or ocean-going passenger routes are members of Cruise Lines International Association (CLIA).

Cruise Ships

Until the 1930s, steamships provided the only means of long distance transport between the major continents. The growth of air travel, especially of inclusive air tours, had a severe impact on the shipping lines. In the post-war years they were faced with increasing competition from the airlines, rising operating costs and growing obsolescence in their shipping fleets, and very high rebuilding/refitting costs. Most companies chose to diversify into other areas of activity and now those that remain have turned increasingly to the cruise line business. This is the luxury end of the tourist market. For example, only 4% of the population of the United States has taken a cruise, but the majority of the 4% is repeat business. The tourists on a cruise ship are not just buying a trip from A to B, they are buying a stay at a floating resort, with a level of service and accommodation comparable to the best resorts and hotels. The appeal of the cruise is that it is an all-inclusive package with accommodation, meals and entertainment all included in the price of a ticket.

In the past 10 years, the cruise lines have introduced innovations and special interest packages to appeal to a wider clientele. Most cruise lines offer a fly-cruise deal, for example where passengers fly out to the Caribbean before joining the cruise ship in the West Indies. The most prestigious is probably the Cunard package which involves flying out of Britain to the United States on Concorde and returning on the QE2. The appeal to passengers of these fly-cruise packages is that in the past, when cruises started at Southampton or New York, it took several days of sailing through cold waters, and possibly rough seas, before warmer waters were reached. Now tropical sunshine and warm waters are just several hours' travel away.

In order to appeal to a younger clientele, many cruise ships now offer full spa and fitness facilities as well as a wide range of sporting activities. For example, the Norwegian Caribbean Lines offer snorkelling and scuba diving lessons on board by qualified instructors; golf and tennis clinics are available on many ships. Some companies offer unique cruises, for example, the Sun Line have an Amazon River Cruise that includes a performance at the Opera House Manaus and their Transatlantic Grand Cruise begins in Athens and ends in Fort Lauderdale, with stops in the eastern and western Mediterranean and the Caribbean. The three main regions for cruise trips are the Caribbean, the Mediterranean and the Far East. The cruise market is dominated by United States tourists, who account for 80% of all cruise passengers, although the headquarters of the main cruise line companies are based in Europe. For Caribbean sailings many lines now fly passengers to San Juan, Puerto Rico or Jamaica or Barbados, or cruises begin at the Florida Ports.

South Florida ports of Miami, Port Canaveral, Tampa, Port Everglades, and Palm Beach embarked more than 1.8 million people on cruises in 1986 (*Travel Weekly,* June 23, 1988). The west coast cities of Los Angeles, San Francisco and San Diego are attracting more cruise lines and are beginning to rival the Florida based lines, especially for Mexico and Panama Canal cruises.

In the Pacific, more cruise lines are offering seven day cruises from Hong Kong and the ships of the Holland America, Cunard, Royal Viking and P&O Lines offer larger cruises calling in at Hawaii, Tahiti, New Zealand, Australia and Japan.

In Europe, DFDS Danish Seaways took over Tor Line and the West German Prinsferries in the early 1980s and built up a separate inclusive tour operation of short cruises outbound from UK ports to Scandinavia. These now account for 100,000 passengers a year out of a total of 1.2 million carried. About 30,000 of these are from the USA (*Travel and Tourism Analyst,* 1987) and 45,000 from the UK.

Cruise ships are very labor intensive and average about one crew member for every two passengers. In other words, a ship carrying 800 passengers should have about 400 crew members. Cruise ships vary in size from the relatively small ship carrying 100 passengers to the luxury liner carrying 900 to 1,000 passengers, with theaters, casinos, swimming pools, shops and other onboard entertainment facilities. In 1987, the Royal Caribbean Cruise Line put into service the Sovereign of the Seas at 74,000 gross tons. It can carry more passengers (2,690) than any other cruise ship now in service. In gross tonnage it outweighs the Cunard's Queen Elizabeth 2 by 7,000 tons and the Norway (formerly the France) by 4,000 tons. Even larger cruise vessels are planned. World City Corporation announced plans in 1988 for a $1 billion 250,000 ton, 5,600 passenger ship to be called the Phoenix.

Passenger Ferries

The first steam passage of the English Channel was in 1816 and the first regular steamer service in 1820. By the 1830s about 100,000 passengers were using the cross-Channel Ferries and, by 1882, this had increased to 500,000. The present-day cross channel traffic carries 2.3 million passengers a year (Table 14). between seven different English ports and France, and on the east coast three ports operate ferry services across the North Sea (Figure 28 on page 93).

In the United States, with the exception of the Mississippi river cruise lines and the Great Lakes cruise ships, there has not been a similar massive development in ferries linking different parts of the country. The American seamen's unions and restrictions by intracoastal transportation laws, which prohibit traffic between USA ports, have prevented any development of shipping links.

The other main concentration of ferry routes is in the Mediterranean, particularly the links between mainland Spain, France, Italy and Greece and the islands that form part of their jurisdiction, where there is an extensive network of ferry links. Greece is a good example. There are over 20 main islands in the Aegean and Ionean seas, and dozens of smaller ones, and all of them rely on ferry services to bring in supplies and essential goods and, of course, tourists. The ferry may be a car ferry of several thousand tons or an ultra-modern hydrofoil providing a link between an airport and surrounding islands.

There are several key factors that determine the viability of ferry services:

(i) They need to be equipped to deal with large numbers of passengers and their cars;

(ii) They need to be equipped for a fast turn-round at their destination port at either end of the ferry link so as to increase the number of sailings during the peak season;

(iii) They require a roughly equal flow of traffic in both directions so that they have no 'dead' journeys;

(iv) They need to be on routes that provide a good year-round flow of traffic.

The cross channel routes are all operated by roll on/roll off ferry services which minimize the time spent in port and provide a fast efficient service for car travelers. Over 3 million Britons take cars abroad each year and the only threat to the cross channel ferry services is the advent of the Channel Tunnel. In addition to the conventional ferry services, jet foil, hydrofoil, and hovercraft services offer highspeed water-borne links between Britain and the Continent.

Great improvements in the efficiency of ferry operations have occurred over the past 25 years. In 1953 it took up to 2½ hours for a small drive-on drive-off ship with a stern door to unload and re-load in port. By 1962 a drive through ship with 120 cars and 180 passengers took 1½ hours. Today a ferry taking 350 cars and 1,350 passengers can be turned round in 1 hour.

Table 14:
Growth of Channel/North Sea Ferry Traffic 1975 – 1985

Year	1975	1976	1977	1978	1979	1980	1981	1982	1983	1984	1985
Passengers (millions)	13.89	14.78	16.09	17.4	18.73	20.89	22.6	23.62	23.86	23.17	23.24

Source: Port Authority Figures and estimates from ferry companies)

Figure 28: Sealink route map

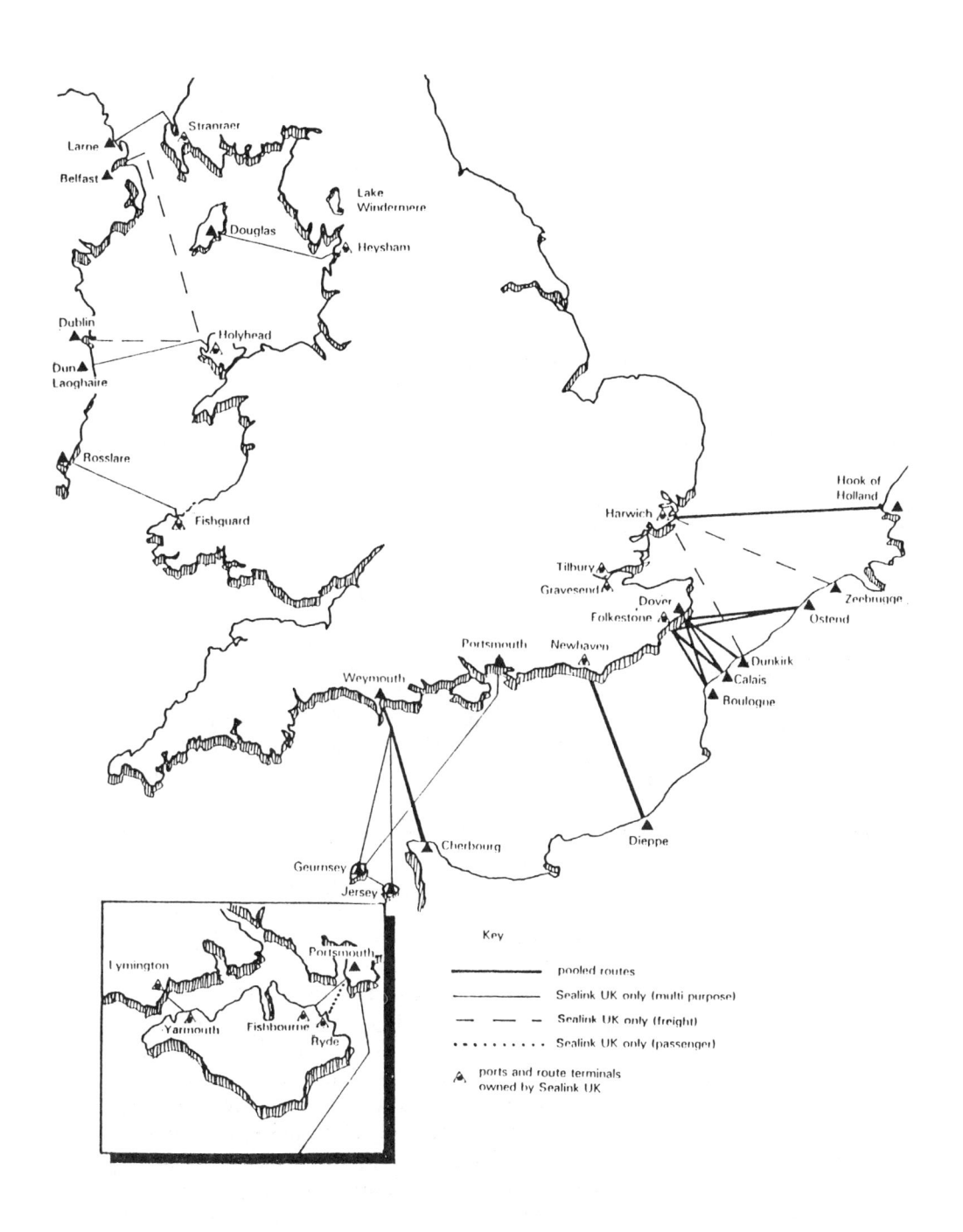

The English Channel and North Sea crossings from the UK to the continent carried an estimated 23 million passengers in 1985. Most of these were car-based holidaymakers. In the late 1950s there were just four car ferries operating. There are now over 200 ferry services around North West Europe, most of them serving the UK. In the 1970s, there was a steady growth in passenger traffic through UK ports and the number of passengers almost doubled between 1975 and 1985 (Table 10). The Channel ferries, which account for about 75% of total crossings from the UK, are dominated by two companies, Sealink and P & O European ferries (formerly Townsend Thoresen). In recent years, both companies have been engaged in fierce competition to protect and increase their market share in the face of the forthcoming threat of the Channel Tunnel.

Impact of the Channel Tunnel

The approval of the project to build a Channel Tunnel, scheduled for completion in 1993, will have a significant impact on ferry traffic. This is at a time when several ports, in particular Dover, have invested many millions of pounds in development programs. Eurotunnel are forecasting a London to Paris journey time of 3 hours 15 minutes compared to 6 hours 45 minutes for a ferry crossing. This reduction in travel time, together with a probable very competitive price, will pose the most serious threat ever to the viability of these ferry services. Although Eurotunnel expect to create new markets as a result of the new fixed link, it is difficult to estimate how much of the traffic generated will be captured from existing ferry or airline routes.

Air Transport

This has been the most rapidly expanding transport sector over the past 30 years and is now the main form of long distance travel. The great increase in inclusive package tours abroad has been largely due to advances in aircraft design and performance, with the long-haul market now dominated by wide-bodied jets carrying over 500 passengers at speeds averaging 600 mph for several thousand miles, and smaller capacity jets for the short-haul routes.

Between 1974 and 1984, the number of airline passengers carried world-wide increased by 66%, with the main increase occurring between 1974 and 1986 (Fig 29 on page 95). During the same period, the number of passenger kilometres almost doubled (Table 15 on page 96). The market share was redistributed, over this period, with a decline in the North American and European share and a rapid increase in the airlines of East Asia and the Pacific (Table 16 on page 96).

During the 1950s and 1960s, air passenger traffic increased in volume by 15% per year, encouraged by increasing market demand and technological developments in aircraft design which increased the speed, range and passenger capacity of aircraft. Table 17 summarizes these developments since 1940.

In the 1980s, the impact of deregulation on the US market, and moves to liberalize air fares in the European and transatlantic markets, have meant that airlines need to be much more flexible in the face of changing consumer demand. However, current forecasts indicate that the passenger travel market will rise by

Figure 29:
GROWTH IN INTERNATIONAL AND U.S.
AIR TRAFFIC 1974–1986

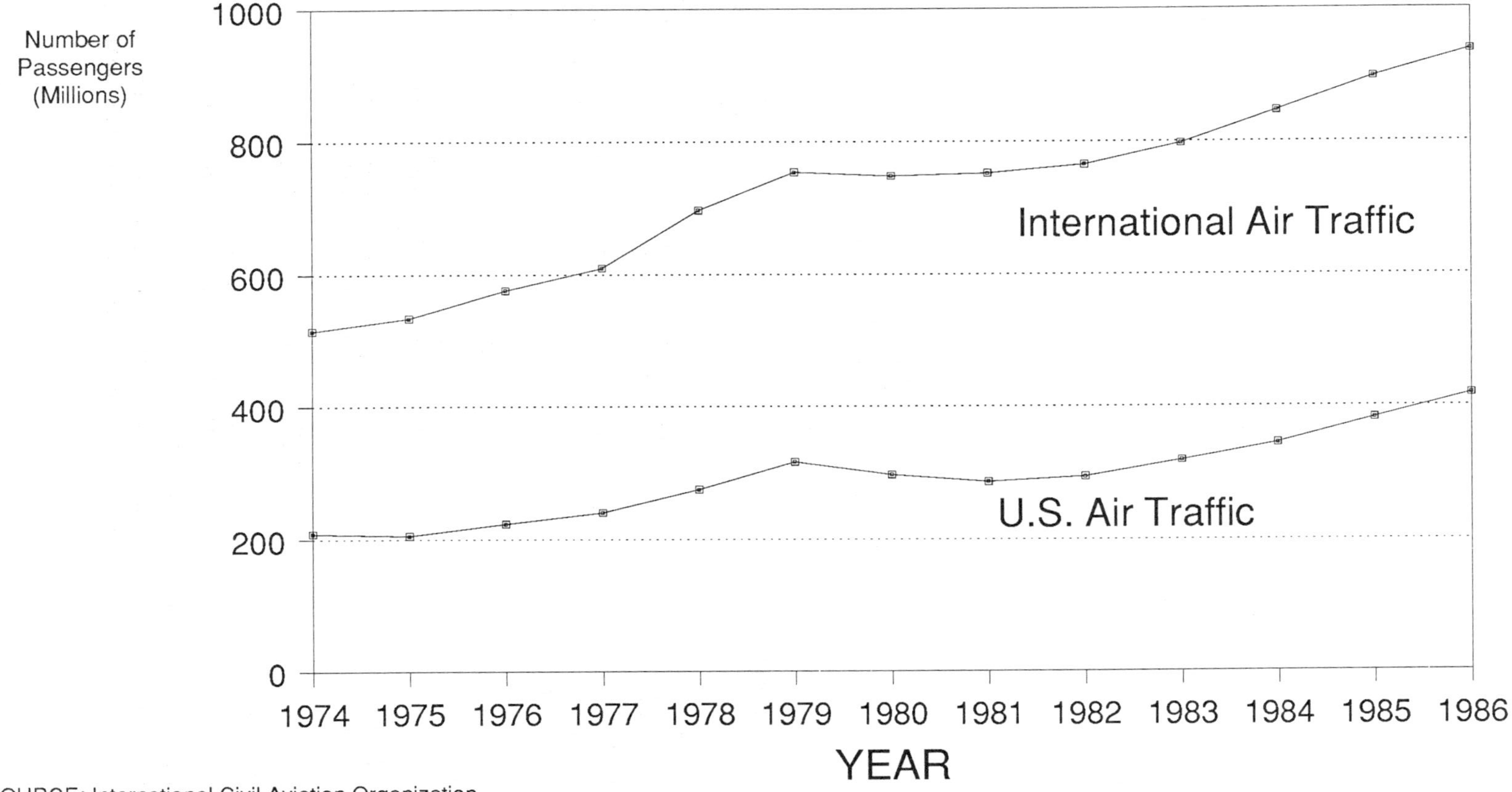

SOURCE: International Civil Aviation Organization and U.S. Federal Aviation Administration

Table 15:
World Scheduled Domestic and International Air Traffic (1974-1984)

Year	Number of passengers (millions)	% change	Passenger/ kilometres (millions)	% change	Load factor
1974	515	..	407,000	..	59
1975	534	3.6	433,000	6.4	59
1976	576	7.8	475,000	9.7	60
1977	610	5.9	508,000	6.9	61
1978	697	14.2	582,000	14.5	65
1979	754	8.1	659,000	13.2	66
1980	748	−0.8	677,000	2.7	63
1981	752	0.5	695,000	2.6	64
1982	764	1.6	710,000	2.1	64
1983	796	4.1	738,000	3.9	64
1984*	860	8.1	780,000	5.7	65

* estimates

Source: ICAO

Table 16:
Scheduled Traffic of Commercial Air Carriers: Tonne-Kilometres Performed by Region (1979 to 1983)

ICAO statistical region of	Total Tonne-Kilometres Performed (Millions)					
	1979	1980	1981	1982	1983 preliminary	83/79 Variation %
Europe						
Total	43,010	44,755	46,935	46,870	48,785	13.42
Passengers	31,560	32,835	34,580	34,505	35,150	11.37
Middle East						
Total	3,840	3,925	4,220	4,625	5,390	40.36
Passengers	2,505	2,550	2,765	3,025	3,465	38.32
Asia and the Pacific						
Total	17,870	20,055	22,335	23,860	25,155	40.76
Passengers	12,750	14,175	15,645	16,555	16,875	32.35
Africa						
Total	3,215	3,540	3,930	4,085	4,220	31.25
Passengers	2,430	2,700	2,965	3,055	3,080	26.74
North America						
Total	52,535	51,455	50,305	50,955	54,215	3.19
Passengers	41,290	49,310	39,155	40,065	42,425	2.74
Latin America						
Total	6,395	6,980	7,310	7,280	7,150	11.80
Passengers	4,890	5,325	5,515	5,355	5,395	10.32
Total ICAO States	126,870	130,710	135,035	137,675	144,915	14.22
Passengers	95,420	97,895	100,625	102,560	106,390	11.49

Source: *ICAO Statistical Yearbook — 1983*

Note: 'Totals' indicate tonne-kilometres attributable to passengers, freight and mail.
'Passengers' indicate tonne-kilometres attributable to passengers and their baggage.

Table 17: **Aircraft Operational Characteristics 1940 to 2000**

Year	Type	Range (miles)	Speed (mph)	Capacity (seats)	Engine (type)
1940	DC-3	1,510	210	28	Piston
1950	DC-6	3,000	316	108	Piston
1960	B707	6,110	600	189	turbofan
1970	B747	7,090	608	350	turbofan
1980	Concorde	3,970	1,400	144	turbojet
1990	B747-400	8,000	620	414	turbofan
2000	B747-500	8,500	620	500	turbofan

Source: Travel and Tourism Analyst

about 5 per cent per annum up to the year 2000, when annual passenger movements will be rapidly approaching the 2 billion level.

There are over 7,000 aircraft currently in service in the world's airlines fleets, and about 40% of these are short to medium range aircraft with less than 125 seats, many of which, such as the BAC 1–11, are no longer in production. 25% of the world's aircraft are short to medium haul types carrying up to 185 passengers. The long-haul market, epitomized by the 747, accounts for 20%.

However, nearly 50% of the world's fleet is over 12 years old and some 2,000 aircraft (i.e. 28% of those in use) are approaching the end of their working life. Renewal of aircraft is now a major issue with many fleets, especially those in the less developed countries of Africa, South America and Asia. Table 18 below outlines estimates of expected aircraft requirements up to 1995.

Table 18:
Estimates of commercial jet aircraft requirements 1985 to 1995

Aircraft Manufacturer	Boeing	Airbus	McDonnell Douglas
Type			
Narrow bodies			
Short range	—	1,134	815
Short/medium range	—	1,719	1,347
TOTAL	2,560	2,853	2,162
Wide bodies			
Short/medium range	—	2,509	1,150
Long range	—	894	703
TOTAL	1,179	3,403	1,853
Overall Total	3,739	6,256	4,015
Assumed RPM growth (% per year)			

Source: *Flight International* March 15th 1986

The growth in traffic led to a growth in competition between airlines and they had to adapt fares and products to market needs to achieve better capacity levels in their aircraft. As Table 15 shows, load factors rose from 59% in 1974 to 65% in 1984 (seats sold as a percentage of seats available). One of the main means of increasing capacity levels has been to offer discounts in air fares for advance bookings (APEX, Advance Purchase Excursion or Super-APEX), seasonal discounts, and very competitive fly-drive packages with substantial discounts for car hire. All of these variations in pricing relate to scheduled services, and they have been very successful. In the United States, the scheduled airline industry is very well developed. Due to the size of the country the airplane has historically been very important in mass travel for business and pleasure (Table 19). A recent poll by the Gallup Organization (*Travel Agent,* Oct. 19, 1987) found that the number of people who have flown on a commercial airline has increased from 49% of the population in 1971 to 72% in 1986. In 1986, U.S. Airlines carried more than 430 million passengers, 42% of all the world's air passengers (*Travel and Tourism World Yearbook,* 1987).

Table 19:
IATA Members' Rankings — Scheduled Airlines, 1987
(scheduled passenger-kilometers flown)

International Airline Rank	Millions	Domestic Airline Rank	Millions	Total Airline Rank	Millions
1. British Airways	44,085	1. United Airlines	89,075	1. United Airlines	106,685
2. Japan Air Lines	34,821	2. American Airlines	78,427	2. American Airlines	91,329
3. Pan American	33,519	3. Continental Airlines	52,929	3. Continental Airlines	62,931
4. Lufthansa	29,048	4. Eastern Air Lines	52,135	4. Eastern Air Lines	58,103
5. Air France	24,481	5. TWA	33,693	5. TWA	53,452
6. Qantas Airways	22,709	6. Air Canada	10,551	6. British Airways	46,299
7. KLM	21,797	7. Japan Air Lines	9,181	7. Japan Air Lines	44,002
8. TWA	19,759	8. Pan American	8,474	8. Pan American	41,992
9. United Airlines	17,609	9. Indian Airlines	8,110	9. Lufthansa	31,771
10. Iberia	14,909	10. Canadian Airlines Int'l	7,559	10. Air France	31,440
11. Alitalia	13,532	11. Air France	6,959	11. Qantas Airways	22,709
12. Swissair	13,519	12. TOA Domestic	6,537	12. KLM	21,801
13. American Airlines	12,902	13. Ansett Airlines	5,706	13. Air Canada	21,165
14. Air Canada	10,614	14. Australian Airlines	5,432	14. Iberia	19,404
15. Saudi Arabian Airlines	10,342	15. Saudi Arabian Airlines	5,297	15. Alitalia	18,094
16. SAS	10,155	16. Aeroméxico	4,701	16. Saudi Arabian Airlines	15,640
17. Continental Airlines	10,002	17. Alitalia	4,562	17. Canadian Airlines Int'l	15,479
18. British Caledonian	8,559	18. Iberia	4,496	18. Swissair	13,724
19. Air-India	8,335	19. VASP	4,231	19. SAS	13,207
20. Air-New Zealand	8,036	20. VARIG	3,795	20. VARIG	11,669
21. Canadian Airlines Int'l	7,919	21. P.T. Garuda Indonesia	3,594	21. P.T. Garuda Indonesia	11,104
22. VARIG	7,874	22. Mexicana	3,242	22. Mexicana	9,736
23. P.T. Garuda Indonesia	7,510	23. Transbrasil	3,114	23. Air New Zealand	9,563
24. Philippine Airlines	7,486	24. SAS	3,053	24. Philippine Airlines	9,260
25. El Al	7,284	25. Aerolineas Argentinas	2,926	25. British Caledonian	8,834

Source: International Air Transport Association (IATA)

To understand the commercial aviation industry in the United States, several distinctions are necessary. The U.S. airline industry is privately owned and operated for a profit. There are no national flag carrying airlines operated and subsidized by the government that are common in many other countries. Since a company's directors must report to stock holders and competition is always present, there must be a continuous striving to cut operating costs, increase market share and perhaps, as some companies have done, to diversify into other business. The U.S. airlines are classified according to the size of annual revenues but essentially there are three types, trunk line or long haul carriers, commuter lines that feed the trunk line carriers at major airports or hubs, and charter or supplemental air carriers. The latter carriers are not as prominent in the United States as they are in Europe where the greatest increase in air traffic since 1970 has been in the air charter business as inclusive air tours have grown.

The tour operator prepares sample brochures for specific tours and then forwards this to one of the IATA member carriers (normally the one that will be used for the charter) for approval. The carrier then assigns an IT (Inclusive Tour) code number which must appear on the air ticket in order to qualify for the tour commission. Tour operators take advantage of the unsold capacity in existing aircraft owned by the airlines, who in turn wish to fill as many seats as possible and to avoid 'dead' legs on an airline route where few passengers may be travelling.

Charter Flights

The early charter flights in the 1960s took several forms because of existing regulations which limited the operations of charter carriers in Britain and the United States. There were the 'one stop inclusive tour charter' (OTC) the 'inclusive tour charter' (ITC) and the advance booking charter (ABC), as well as special interest 'affinity' groups which were set up simply as a means of obtaining low-cost air fares. The rules for these charters were constantly abused and ignored (especially for the affinity groups) since government agencies regulating the operations of air carriers lacked the manpower to police them effectively. By the 1970s, both the British and United States governments realised the ineffectiveness of these regulations and introduced less stringent regulations for air charters.

The pioneering firms in the tour operations business chartered aircraft on an *ad hoc* basis as part of a particular tour package that they put together, relying on a full aircraft to increase their load factor, reduce costs per passenger mile and thus dramatically lower air fares compared with scheduled services. Charter companies also reduce their operating costs by having fairly small numbers of administrative staff, usually located in offices out of the city center. They rely on advertising and promotion being handled by the tour operator and travel agent. Moreover, because they are not committed to operating a scheduled service, they can cancel flights at short notice if insufficient seats have been sold, or combine two flights on the same aircraft to make a flight viable. Scheduled flights will have precedence in using the main airports for departures and arrivals, so charter flights are often late at night or early morning, even for short haul routes. So, although charter flights offer bargain fares, they do so with several strings attached. Charter traffic grew rapidly. In 1963, 630,000 Britons were flying on inclusive charter tours; by 1971 this had increased to 2,482,000 and by 1981 to over 5 million. In 1987 over 8 million Britons took advantage of inclusive air charter tours.

There are now five main airlines flying charter package holidays mainly to the mass market destinations around the Mediterranean, and almost all using Boeing 737s or 757s for these short-haul flights. These airlines and their airline codes are:

(i) Britannia Airways (BY)
(ii) Orion Airways Ltd (KG)
(iii) Air Europe (AE)
(iv) Dan Air (DA)
(v) Monarch Airlines Ltd (OM)

They normally fly from Gatwick or Luton and the main regional airports such as Manchester or East Midlands. Outside of the schedule services, tour operators must also obtain a license to operate inclusive air tours as a safeguard for passengers who could be stranded abroad if a company collapsed during the holiday season.

A list of charter airlines in North America is difficult to obtain and verify. Many operate on a narrow profit margin and their economic viability from year to year is unstable.

To sum up, since 1945, the air transport has been regulated in three ways:

— at international level with IATA and the International Civil Aviation Organization (a UN body);
— at national level by state control over fares and freight cargo rates offered to the public;
— bilateral agreements between governments covering specific routes, the number of flights on these routes, and the airlines who can fly them.

Although concern over safety standards and the financial viability of airlines is as strong as ever, there has been a general move during the 1980s to relax controls over fares, capacity, markets and frequency of flights in an effort to increase competition, in the belief that market forces will create the best environment for air travelers. This move is referred to as 'deregulation'. However, this raises the broader issue of the function of air transport. Is it a public service, a strictly commercial activity, or a compromise between the two?

Deregulation

At the international level, the first moves to deregulate air fares were initiated by the United States in the late 70s and early 80s. Unfortunately, this was a period of rising costs and declining profits for all international airlines and this led to concerted opposition to wholesale deregulation as airline financial losses were growing. The main problem with applying deregulation internationally is that it affects national airlines of countries in different stages of development. Some countries may provide services as a means of generating foreign exchange, providing tourist access as a national flag carrier, or generating foreign trade, and may not operate at a commercially viable level. Some of the developing countries come into this category and they may feel unable to compete with the larger well-established international carriers based in Britain or the U.S.

In the United States cargo deregulation was introduced in December 1977, followed by passenger deregulation in November 1978. Although this only affected internal domestic flights, the U.S. began to negotiate deregulated bilateral agreements for international services, coming into direct conflict with IATA which opposed complete deregulation. Within the United States, the whole regulatory system was further relaxed when the Civil Aeronautics Board was abolished in 1984. It is too early to predict the long-term impact of deregulation in the United States, but it already appears to be having the following impacts on domestic air services:

— an expansion in small and medium sized regional and local airlines;
— more airline bankruptcies as competition intensifies;
— a growth in commuter services;
— fare wars;
— mergers between airlines in the face of increased competition;
— accelerated development of hub and spoke interchanges;
— commuter lines sharing code designations with larger lines;
— consumer services strained;
— 80 – 85% of all passengers flying on discounted tickets;
— one airline may dominate traffic into and out of one city hub and fares are high.

In 1978, ten major carriers dominated US domestic traffic, accounting for 88% of the market share. By 1984, this group had shrunk to nine and their market share to 75%. Fifteen new airlines were started up, although they accounted for less than 5% of all traffic (Pryke 1987). Most of the newly certified carriers were located at secondary airports such as Midway, Chicago or Newark, New Jersey, and many offered limited amenities, preferring to compete with low fares. One structural development that has emerged with deregulation is the appearance of hub-and-spoke networks, with airlines increasingly basing their activities at a limited number of major airports.

The long term effect may well be that, although fares may drop in the short-term, mergers will mean that much domestic traffic will be in the hands of a few large companies who will squeeze out the smaller operators.

Eight major airlines controlled 93 percent of the air traffic in 1988, while in 1978 twelve carriers controlled the same proportion. The top eight airlines in 1988 by revenue passenger miles, (one RPM equals one paying passenger flown one mile) and their rank in 1978, are as follows:

	1978	**1988**
United	1	1
American	2	2
Delta	5	3
Continental	9	4
Northwest	11	5
TWA	3	6
Pan Am	6	7
Eastern	4	8

(Source: *Travel Industry World Yearbook*, 1988)

Texas Air Corporation owns Continental and Eastern; if these two companies were considered as one airline, it would be the largest with about 19 percent of the market.

In Britain, there has been increasing emphasis on competition between airlines and, since 1983, talks have taken place within the European Economic Community to liberalize air fares throughout Europe, although this has met strong opposition from several national carriers and it will be a slow and gradual process.

The London *Sunday Times* (November 16, 1986) published a comparison of air fares between points in Europe and the United States. The distance between New York City and St. Louis, Missouri is 894 miles. It is 895 miles between London and Rome. The cost per mile between the U.S. cities is ⅓ of the cost between the European cities ($148 compared $384). Flying in Europe is, on the average, twice as expensive on a per mile basis as in the United States and helps to explain how air travel has increased with deregulation. Fortunately for the Europeans, there is an alternative, a well developed and efficient railroad system.

U.S. citizens may fly inexpensively but must also contend with traffic congestion to reach the airport, crowded terminals and delays. In the United States other than airport buses, railroad mass transit facilities to most large airports are just beginning to be developed. European countries have had more foresight and implemented intermodal transport interchanges at airports, inner cities and suburbs. Of the world's top 10 airports by passengers enplaned, only two are outside the United States--Heathrow (London) and Tokyo International. Both of these terminals can be reached by rail. O'Hare International (Chicago) is the world's leader with 53 million passengers in 1986 (*Travel Industry World Yearbook,* 1988).

The overall efforts to increase deregulation on international routes are likely to continue, albeit slowly. One benefit of the increased competition created by deregulation is that it forces airlines to be more efficient by scaling down their operations, improving productivity, aircraft load factors and their attractiveness to the traveler, particularly the business traveler.

It has become increasingly evident that the commercial air transport system at major world air terminals is congested to the point of questionable safety standards. The air passenger, during holidays and high season vacation periods, must contend with crowded terminals and departure delays to the point that travel can be truly interpreted as travail. A strike by air traffic controllers may also throw the system into chaos as the short news item in *U.S.A. Today,* July 18, 1988 relates:

> CROWDED SKIES: An expected one-day strike today by French air traffic controllers was called off Sunday by two of three unions. But Europe's air traffic is likely to remain snarled; travelers reported delays of up to 24 hours in Britain.

Air traffic controllers in North America and Western Europe are overwhelmed by the number of aircraft in the skies above the terminals. To monitor this traffic, in order to maintain safe traffic patterns in three dimensional space, has at times become a true nightmare. Inclement weather taxes the system even more. More airports are needed, as well as more controllers on the ground. The future may prove that travel by air will at times be limited by human capabilities to ensure safe travel, and this includes halting terrorism.

Future Developments in International Air Travel

The major factors likely to influence international air transport are in the areas of aircraft technology, operations and distribution systems. Improvements in the operating efficiency of engines will help reduce fuel consumption as will the greater use of composite materials in airframe construction, together with more sophisticated flight systems which will make aircraft easier to fly. Estimates of operating costs vary, but the new generation of engines in use in the 1990s are likely to have cost savings 10% lower than existing versions. The main body of the Boeing 767 has only 3% composite materials but this gives it a weight saving of 630 kg, equal to the weight of 8 passengers. By 1992, composites such as carbon-fibre thermoplastics could cover up to 30% of the surface area of new aircraft, with corresponding savings in the payload cost. Improvements in on-board computers and display technology are likely to give volume savings of 60% and weight savings of 70% in the flight decks of the 1990s aircraft. Miniaturization will also bring in small personal video screens for in-flight movies and individual passenger entertainment systems.

These technological advances will bring very real cost savings to those airlines who invest in the new aircraft types and, assuming that deregulation produces a more liberal air transport environment worldwide, the airlines will be able to pass on these savings to their customers in the form of reduced fares, in order to maintain their market share. For example, Northwest Orient, which has purchased up to 100 Airbus 320-200 aircraft, estimate that their fuel consumption will be 50% lower per seat than the existing fleet. This will enable the company to operate more effectively in a very competitive US market.

The increasing use of non-stop long range aircraft, such as the Boeing 747 – 400, is likely to give rise to strategic hub international airports similar to the pattern now emerging in the US domestic market. London, New York, Tokyo and Los Angeles are likely to emerge as world hubs.

ASSIGNMENT

1. Outline what you consider to be the impact of deregulation on:
   a) Domestic coach operations;
   a) Domestic air travel;
   a) International air travel.

2. Describe the impact of changing travel preferences on the traditional holiday resort.

Chapter 7
The Lodging Sector

Learning Objectives: After reading this chapter you should have an understanding of:
— the main components of the accommodation sector;
— how these components operate;
— changes in accommodation preferences since 1970;
— the main companies in this sector;
— the distribution of accommodation in the USA;
— recent trends in this sector.

Introduction

Jobs provided by the lodging sector form a major element of the tourist industry in the United States and Britain. In the United States out of almost five million people employed in the industry, 1.5 million are associated with lodging. In Britain the ratio is higher than the United States — 900,000 in accommodation and catering out of 1.5 million employed in the tourist industry. In 1986, in spite of some regional decline in hotel occupancy rates, the industry added 100,000 employees, while in Britain 92,000 jobs were created between 1982 and 1985.

Providing lodging for the traveler is the most important and largest part of the facilities and services component of the tourist industry. Fifteen percent of all expenditures in domestic travel can be attributed to the lodging market. The World Tourism Organization estimated that the U.S. and Canada had 2.8 million lodging rooms in 1986. Europe had 5.0 million rooms. Combined, these two world regions had 78% of all rooms in the world. The average occupancy rate in the world in 1986 was 64.5%, a ten year low, while the average room rate was $53 per room (Horwath & Horwath World Wide Hotel Industry, 1987) (Table 20).

The lodging sector has also demonstrated its resilience in times of economic recession and its ability to recover more quickly than many other tourism-related activities. Although these figures refer to the commercial accommodation sector, it is important to have an understanding of all types of accommodation used and their importance to the tourist industry or the economy of a tourist region.

During the eighteenth and nineteenth centuries, accommodation mainly consisted of coaching inns, boarding houses, and houses let for the 'season', with the emergence of 'grand hotels' following the development of the railways. Few major resorts were without at least one luxury hotel. The growth of mass tourism and the spread of holidays with pay saw the emergence of smaller hotels and boarding houses catering for the summer trade and, in the 1930s, the development of new types of accommodation including camping, caravanning, youth hostelling and holiday camps. Post 1945 developments have included a mix of commercial ac-

Trends In Performance Measurements—Worldwide Hotels

Table 20:

	All Hotels		Africa and the Middle East		Asia and Australasia		North America[2]		Europe		Latin America/ Caribbean[2]	
	1985	1986	1985	1986	1985	1986	1985	1986	1985	1986	1985	1986
Percentage of Occupancy	67.1%	64.5%	61.8%	55.9%	68.3%	67.9%	67.0%	68.4%	67.1%	62.9%	67.9%	63.4%
Percentage of Double Occupancy	35.6	36.2	19.8	21.8	51.9	45.6	48.9	46.6	33.7	31.6	46.3	70.4
Average Room Rate												
Per Room	$45.17	$56.72	$54.24	$58.72	$43.19	$51.65	$50.85	$61.40	$40.18	$51.99	$46.34	$55.56
Per Guest	32.38	43.79	43.67	50.23	31.41	36.15	35.40	43.73	30.49	41.40	29.23	39.43
Income Before Fixed Charges												
Ratio to Room Sales	43.7%	43.4%	42.6%	43.6%	49.7%	45.4%	39.4%	38.3%	45.5%	53.9%	42.1%	43.2%
Ratio to Total Sales	23.1	22.9	21.4	18.9	25.7	20.3	22.9	23.2	23.5	26.3	23.3	24.4
Number of Times Average Rate Earned	116	107	111	89	120	108	103	100	125	128	105	112
Composition of Sales[1]												
Rooms	53.1%	56.0%	45.9%	53.1%	53.3%	50.8%	60.1%	63.9%	50.1%	50.3%	55.9%	55.4%
Food	26.8	24.6	28.5	21.6	27.2	27.7	23.4	21.8	29.5	29.2	23.4	22.8
Beverage	12.2	10.7	10.5	8.3	10.7	10.3	10.8	8.6	14.8	14.7	10.2	9.6
Telephone	3.6	3.7	6.4	7.1	3.8	3.8	2.5	2.5	2.9	2.9	4.7	4.2
Minor Operated Departments	2.3	2.2	5.8	3.5	2.6	4.1	1.7	1.5	1.4	1.4	2.3	3.2
Rentals and Other Income	2.0	2.8	2.9	6.4	2.4	3.3	1.5	1.7	1.3	1.5	3.5	4.8
Total	100.0%	100.0%	100.0%	100.0%	100.0%	100.0%	100.0%	100.0%	100.0%	100.0%	100.0%	100.0%
Amounts per Available Room												
Total Sales	$20,929	$24,329	$25,940	$22,694	$21,444	$25,142	$21,077	$23,354	$20,460	$25,492	$19,555	$23,979
Income Before Fixed Charges	4,543	5,790	4,067	4,379	4,202	5,174	4,377	5,397	4,784	7,168	4,174	5,373
Net Income or (Loss) Before Income Taxes	2,159	1,626	2,669	1,874	1,566	1,608	931	672	2,841	3,743	2,143	1,887

[1] Based on arithmetic mean; all other figures medians.
[2] 1985 figures included Caribbean properties in the North American section.
Source: Worldwide Hotel Industry 1987, Horwath and Horwath International.

tivities such as villa holidays abroad, time-share holidays, consortia marketing country cottage or farmhouse holidays; and non commercial activities such as visiting friends and relatives (VFR) and house exchange schemes, as well as the growth in the ownership of second homes.

Structure of the Lodging Sector

The American Hotel and Motel Association (AHMA) classifies the industry according to transient hotels, all year round resort hotels, seasonal resorts, residential hotels and condominium hotels. The largest group is the first, the transient hotel, which includes motels that since World War II have been built at the interchanges on the interstate highway system. This growth was spearheaded by the Holiday Inn Company (now Holiday Corporation) in the early 1950s. The inner city is the major location for residential hotels and, of course, transient center city hotels. Large center city hotels provide accommodation for businessmen and convention attendees. Suburban hotels and motels have grown along the highway beltlines, encircling large cities, to service the transient traveler and, because there are many businesses and corporations that have moved to the suburbs, the traveling business person. Major airports have been growth areas in the last decade selling rooms to airline employees on stopovers, travelers, and providing meeting facilities for small groups near the transport interchange. Resort hotels have generally developed in peripheral locations to population centers but, in recent years, the resort concept has been applied to hotels in cities to attract vacationers as well as the business person (Figure 17 on page 52). The 1986 Laventhol and Horwath summary of the U.S. Lodging Industry provides a profile of the location of establishments that cooperated in the accounting firm's survey:

Location	**Percent**
Center City	30.6
Surburban	24.7
Airport	11.5
Highway	16.1
Resort	12.0
Not Reported	5.1

The composition of sales at these properties is consistent, regardless of the above locations. Room sales constitute 65 percent of total sales, food 21 percent, beverage 8 percent, telephone 2 percent and other 3 percent. The source of business for all lodging establishments is primarily from domestic visitors — 92 percent. Hotels in the northeastern states have the highest proportion of foreign clients — 11 percent, while the North Central and Western regions have the lowest proportions — 7 percent. Unless a hotel does a specific survey as to why a guest is there, when they appear at the check-in or reception desk, it is impossible to separate leisure guests from other visitors. In general, surveys of this type have found that 40-50 percent of guests are business or government travelers, 25 – 35 percent are tourists and the remaining proportions are convention and other trip purposes. The location of the accommodation will dictate a varience in these proportions with the tourist visitors' percentage higher in the summer in resort hotels and accommodations located along highways.

Hotels, motels and motor hotels are dominated by large corporations. Some of the largest domestic chains and the number of hotels and motels operated in each chain are listed in Table 21. Listing hotel chains by number of establishments is misleading as to actual magnitude of a chain. For example, the Sheraton Corporation operates at 503 locations but, in terms of the number of rooms, the hotel chain is almost of the magnitude of Best Western International Inc.

Table 21:
Major UK Hotel Chains

Hotels operating in UK in Top 100	World Rank*	Total Rooms	Great Britain Hotels	Rooms
Holiday Inns	1	312,426	17	3,785
The Sheraton Corp	2	118,584	3	1,415
Ramada Inns	3	95,198	1	200
Trusthouse Forte	5	74,568	208	20,950
Marriott Corp	9	48,408	1	274
Novetel SIEH	11	46,253	5	1,088
Intercontinental	14	39,533	8	2,995
Hilton International	17	33,034	2	1,120
Hyatt International	23	13,826	1	228
Crest Hotels	29	12,220	54	8,184
Dunfey Hotels	36	10,929	1	800
Commonwealth Holiday Inns	42	9,648	—	—
Four Seasons	60	6,639	1	220
Penta Hotels	63	6,037	1	900
Thistle Hotels	78	4,963	39	5,952
Comfort Hotels	81	4,820	22	2,900
Taj Hotels	84	4,638	2	—
Ladbroke Hotels	86	4,600	32	3,500
Hotel Groups in UK				
Queens Moat			55	4,432
Mount Charlotte			43	5,300
Embassy Hotels			42	3,561
Swallow Hotels			31	3,000
Virani			19	2,200
Rank Hotels			5	2,074
Reo Stakis			24	2,000
De Vere Hotels			14	1,560
Norfolk Capital			10	1,000
Imperial Hotels			34	1,000
Metropole			5	2,000
Sarova			7	1,000
Seaco (Distinguished Hotels)			6	816
Savoy			4	636
Gleneagles			4	650

*According to the World's Top 100 Hotel Chains, prepared by Hotels and Restaurants Internationals.

The accommodation sector in the United Kingdom is divided into two components; the first is serviced accommodation and the second is called self-catering. Essentially meals are not included in the price of a room and spartan kitchens are available for the guests to prepare or cater for their own needs. In North America, as in Britain, self-catering lodging is most common in resort areas. The budget motel in the United States with no room service, no restaurant, and few room amenities is an innovation not emulated in Europe.

In the U.K. and the United States, commercial serviced accommodation is dominated by the hotel/motel sector. The types of companies operating in this sector cover the whole range from multi-national companies to franchises, cooperatives or sole owners. The Catering Intelligence Unit (CIU) of the Consumer Industries Press estimates that there are now 145 hotel groups in the U.K. operating 2,000 hotels with a total of 146,000 bedrooms. Table 21 on page 108 outlines the share of the British hotel market, and emphasizes the importance of the international hotel chains. Two of the top three companies are U.S. based, and have developed the system of *franchising* where the person operating the hotel pays a fee and royalties for using the brand name and marketing back-up of the parent company. Trusthouse Forte, Crest Hotels (owned by Bass PLC) Thistle Hotels (owned by Scottish and Newcastle), Holiday Inns and Ladbroke Hotels are the main companies with overseas interests. The Hotel Development Incentive Scheme (1969–73) which arose from the 1969 Development of Tourism Act, encouraged several companies with broad interests in leisure activities to invest in the tourist industry. Bass PLC acquired the Crest Hotel group; Scottish and Newcastle, the Thistle Hotels; and Ladbrokes established their own hotel chain. Since the end of this scheme in 1973, few new hotels have been built. However, the UK hotel market has remained fairly unchanged during the 1980s and, faced with increasing competition for a share of this market, a number of new companies have emerged as well as consortia of independent hotels who have combined their marketing operations. Examples of new companies in the 1980s include the Queens Moat Hotels (55 hotels) and the Virani Group (19 hotels). The independent hotels who have formed marketing consortia have gained access to national and international markets through joint promotions. Table 22 below shows the main hotel marketing consortia operating in Britain.

Table 22:
Hotel Marketing Consortia Operating in Great Britain

	World Rank*	Total Rooms	Great Britain Hotels	Rooms
Best Western	1	216,640	170	8,000
Leading Hotels of the World	7	44,000		
World Hotels	10	18,500		
Minotels	13	12,972		
Consort Hotels	20	5,000		
Exec Hotels	33	1,900		
Prestige Hotels	34	1,712	22	1,712
Guestacom	37	863		
Inter Hotels			103	n.a.

*According to the Top 37 International Consortia prepared by Hotels and Restaurants International.

The lodging industry in the United States has enjoyed a mixed up and downward growth and decline on a regional basis since the first energy crisis in 1975. The current popular term in the industry is 'overbuilt' but the reality may be the result of the cyclical nature of the industry. The Federal Economic Recovery Tax Act (ERTA) of 1981 created investment tax credits and shorter depreciation schedules and thus provided new incentives for lodging development. The result was 500,000 new hotel rooms and a drop to 65 percent in the average occupancy in 1985, down one percent from 1984 (Travel Industry Yearbook, 1987). Japanese and European hotel chains are making many lodging investments in the United States. The Japanese in particular have been making investments in the Hawaiian

Islands for many years, with about 40 hotels. Investments are very substantial, particularly when it is realized that the cost to construct one new hotel room in the 1980s is about $100,000. British Bass PLC Company now owns the international assets of Holiday Corporation and Britain's Ladbrook Group owns Hilton International (Travel Industry World Yearbook, 1988).

The *self-catering sector* has grown in importance over the past 30 years at the expense of the unlicensed hotel and guest house sector. This includes rented accommodation, caravans, and tented camp sites. In 1957, 15 per cent of British holidaymakers used self-catering accommodation and 31 per cent stayed in unlicensed hotels and boarding houses. By 1971, these proportions were reversed and, by 1981, over 36 per cent of Britons used self-catering accommodation on holidays in Britain.

Self-catering accommodation can take several forms. It can be:

— rented holiday flats, cottages or houses
— rented caravans
— rented tents
— holiday camps

Most of this self-catering accommodation is located on or close to Britain's coast, reflecting in part the long-standing preference for seaside holidays by most domestic tourists. The rapid growth and spread of coastal caravan and camping sites during the 1960s and 1970s gave rise to a range of conflicts and these are discussed in more detail in Chapter 12.

The answer to self catering, and to less expensive accommodation, in the U.S. has been the development of the budget motel, the all-suite hotel, resort condominium and the revival of bed and breakfast accommodations. According to USTDC National Travel Survey in 1986, only 5 percent of all vacation person-trips were spent in a rented cabin, condominium or vacation home.

Farm-based accommodation has grown in importance over recent years as farmers have turned to other activities to supplement their incomes, and development grants have been made available through the tourist boards, notably the West Country Tourist Board and the Wales Tourist Board. This accommodation may be serviced or self-catering. Accommodation in farm premises consists of rooms let either in the main building, where the farmer and his family live, or in another structure that has been converted from agricultural use to holiday accommodation. Letting of farm cottages is also popular, as is the development of small touring caravans or camping sites.

Although comprehensive and reliable statistics on farm tourism are not yet available, what is clear from the data that does exist is that, in most EEC countries, it has already established itself as an important element in the rural economy. Most of the information outlined below has been drawn from papers presented at the Marienhamn Symposium in 1982.

— *France* There is a long tradition of farm tourism in France dating back to 1955 when the policy of *gites ruraux* was established. The amount of rural farm accommodation almost trebled between 1973 and 1981 from 9,978 units to over 25,000. About 150,000 beds are provided in this sector with an estimated 7.5 million overnight stays.

— *West Germany* Farm Tourism has a 12 year history in West Germany with almost 25,000 farms now offering tourist accommodation. Recent surveys by the University of Munich have shown that about 3 million West Germans are interested in spending their holidays on farms.

— *Ireland* Farm tourism was developed in the early 1960s and the first listings contained only a few farm premises. The 1982 guide contains over 500 farmhouses offering tourist accommodation and a further 500+ farm cottages.

— *United Kingdom* A conservative estimate suggests that 10,000 farms offer farmhouse accommodation and a further 10,000 offer self-catering accommodation. A further 5,000 farms provide camping and caravanning facilities.

— *Denmark* To date (1979) only 500 farms provide for tourists and no capital grants are available. However, the marketing of farm tourism is heavily subsidised by the Danish Tourist Board who are also involved with the promotional literature.

No information is available on the extent of and growth in farm tourism among the other Member States of the European Economic Community. The summary report of the Marienhamn Symposium concludes that most of the farms depending on non agricultural income are interested in farm tourism (i.e. 40 to 60 per cent of all farms) and some regions, particularly in Scandinavia, show a very high growth rate in this activity. Farm tourism has not yet developed in Italy or Greece.

In the United States, farm and ranch vacations are also growing as overnight accommodation sites but, more importantly, as vacation destinations for a week or longer. There are at least 500 such sites in the U.S. and Canada. They are centered in the states of Pennsylvania, Ohio and Iowa for farm vacations and in Wyoming, Montana, Colorado and Arizona for ranch vacations. This segment of the vacation industry, consisting of individual farm and ranch owners, is not well documented.

In the non-commercial accommodation sector, visiting friends and relatives (VFR) is taking a growing share of the accommodation market. In 1961 visiting friends and relatives accounted for 32% of accommodation used. By 1980 this had increased to 43% of accommodation used by British Tourists. In the past the VFR market has been neglected as a segment of the total market but it is important also when marketing to overseas tourists. In 1978, 40 per cent of overseas visitors to Britain stayed with friends and relatives. In the United States, 47% of vacation person trips in 1986 were spent in the homes of friends or relatives. According to the U.S. Travel and Tourism Administration's In-Flight Survey of International Air Travelers in 1986, 15% of overseas visitors to the U.S. stayed with friends and 21% stayed with relatives.

The growth in the ownership of private trailers (caravans to the British), trailered tent campers and recreation vehicles, has made mobile vacations available to people in the United States and Western Europe. In 1987, 3.9 million overnight stays were made by tent campers in the U.S. National Parks and another 4 million camped in recreation vehicles. In the United States there were more than 48 million camper nights in state parks in 1982, 57 million visitor days at U.S. Forest Service campsites and another 9 million visitor days at campsites operated by the Bureau of Land Management. According to the National Campground Owners Association, there are an estimated 10,000 privately operated campgrounds and 947,000 campsites in the United States, some that are franchised such as Campgrounds of America with 600 properties, and Yogi Bear's Jellystone Park Camp-Resorts with 80 properties.

More recent trends include national and international home exchange schemes where, for a small annual fee, individuals can exchange houses for the holiday period, and time-share developments where purchasers can buy exclusive use of a property for a specific period of the year. This development is discussed in more detail in Chapter 13.

Classification systems or grading of service in the United States and the United Kingdom are voluntary, unlike many European countries that have compulsory classification systems. The international traveler moving from country to country must become familiar with the system used in each country. A three star hotel in one country may be comparable to a two star hotel in another.

There is no statutory registration system for hotels in the U.K. although from January 1987 the National Tourist Boards for England, Scotland and Wales have introduced a new Crown Classification system. It covers *serviced accommodation* and includes all types of serviced establishments, from those listed for simple accommodation to five crowns for top class accommodation. Previous attempts at voluntary classification were unsatisfactory because they relied on facts supplied by the owners/managers themselves without any checking. The new Crown system will ensure that no classification will be granted until a verification check has been carried out. Subsequent checks will be made on an annual basis. From 1987 onwards, only those premises classified by the tourist boards will be included in their accommodation guides. The tourist boards hope that by introducing one scheme common to all serviced accommodation in Britain they will help the industry to market itself more effectively at home and overseas. By the end of 1986 over 10,000 establishments had been classified under this scheme.

The Automobile Association (AA) and the Royal Automobile Club (RAC) also operate their own classification schemes. Until the introduction of the Crown scheme, the star rating awarded by the AA has been one measure of the quality of the serviced accommodation sector. Nearly 80% of the entries in the AA guide are in the 2 and 3 star categories — 6% are 4 star and under 1% are 5 star.

The American Automobile Association (AAA) provides a lodging rating in directories provided to members. A five diamond rating is reserved for a very select group of the 20,000 motels, hotels and resorts inspected each year for the AAA membership of 28.5 million. Properties that request listing in the guidebooks must agree to an inspection of more than 200 separate items. In 1988 forty properties in the United States, four in Canada and three in Mexico, were granted the coveted five diamond rating for exceptional restaurants, rooms, and service staff. The Mobil Travel Guide provides a similar rating based on a star system. The 'best in the country' five star rating was granted in 1988 to twelve resorts, two motels, seven hotels and ten restaurants, a category not included by the AAA. The Arizona Biltmore, a resort hotel in Scottsdale, has been given the five star rating for 29 consecutive years. Most middle class travelers find two and three star or diamond ratings very satisfactory and compatible with travel expenses. In the United States, unlike many other countries, rooms with private baths are the rule rather than the exception, even for the lowest ratings.

Problems Affecting the Accommodation Sector

The owner or manager working in the accommodation sector is working in a highly competitive commercial environment, and has to deal with several issues that can affect the success of his operation.

These include:

- the seasonality of hotel occupancy rates
- the cost and availability of manpower
- the supply of raw materials
- the availability of new technology
- interest rates and taxation policy

The domestic holiday market is still heavily concentrated in the period between June and August, and the accommodation sector faces the dilemma of gearing up to meet peak-season demand and then having under-used resources for the rest of the year.

To offset this seasonal peaking, the British Tourist Authority introduced 'Operation Off-Peak' in 1972 with the aim of encouraging operators to put together development packages that would promote overseas visitor numbers during the trough periods — particularly the autumn and winter months.

Hotels in the United States and Canada also offer off-season and weekend rates and the competition between major lodging companies to increase occupancy is very intense in some areas.

New technology is playing an increasingly important role in the accommodation sector. A Gallup survey for the *Caterer and Hotelkeeper* in 1983 found that more than a third of hotels with 3 stars or more, regardless of size, possess computers. These are used for a wide range of functions including:

- Front office activities — reservations, accounting, ledgers, credit control;
- General office activities — financial control, day-to-day accounts, purchases, invoices, credit control;
- Room service accounting;
- Restaurant/meals and drink accounting;
- Telephone accounts.

Hotels that form part of a chain may have their activities linked by computer networks and the General Management/Boards of Directors can receive up to date information on the performance of individual hotels and consortia of hotels. Clearly, staff working the front office or finance and accounting divisions of an hotel will have to have training in computer applications and usage, particularly data-base packages, viewdata systems, and spreadsheets.

Hotels that are part of a large chain (company owned and operated) or franchised system (which leaves management decisions to the private owner) have many advantages. In the United States, the major advantage is the tie-in with a nation-wide reservation system. Other advantages include regional and state advertising and image promotion, inspection systems providing quality control, contact with package tour companies, bulk purchases of supplies, listings in travel guides, and, frequently, a lobbyist in Washington, D.C.

Table 23:
Top 25 U.S. Lodging Chains, 1986

	U.S. Properties		Foreign Properties	
	Number	Rooms	Number	Rooms
Holiday Corporation	1,623	303,044	201	47,495
Holiday Inns & Crowne Plazas	1,440	269,543	201	47,495
Embassy Suites	73	17,254	0	0
Hampton Inns	106	13,394	0	0
Harrah's	4	2,853	0	0
Best Western International Inc.	1,905	174,059	1,441	81,554
The Sheraton Corporation	503	144,170	127	48,342
Quality International Inc.	928	110,678	100	10,442
Comfort Inns	400	36,921	19	1,197
Quality Inns	478	60,571	76	8,734
Clarion Hotels/Inns/Resorts	32	10,394	5	511
Comfort Suites	8	1,231	0	0
Quality Suites	10	1,561	0	0
Hilton Hotels Corporation	271	97,535	1	622
Hilton Hotels	271	97,535	0	0
Conrad International Hotels	0	0	1	622
Marriott Corporation	235	88,960	13	4,988
Marriott Hotels & Resorts	194	82,736	13	4,988
Courtyard by Marriott	40	6,000	0	0
Marriott All - Suites	1	224	0	0
Ramada Hotel Group	507	85,600	64	14,400
Ramada Inns	442	66,300	18	2,500
Ramada Hotels	53	13,000	31	7,600
Ramada Renaissance Hotels	12	6,300	15	4,300
Days Inns of America	439	65,770	4	488
Howard Johnson Franchise Systems, Inc.	445	53,556	13	1,549
Hyatt Hotels Corporation	84	46,391	42	15,167
Motel 6, Inc.	409	45,793	0	0
Travelodge/Viscount Hotels	420	32,297	27	2,111
Exclusive	4	1,501	1	315
Viscount	12	3,431	1	238
Travelodge	404	27,365	25	1,558
Econo Lodges of America, Inc.	394	31,807	2	137
Super 8 Motels, Inc.	402	25,655	2	99
La Quinta Motor Inns Inc.	188	23,674	0	0
Radisson Hotel Corporation	97	23,662	35	7,941
Plaza Hotels	10	3,715	0	0
Suite Hotels	6	1,368	0	0
Hotels	34	9,446	35	7,941
Inns	17	3,520	0	0
Resorts	6	1,111	0	0
Colony Resorts	24	4,502	0	0
Westin Hotels & Resorts	31	18,875	30	13,757
Red Roof Inns, Inc.	171	18,708	0	0
Rodeway Inns International, Inc.	152	18,190	0	0
Hospitality International Inc.	263	17,922	3	220
Scottish Inns	107	6,394	0	0
Red Carpet Inns	120	8,928	0	0
Master Host Inns	23	2,314	0	0
Master Host Resorts	13	286	3	220
Embassy Suites	73	17,254	0	0
Preferred Hotels Worldwide	46	13,227	27	6,995
Omni Hotels	30	13,034	3	1,355
Omni Hotels	22	10,228	0	0
Dunfey Hotels	8	2,806	0	0
International Hotels	0	0	3	1,355
Knights Inn	110	12,200	0	0
The Residence Inn Co.	87	10,476	0	0

Source: Lodging Hospitality.

Recent Trends in the Lodging Sector

The hotel sector has withstood the recession years quite well, by adapting to changing trends, identifying new markets, better market segmentation and more efficient management. The growth in the numbers of foreign tourists during the 1970s and 1980s has clearly helped the hotel sector, and the numbers of foreign visitors to the U.K. is expected to continue to grow during the 1980s.

Likewise, in the United States foreign visitors are expected to increase. Hotel demand will increase at major entry gateways and at attraction complexes that are known overseas, such as Disneyworld.

The lodging industry in the United States has reached a mature stage of development. Large companies have been initiating methods to segment the industry. One method is to increase the amenities provided for the guest, depending upon the type of market. For example, Motel Six has now installed a reservation system and added more free luxury items in rooms. Other hotels have added exercise rooms, enclosed swimming pools for year around use, or even lighted tennis courts. The trend towards market segmentation is exemplified by the names of the properties (Table 23). Holiday Corporation has very upscale properties called Crowne Plazas and their highway transient properties, affordable to the middle class, are now labeled Hampton Inns. Upscale lodging can be identified by titles such as Courtyard by Marriott, Ramada Renaissance, and Travelodge Exclusive. With segmentation, product marketing becomes more important and the focus, according to Laventhol and Horwath, has shifted from the operational to that of marketing.

A relatively new form of segmentation in large cities has been development of all-suite hotels. In locations with high business clients, a suite of rooms for group meetings is highly desired and hotels of this type have occupancy rates above the national average. There are currently (October 1987) about 750 such hotels in the USA. According to the Laventhol and Horwath survey these 'all suite' hotels are generating much higher occupancy levels than any other hotel product, and their attraction is that they can be designed to cater for a wide range of different market segments from the business traveler to the family on vacation.

Some lodging corporations have acquired properties by mergers, such as Mariott's acquisition of Howard Johnson from Imperial Group Ltd. in 1985. Laventhol and Horwath believe that consolidations of this type may continue, partly due to market segmentation, as one company purchases another that has experience in a particular market area or as companies seek to control the best real estate sites. Location of a hotel or motel is a major key to success and quality locations are in short supply.

The marriage between airlines and hotel operations, which was common prior to airline deregulation, did not prove successful. Allegis Corporation's (United Airlines) venture into the ownership of Westin Hotels, and its mid-1980s purchase of Hilton International and Hertz Rental Car, were intended to offer the United Airlines traveler a complete line of travel services. In theory this was a good idea, but the highly competitive nature of the airline industry, plus an overcapacity of rooms in the U.S. lodging industry, proved the theory unsound.

As Table 24 shows, there are around 24,000 hotels in the USA almost evenly divided into chains and independent operators. The majority of the independent operators have under 300 rooms, with 30% having less than 75 rooms. These smaller hotels are mainly catering for the cheaper end of the market. In contrast, only 9% of the chains operate hotels with under 75 rooms and 58% of the chains are hotels with 150 rooms or more.

Table 24:
The US Hotel Industry 1986

	Hotel Chains	Independent Hotels
No. of Properties	11,683	12,236
No. of Rooms	1,678,935	971,303
Number of rooms	%	%
Under 75	9.0	30.6
75 – 149	32.3	25.5
150 – 299	30.8	20.9
300 – 600	18.0	14.2
Over 600	9.9	8.2
TOTAL	100.0	100.0

(Source: *Laventhol and Horwarth, US Lodging Industry,* 1987)

One main trend between 1982 and 1986 was the shift in location of the independent hotels, with a 10% growth in resort locations while the chains show no significant difference between city center, airport, suburban or resort locations. (Laventhol and Horwarth 1987).

An analysis of the market segments catered for between 1982 and 1986 shows that the independent US hotels developed more business in the general tourism sector while the chains saw a small growth in the business/conference market (Table 25).

Table 25:
Market Share of US Hotels 1982 – 86

Market Segment	All	1982 Independent	Chain	All	1986 Independent	Chain
General Tourist	34.0	41.6	31.0	35.1	49.0	29.9
Business	44.2	37.8	44.9	38.8	27.5	44.0
Conference	15.7	15.3	17.6	18.1	17.1	18.2
Other	6.1	5.3	6.4	8.0	6.4	7.9
TOTAL	100.0	100.0	100.0	100.0	100.0	100.0

The growth in numbers of incoming tourists since the mid 1980s, due in part to the lower value of the US dollar, has greatly benefited the US hotel industry. The upturn in the domestic economy has also helped the domestic tourist industry and the general growth in incomes will encourage the spread of mini breaks and second or third vacations each year. All these factors will help improve occupancy rates and profitability in the US hotel industry. Laventhol and Horwath estimate that there will also be a growth in new types of hotel and a general growth in the major chains at the expense of less successful hotel operators, either the small chains or the independents. Those hotels located in the sunbelt resorts with a good year-round climate should benefit from the general growth in the US travel and tourism market.

Holiday Camps

A trend in Europe is for more people to go on vacations which do not need serviced accommodation. The Holiday Camp is unique to the United Kingdom and a trend-setting type of holiday. There are no comparable examples in the United States but this does not mean that a derivative of the holiday camp may not manage to cross the Atlantic. The holiday camp was pioneered in the 1930s, by Billy Butlin and Fred Pontin, and by 1939 there were about 200 permanent camps scattered around the coast of Britain. During the 1950s and 1960s, these holiday camps came to be concentrated into about 150 main centres and the majority are now controlled by four major companies — Rank, Bass, Ladbrokes and Grand Metropolitan (owned by Mecca Leisure).

In the 1950s, these holiday camps tended to attract a largely regional and working class clientele and their canteen-style catering and range of entertainments reflected this client group. The growth of cheap inclusive tours in the 1960s was aimed at this same market segment and the numbers of visitors to the holiday camps began to decline or fall off during this period. In response to this they have changed their mode of operation, improved their range of amenities and aimed for a greater marketing mix. The emphasis is much more on self-catering, based on small blocks of chalets or bungalows, with an image that is quite different to the traditional holiday camp of seaside chalets, bars and dance halls.

On the continent, a Dutch company has pioneered a new concept in holiday villages. The company is called Center Parcs (formerly Sportshuis Centrum) who started in the early 1970s as a chain of shops selling camping and caravan equipment. They have developed the concept of bungalow parks, usually set in a landscape of trees and lakes and focused on a large central complex of covered all-weather tropical pools. Water temperatures are around 78°F and they have wave machines, water shutes, saunas, solariums, bars and creches, all part of the main pool complex. There is also a whole range of indoor and outdoor sports activities. There are now 8 sites in Holland and one in Belgium (Fig 30) and they are planning 6 developments in Britain by the mid 1990s, with the first near Sherwood Forest. They are open all year round and have occupancy levels of over 95% over a 52 week period.

How do they do it? Well, clearly they have got the product right. The pool complex is the major attraction, particularly for families with children. They have gone for particular market segments for particular times in the year. So, outside of the main school vacation times they aim to attract families with pre-school children and older people who no longer have children. In Holland, over 70% of bookings are repeat visits.

Figure 30: Location of Centre Parcs developments in Holland and Belgium

They also carry out regular surveys of their visitors to determine their likes and dislikes, and have a special staff training program for hospitality. In addition, they advertise widely in newspapers, magazines and on the TV and radio. Another mark of a successful product is a large number of repeat visits and nearly half of their visitors are on repeat visits.

The concept of all-weather tropical environments with de luxe accommodation and a wide range of water-based recreation facilities appeals to several market segments and appears to be attracting new people to the bungalow park in considerable numbers. The additional appeal of these leisure complexes is that they can be enjoyed in all weather and all seasons.

Tourism is now an international activity and, if accommodation stock is not modernized and comparable to standards in the best resorts overseas, and marketed imaginatively, it will lose its market share to new types of accommodation being developed.

ASSIGNMENT

Produce a proposal (for a major multi national company with a wide range of business interests) setting out:
a) the optimum locations for lodging development in the U.S.A.
b) the types of development.

Justify the reasons for your decisions.

Chapter 8

Federal, State, And Regional Roles

Learning Objectives: After reading this chapter you should have a clear understanding of:
— the main aspects of public sector tourism;
— the role of the State Tourism Offices;
— the development and future of public sector tourism;
— interface of public sector with the trade.

Tourism is the mixed economy in action, and nowhere is this more evident than in the promotion of tourism where the public sector plays a major role. An important part of the promotion and marketing of individual resort towns, and indeed of a tourist destination generally, is done by public sector bodies — yet the product being sold is largely run and owned by the private sector. Why is this? How has this come about?

There are at least five sound reasons why public sector bodies promote tourism:

(i) it can make a significant contribution to the overall economic activity of a country, region or town;

(ii) it can create new jobs;

(iii) it can make a significant contribution to the balance of income over expenditure — for a city, region or country.

(iv) synergy, i.e. the working together of corporate organizations and regional/national bodies to produce an effect greater than the sum of their individual effects.

(v) they can control the development of tourism by sponsoring projects in areas of high unemployment and by directing new developments away from environmentally sensitive areas.

Unlike many other countries, government in the United States at all levels has traditionally ignored the travel and tourism industry, believing that the development of tourist attractions, service facilities and mass transportation modes were the responsibility of private enterprise. Governments in the United States have passed laws to enforce, regulate and protect the public health, safety, and consumers of the travel industry. It is true that the public sector has financed public utilities and protected national resources by establishing national and state parks, forests and reservoirs that constitute major resources for travel and recreation. In addition, government has planned and developed highways, harbors, and major airports, but has provided less leadership and funds for planning and developing tourist attractions and service facilities such as hotels. There are exceptions; for example in the 1950s, Oklahoma, Kentucky and Ohio financed and developed resort hotels adjacent to large reservoirs. The legacy for this action was established by the Federal government by allowing the railroads to build hotels in many national parks in the early 1900s; but it was still the responsibility of the railroads to operate the hotels and promote travel to the parks.

The automobile and the improvement of highways expanded the horizons of the domestic traveler. State governments and petroleum companies, seeking revenue from the traveler, encouraged travel by promotional activities of various types. The publication and free distribution of highway maps was the most common item of promotional literature. The Federal government did not become involved in travel promotion until a few years prior to World War II. A Bureau within the National Park Service was established in 1937 to encourage travel to the parks and a Domestic Travel Act was passed by Congress in 1940 to further this program. World War II curtailed the program and it was not renewed after the war.

Travel of Americans overseas was encouraged in the 1950s as a means to help foreign governments to rebuild. The premise was that the money spent by Americans overseas would be returned when these countries were able to purchase our manufactured goods. The Eisenhower Administration encouraged foreign travel with a 'Visit USA' in 1960 and recommended ways to reduce international barriers to leisure travel in a 1958 report. No provisions were considered to promote travel to the U.S. and no governmental guidelines included planning or economic development incentives. By 1960 the U.S. had a travel deficit of more than one billion dollars. The Office of International Travel in the Department of Commerce had a budget of less than $50,000.

The international Travel Act of 1961 established the U.S. Travel Service in the Department of Commerce with a budget of $2.5 million to promote the U.S. overseas and hopefully reduce the travel deficit. The travel deficit continued to increase to $2 billion and, by 1968, President Johnson proposed a plan to discourage U.S. travel overseas by taxing international tickets and travel expenditures and reducing duty free allowances of returning tourists. These measures were not undertaken. In 1970, amendments to the Travel Act of 1961 authorized matching funds to states and non-profit organizations for schemes to promote travel to the United States. It was proposed at the time that a National Tourism Administration be established with four bureaus to include research and planning; information and promotion; facilities, and regional tourism development. The bill did not pass.

A National Tourism Resources Review Commission Report was completed in 1973. *Destination U.S.A.* was published in six volumes and, for the times, was a landmark study focusing on a little understood industry. It recognized that there were more than 100 programs relating to tourism in more than 50 different Federal agencies. No program or agency had any sweeping powers to plan or guide the industry. The International Travel Act of 1961 was once again amended, giving the Secretary of Commerce latitude to promote domestic travel as well as international travel, but the budget to do this was inadequate. *Destination U.S.A.* fostered a Tourism Policy Study in 1974 that stated that tourism impact was not only economic but provided intangible educational, health and social benefits.

By 1979, a National Tourism Policy Act had passed in the Senate with the backing of senators from states that relied on tourism as a source of revenue. Also in 1979, the Senate created a travel industry advisory committee and the House of

Figure 31:

Travel Generated Employment – 1985
Share of Total State Payroll Employment
(Percent)

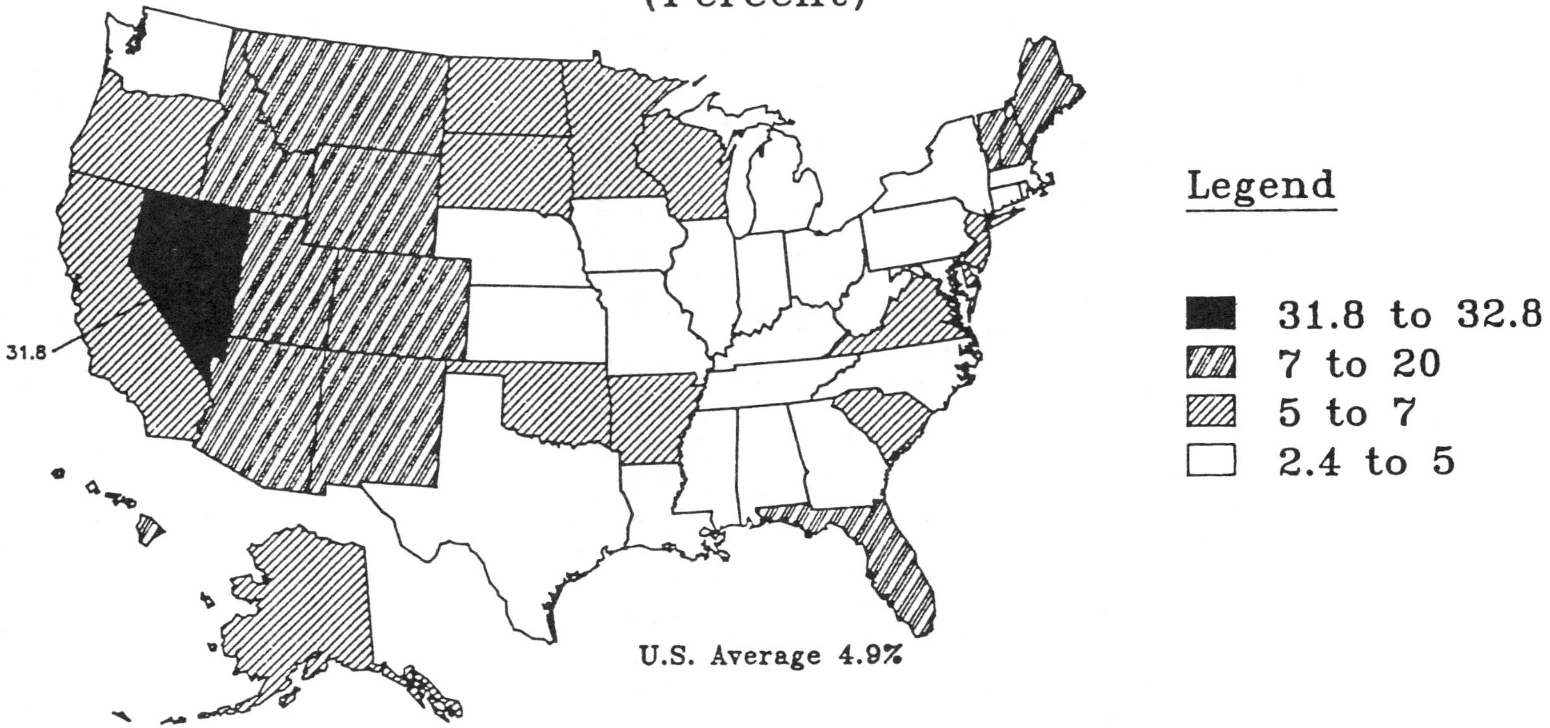

Legend
- ■ 31.8 to 32.8
- ▨ 7 to 20
- ▧ 5 to 7
- ☐ 2.4 to 5

31.8

U.S. Average 4.9%

Source: U.S. Travel Data Center, *Impact of Travel on State Economies 1985*, Washington, D.C.

Representatives a Congressional Travel and Tourism Caucus. The awareness of tourism as an economic force was building and a need for a national policy became more apparent. In 1981, the Policy Act had the approval of the House of Representatives and was signed by the President. This Act changed the name of the U.S. Travel Service to the U.S. Travel and Tourism Administration (USTTA) with a position for an Under-Secretary of Tourism within the Department of Commerce.

The Reagan Administration's efforts to reduce the Federal budget in the 1980s called for a reduction in the appropriation for the USTTA. Congress vetoed the President's recommendation and saved USTTA's program, even if funding of $8 to $12 million dollars a year was meager, compared to the spending of other countries. In 1985, Italy spent $100 million to promote travel, Greece $76 million and the United Kingdom $43 million. Twenty-three nations spent more than the United States for travel promotion in 1985 (USTDC, 1987).

The U.S. Travel Data Center (USTDC) has emphasized that, in some years, Canada's market development budget just for the U.S. has exceeded the entire U.S. government expenditure for marketing travel. In 1983, the U.S. spent a paltry $8.1 million dollars. The U.S., in 1985, was ranked first among nations in international visitor receipts, or 6.5 percent of the total, and yet it was the only nation with high receipts to have a travel payments deficit (USTDC, 1987). Clearly, the U.S. government must take future steps to reduce the travel deficit and still maintain high travel receipts. The U.S. has eliminated visa requirements for a limited number of countries but, in the future, it may take government approved tax incentives before the travel deficit is reduced. Of the 25 countries of the OECD the United States is the only one that does not provide some direct aid to the tourist industry in the form of loans, loan guarantees, subsidies or fiscal incentives (*Tourism Policy and International Tourism.* 1984).

It would be misleading to think that the Federal government is the only institution that spends money to develop foreign travel markets. Promotion dollars for travel to the U.S. are spent by other public and private institutions. In 1986 the 50 states spent $234 million in travel promotion. The top ten states, according to the USTDC, in 1986 were:

	Million
Illinois	$15.5
New York	14.8
Pennsylvania	11.8
Michigan	11.8
Tennessee	10.8
Florida	10.8
Massachusetts	9.4
Hawaii	8.4
New Jersey	8.1
California	7.8

In addition, the travel industry spent $737 million on advertising in U.S. media *(World Travel Overview 1987/1988)*. Most of the state budgets are spent for domestic media promotion. Figures are not available on foreign market expenditures but gateway states and airlines, hotels, and major attractions certainly

Figure 32:

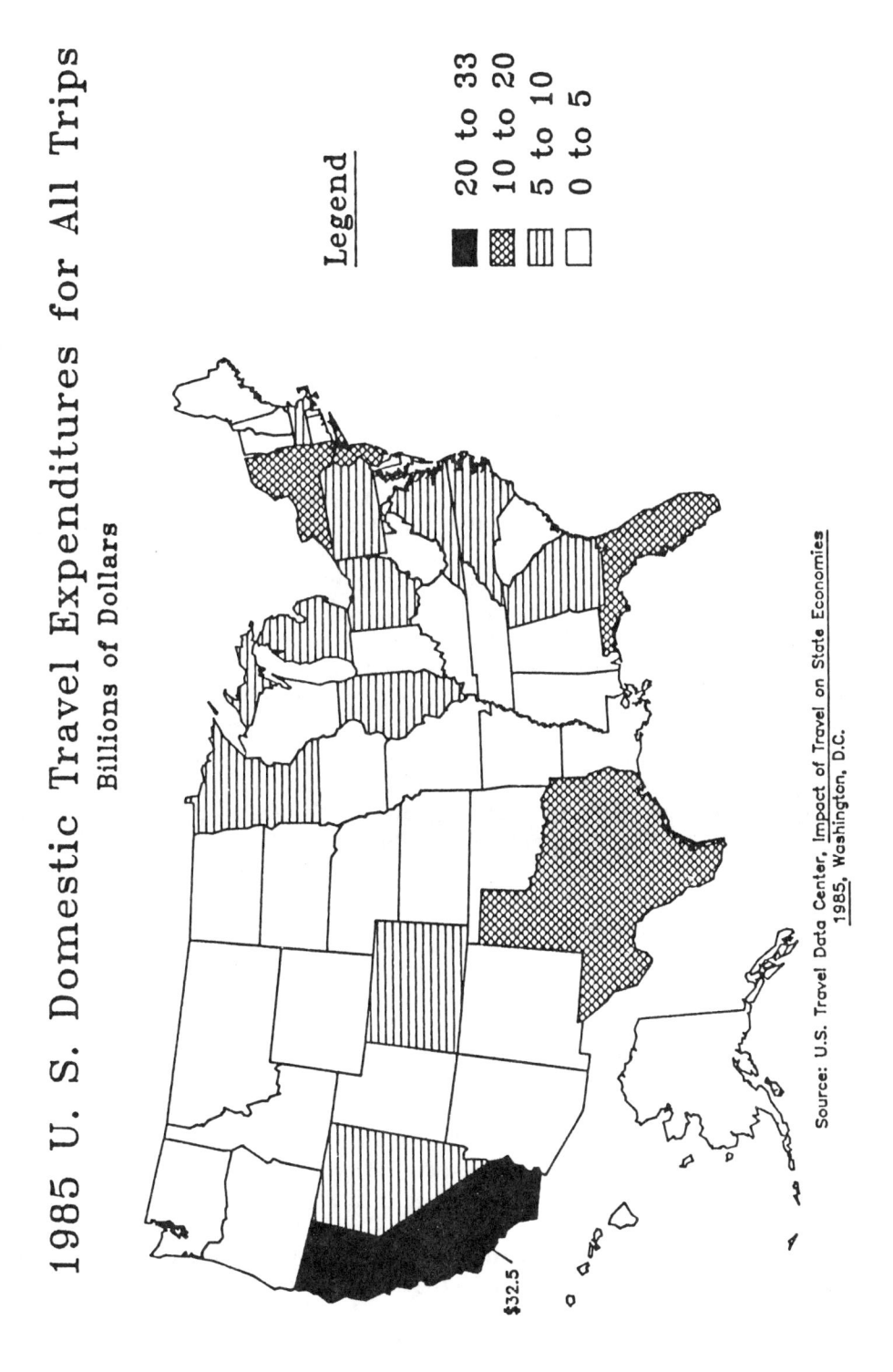

1985 U. S. Domestic Travel Expenditures for All Trips
Billions of Dollars

Legend
- ■ 20 to 33
- ▦ 10 to 20
- ▥ 5 to 10
- ☐ 0 to 5

$32.5

Source: U.S. Travel Data Center, *Impact of Travel on State Economies 1985*, Washington, D.C.

spend considerable amounts to promote in foreign countries. Nine states have become more cognizant of the importance of tourism to their economies as evidenced by recent legislation to delay the fall opening of schools until after the September Labor Day weekend (Figures 31 and 32). Such legislation provides for vacation travel until the first week of September and also allows young adults to hold jobs through the last holiday weekend of the summer. Tourism spokesmen have argued that the tourism spending in this 3 day break produces more travel tax income for the state that can be used to support the school system. The states that prohibit pre-Labor Day school openings are Arkansas, Iowa, Minnesota, Missouri, South Dakota, Texas, Virginia and West Virginia. More states will undoubtedly pass similar legislation.

The British have approached public sector involvement in tourism in a different way. In 1947 the government set up the British Tourist and Holidays Board (incorporating the Travel Association). This new body was the pre-runner of the present-day British Tourist Authority. The Board had 3 main objectives — to rebuild an effective tourist promotion organization; to carry out market research and related studies; and to establish links with other national tourist organizations overseas. In 1948/9 the Board of Trade gave a grant of $914,200 to the Board and this marked an ongoing commitment to the involvement of the public sector in the tourist industry — a commitment that has remained constant over the intervening 30 years. The essential role of this organization was summed up in 1950 when the British Tourist and Holidays Board and the Travel Association divisions were integrated to form the British Travel and Holidays Association. The Association was seen to have 2 main functions — bringing visitors from overseas to this country (the U.K.) and ensuring that they, as well as home holidaymakers, were well received and accommodated and had the best facilities that could be provided.

By 1960, the British Travel Association had offices in fifteen countries throughout the world and there were over 1.6 million visitors to Britain. During the 1960s several regional tourist associations were established with local authority support, including the London Tourist Board and the Lakes Counties Travel Association. However, these associations arose out of a voluntary approach towards developing tourism and it became increasingly clear that, if a major expansion in tourism promotion was to come about, central government must play a greater role.

Development of Tourism Act

In 1969 the British government issued the Development of Tourism Act which contained three main sets of proposals.

Part I established a statutory British Tourist Authority and Tourist Boards for England, Scotland and Wales with responsibility for promoting the development of tourism to and within Great Britain, and to encourage the provision and improvement of tourist amenities and facilities in Great Britain (Figure 33). The English, Welsh and Scottish Boards would have similar functions. In addition each National Tourist Board was given the authority to:

a) promote or undertake publicity in any form;
b) to provide advisory and information services; and
c) to promote or undertake research.

The Act also enabled the British Tourist Authority, after consultation with the English, Scottish and Wales Tourist Boards, to prepare schemes giving grant aid or loans to tourism development projects which, in the opinion of the Board, would provide or improve tourist amenities or facilities.

The British Tourist Authority, and likewise the English, Scottish and Wales Tourist Boards, had the duty to advise any Minister or public body on any matters relating to tourism.

These Tourist Boards received their funding through the Board of Trade and the Chairman and members were appointed by the Board of Trade. So, for the first time, after over 40 years of tourism promotion in Britain, the government established a national organization with a statutory responsibility for the development and promotion of tourism in Britain.

Part II of the Act, which followed from an earlier White Paper on *Hotel Development Incentives,* provided financial assistance for hotel development schemes. This assistance took two forms — grants and loans. Hotel Development Grants were available from the National Tourist Boards — but the hotel had to have at least 10 bedrooms (in Greater London 25 bedrooms) and the grant could only be claimed *after* the completion of the hotel. However, this provision meant that all small hotels were excluded from the scheme. Grants were also available for the extension or alteration of existing hotels, provided at least 5 additional bedrooms were added. The grants would meet 20% of the expenditure or £2,400 per bedroom, whichever was the less. In development areas this grant was increased to 25% of total expenditure.

The National Tourist Boards could make loans of up to $1.2 million to provide new hotels, or extend or improve existing hotels, and would generally lend up to 30% for new hotels and 50% for improvements to existing ones. These grants or loans were directed to the private sector and were not available to local authorities.

At the time this Act was passed, three-quarters of hotel rooms in Britain were over 50 years old and many lacked modern amenities. Before 1969 new investment in hotel development was very limited and confined to a few larger companies. In 1969 new hotel building was producing about 2,000 rooms a year for an annual investment of $35 million. Section I of the *Development of Tourism Act* led to a rapid growth in the hotel industry and, by 1973, over 70,000 additional hotel bedrooms had been provided at a total cost of over $710 million, almost doubling the capacity of hotel accommodation. However, the bulk of these were in London and many of the old traditional resorts still lacked modern hotels. The Hotel Development Grants Scheme was terminated in 1973 and the Section 4 system of grants and loans has largely replaced it. The next section of this chapter discusses the Section 4 scheme in more detail.

Part III of the *Development of Tourism Act* enabled the respective Tourist Boards to maintain registers of accommodation and to introduce classification and grading of accommodation.

In the years since 1969, there has been a massive increase in both international and domestic tourism. In 1969 Britain received over $830 million from spending by overseas visitors. By 1986 this had increased to over $7,250 million, and domestic tourism produced a further $8,700 million. A large measure of this growth is due to the efforts of the National Tourist Boards promoting Britain as a tourist destination and encouraging the development of tourism facilities and amenities throughout Britain.

Figure 33:
Tourist Board Structure in Britain

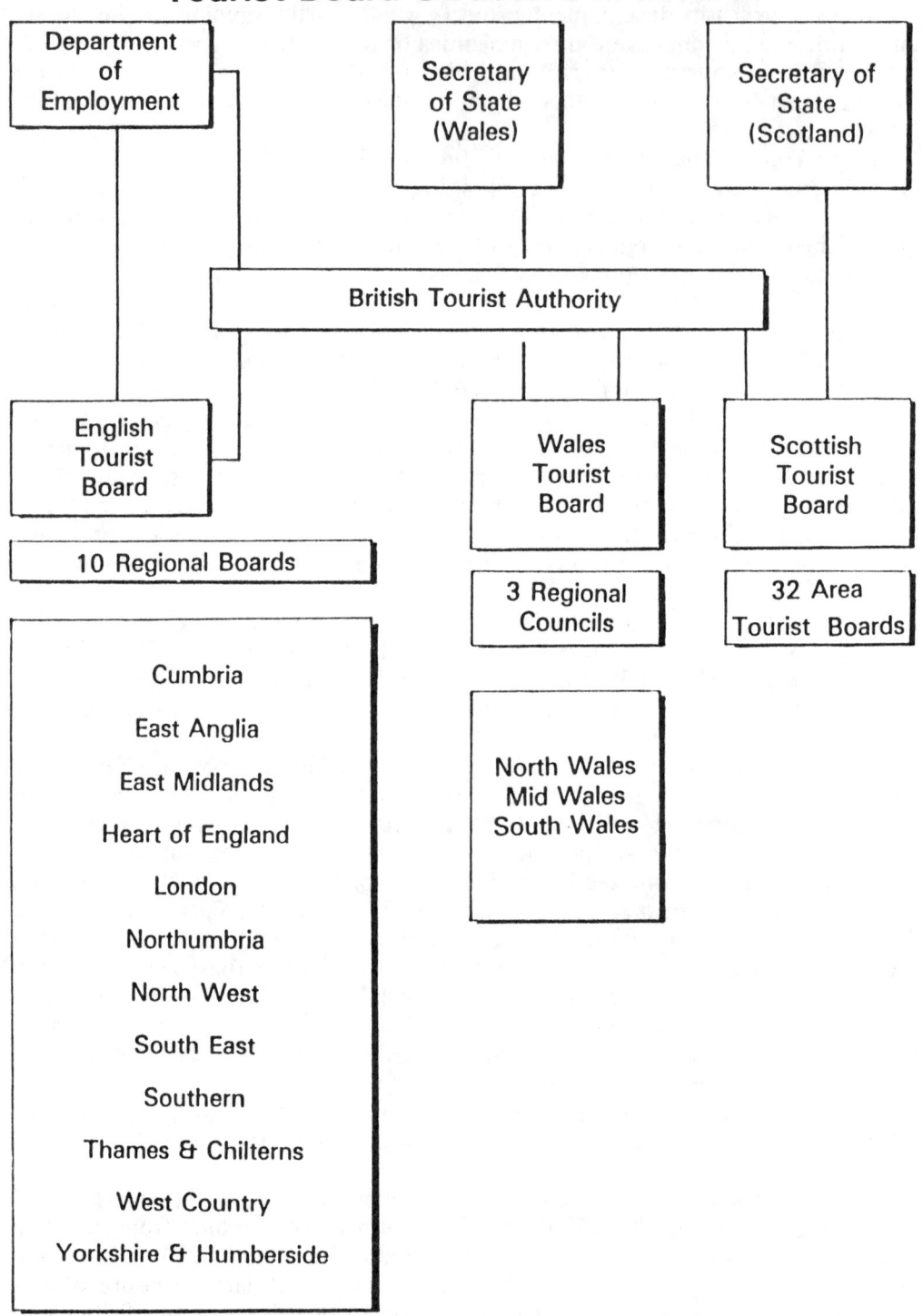

```
┌──────────────┐         ┌──────────────┐         ┌──────────────┐
│ Department   │         │ Secretary    │         │ Secretary of │
│      of      │         │  of State    │         │    State     │
│ Employment   │         │   (Wales)    │         │  (Scotland)  │
└──────┬───────┘         └──────┬───────┘         └──────┬───────┘
       │                        │                        │
       │          ┌─────────────┴────────────────────────┤
       │          │   British Tourist Authority          │
       │          └──┬───────────────┬───────────────┬───┘
       │             │               │               │
┌──────┴───────┐     │       ┌───────┴──────┐ ┌──────┴───────┐
│   English    │     │       │    Wales     │ │   Scottish   │
│   Tourist    │─────┘       │   Tourist    │ │   Tourist    │
│    Board     │             │    Board     │ │    Board     │
└──────────────┘             └──────────────┘ └──────────────┘
┌─────────────────┐          ┌──────────────┐ ┌──────────────┐
│ 10 Regional Boards│        │  3 Regional  │ │   32 Area    │
└─────────────────┘          │   Councils   │ │Tourist Boards│
                             └──────────────┘ └──────────────┘
┌──────────────────────┐     ┌──────────────┐
│      Cumbria         │     │  North Wales │
│      East Anglia     │     │  Mid Wales   │
│      East Midlands   │     │  South Wales │
│      Heart of England│     └──────────────┘
│      London          │
│      Northumbria     │
│      North West      │
│      South East      │
│      Southern        │
│      Thames & Chilterns│
│      West Country    │
│      Yorkshire & Humberside│
└──────────────────────┘
```

ROLE OF THE TOURIST BOARDS

The British Tourist Authority

The main role of the British Tourist Authority is to promote incoming tourism to Britain. In order to do this it has established a worldwide network of 21 overseas offices and employs over 200 staff overseas. It has three primary objectives:

(i)   to increase visitor spending in Britain;
(ii) to increase and spread the overall level of travel beyond London to the regions of England, Scotland and Wales;
(iii) to extend the tourist season by promoting travel in the autumn and winter months.

The BTA works in partnership with the trade and other tourist interests and encourages support from the trade for their promotional work overseas. The BTA's overseas offices work closely with all tourist interests, in the territories for which they are responsible, who wish to market or commission travel products and holiday packages in overseas countries. This may include familiarization trips and educational tours for overseas travel agents, tour operators and their sales staffs. They also run British Travel Workshops which bring together British producers with tourist services and products to sell and overseas buyers — travel agents and tour operators — who are keen to develop their business to Britain.

The English, Welsh and Scottish Tourist Boards

The three National Tourist Boards were all established in 1969 and each was given a remit to encourage tourists to visit and take holidays in their respective countries, and to encourage the provision and improvement of tourist amenities and facilities. Like the BTA, all are financed by a grant-in-aid from central government. The Act also gave powers to the National Boards to establish committees to advise them in the performance of their functions and, in the light of this, the English Tourist Board created twelve Regional Tourist Boards to ensure effective coordination and cooperation on tourism matters at regional and local levels with local authorities and commercial operators. Figure 33 outlines the Tourist Board framework and Figure 34 shows the distribution of Regional Tourist Boards in England.

The Regional Tourist Boards

The Regional Tourist Boards are autonomous bodies and draw their funding and membership from local authorities and commercial tourist operations within their areas, as well as funding from central government via the English or appropriate National Tourist Board. They are autonomous commercial companies, limited by guarantee. A major part of the Regional Tourist Boards, activity is focused on the marketing and promotion of their own regions. Activities will in-

Figure 34:

England's Regional Tourist Boards

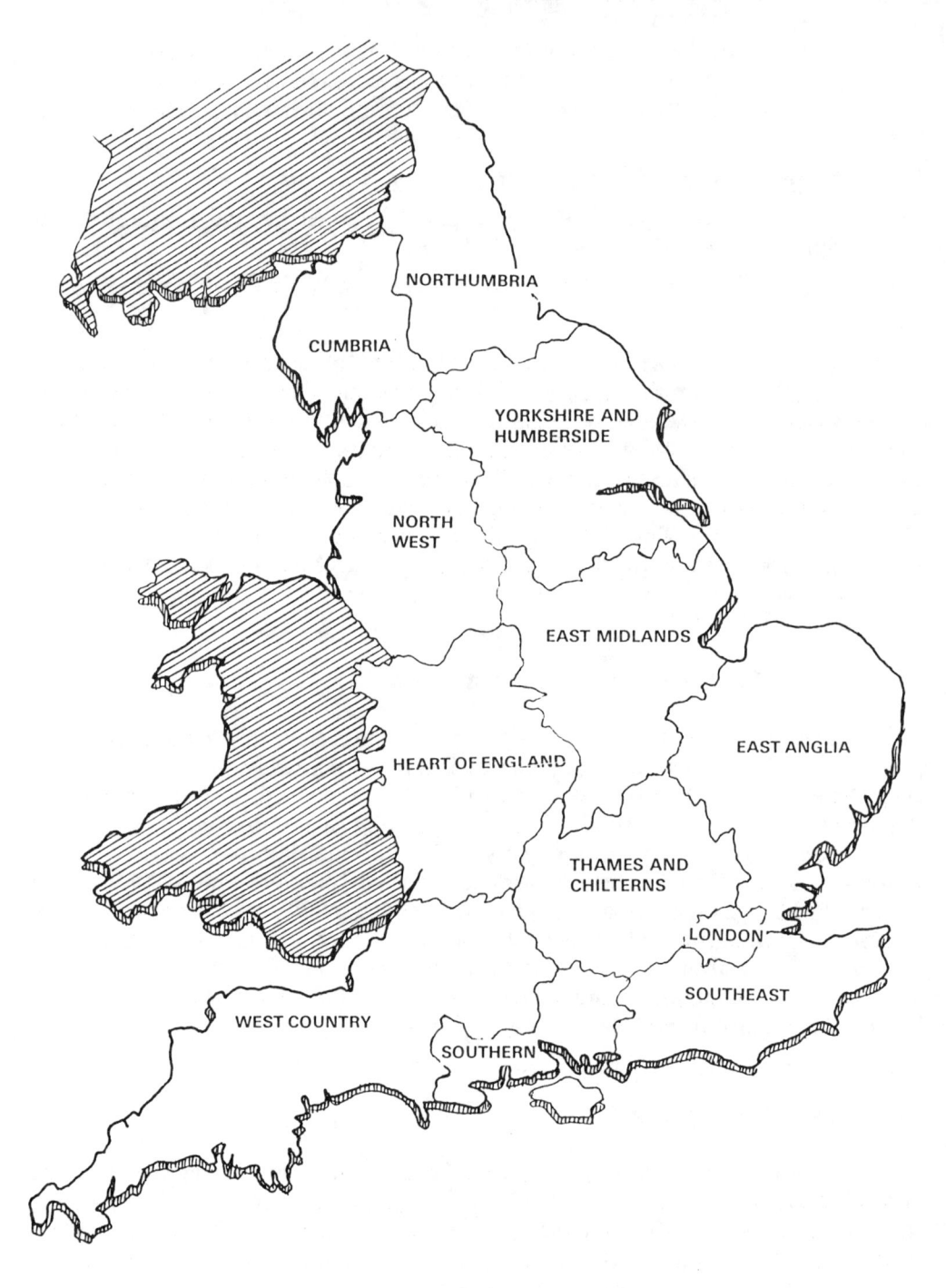

clude the productions of regional accommodation/facilities guides, advertising campaigns, exhibitions and workshops. Most Regional Boards receive their main source of funding from commercial revenue-earning activities, such as selling space, consultancy activities, and so on. Table ... shows the percentage of income from such activities compared with their subvention from the National Board.

The Regional Tourist Boards are closely concerned with the network of Tourist Information Centers throughout Britain (TICs) and generally provide the local contact and distribution for the Boards. In some instances, particularly the more important tourist destinations, the Regional Tourist Boards also provide and staff a limited number of centers to complement those provided by the local authority.

The Regional Tourist Boards are also responsible for the local administration of the Section 4 grant aid scheme for capital projects. Initial applications for assistance are made to the Regional Tourist Board who advise the ETB on particular applications. The Regional Boards now have the delegated authority to recommend for approval grants of up to $180,000 for tourism development projects, although the actual decision-making authority still rests with the English Tourist Board.

A major role of the Regional Tourist Boards is the provision of development advice to commercial operators within their area, and liason and advice on tourism planning and management matters with local authorities. As well as disseminating information about surveys undertaken by the National Tourist Boards, the Regional Tourist Boards also undertake their own surveys and research to provide more detailed local information.

Each Regional Board is also responsible for the preparation and development of tourism strategies for their regions. These will be generally coordinated with strategies prepared by other bodies concerned with tourism and recreation, such as The Countryside Commission, The Sports Council, The Association of District Councils, and so on.

The Regional Tourist Boards have the advantage of both local authority support and backing from commercial tourism operators, and are therefore in a strong position to help individual local authorities in preparing inputs to local structure plans, expressing comment on applications for tourism developments, and providing advice and information during the consultation and submission stages of major plans which affect the Travel and Tourism Industry.

Local Authorities and Tourism

At the most local level many local authorities are directly involved with the tourism industry in a variety of ways. Often they own and manage facilities that are major tourist attractions such as museums, theaters, country parks or historic monuments. They often have their own tourism officers or recreation and leisure officers who include tourism in their remit. All the major resort towns have their own publicity and promotion units either in the Town Hall or in the borough's tourism department. They often set up and run the tourist information centers, manage camping and caravan sites, the beaches and the seafront areas. Some local authorities such as Bournemouth, Brighton and Harrogate, have built large conference centers to promote and encourage business tourism.

The first priority of local authorities is to provide a range of leisure and cultural facilities for local residents. These will vary from outdoor facilities such as playing fields, parks and gardens, golf courses, country parks and picnic sites, to indoor facilities such as sports centers, leisure pools, museums, art galleries, theaters and concert halls. All of these facilities, and their related infrastructure of car parks and amenities, will also attract tourists and will be used by them.

Local authorities also often provide indirectly for tourism by contributing to the income and work of the Regional Tourist Boards, and by giving planning permission or grant-in-aid to tourism development projects. No two local authorities are exactly alike in the way tourism is developed or promoted, and the importance of tourism in the local authority's policy plan will vary depending on whether tourism is perceived as being of value to the local economy. In the early 1980s it was estimated that local authorities were responsible for over 500 art galleries and museums, 700 indoor swimming pools, 600 indoor sports centers and 200 golf courses.

The local authorities provide and resource these facilities in a variety of ways. The public has free access to beaches, picnic sites, country parks, nature trails and so on and while the public doesn't pay directly for these facilities it does so indirectly through the rates. Local authorities also provide other facilities such as leisure pools, marinas and golf courses where there is a direct payment by the user, although this is often highly subsidised.

That tourism is the mixed economy in action is best demonstrated by the major British seaside resorts. Much of the advertising, marketing and general promotional activity is done directly by the local authority, although it is the private sector in the form of hotels, guest houses, coach operators and tourist attractions that benefits from this.

Local authorities spend a considerable amount of money — in excess of $900 million on sport and recreation facilities and about $145 million on cultural activities, shared equally between museums, galleries and theaters. As planning authorities they can assist tourism development projects by making land and/or resources available. They can also give planning approval to private sector tourism developments where they are seen to be for the general benefit of the town or region. Local authorities have very wide discretionary powers and by channelling resources to tourism and recreation they can have a major role to play in developing a town or region as a tourist destination.

Between 1984 and 1987, district councils spent over $770 million on tourism-related projects and over 10,000 new jobs were created both directly and indirectly as a result of this investment. Over the past decade many local authorities, in association with Tourist Boards and various other agencies, have developed tourist facilities based on their cultural, industrial or historic heritage. For example, Torfaen Borough Council, in association with the Welsh Development Agency, the Wales Tourist Board, and the National Coal Board developed the Big Pit Mining Museum. Portsmouth has developed a range of attractions based on the theme of maritime heritage with HMS Victory, HMS Warrior and the Tudor warship Mary Rose as the centerpieces of a former Royal Dockyard. The city is now embarking on a major development program with a $16 million water recreation center; a $180 million marina and a $180 million indoor shopping center.

Local authorities have also begun to realize the advantages of coming together to establish marketing consortia with the common aim of increasing their region's share in the domestic and international tourist market. For example, Devon,

Somerset, Torbay, Exeter and Plymouth have formed a consortium to attract more U.S. visitors to the south west of England. Several local authorities combined to promote nationally the Great English City Break campaign.

Trade/Professional Organizations — The United States

In the United States, the Travel Industry Association of America (TIA) is the largest private organization that promotes tourism. With a small start just prior to World War II, TIA has grown from its original membership of a few state travel promotion members to an association representing the entire travel and tourism industry with a headquarters in Washington, D.C. The objectives of the Association include: promote travel to and within the United States, unify the travel industry on matters of common concern, defend and promote the travel industry as a major factor in the nation's economy, encourage travel between nations, assist the various parts of the industry to improve services to the traveler, and act as a policy spokesman for the industry at various levels of government. TIA is largely responsible for the existence of the US Travel Data Center (USTDC) established in 1973 with funding from the TIA (then called Discover America Travel Organization) and the U.S. Department of Commerce. The Department of Commerce funding was withdrawn after a few years and the USTDC became a part of the TIA. The U.S. Travel Data Center is universally regarded as 'the source' of travel and economic data and analysis for the U.S. travel industry.

Five industry councils are a part of TIA and each is a spokesperson for their particular travel industry component. Each council acts to encourage education programs for their professional memberships and to confront and/or propose legislation that may effect the industry at various governmental levels. The five councils are: National Council of State Travel Directors (NCSTD), National Council of Area and Regional Travel Organizations (CARTO), National Council of Travel Attractions (NCTA), National Council of Urban Tourism Organizations (NCUTO) and, perhaps the most important, the Travel and Tourism Government Affairs Council formed in 1982. This council has representatives from over 30 travel organizations and is the major institution providing a unified travel industry input into Federal Government issues affecting this industry in the United States. Once a year, TIA organizes an international Pow Pow in which wholesale travel companies worldwide come to arrange package tours from abroad to the United States.

There are other specialized industry organizations that have also evolved in the U.S. travel industry. The American Hotel and Motel Association, American Society of Travel Agents, National Restaurant Association, the Air Transport Association of America, National Tour Association, the Recreation Vehicle Industry Association, and the International Association of Convention and Visitor Bureaus are some of the largest and most influential. All of these organizations provide educational and informational services to their memberships and keep abreast of happenings in state and federal government bodies in order to act as industry voices against unfair legislation. All of the organizations have budgets to promote their particular facilities and services to the traveler. Each, in its own way, contributes a piece of the larger pie that collectively is the travel industry.

The American Hotel and Motel Association is composed of members that contribute more than $40 billion annually to the economy and employ 1.4 million people. There are an estimated 2.7 million rooms in 45,000 hotels and motels in the United States, ranging from budget motels to penthouse suites in luxury hotels that may cost $1,000 per night.

The National Restaurant Association, like the Hotel and Motel Association, offers education, research, public affairs and government relations services to its members. In recent years, there have been 10,000 members representing 125,000 establishments that include fast food establishments and exclusive gourmet restaurants.

Trade/professional organizations — United Kingdom

A variety of organizations have evolved to represent the many different interests which make up the tourist industry. They are mainly organized on a sectoral basis, for example the Hotel, Catering and Institutional Management Association (HCIMA), the British Hotels Restaurants and Caterers Association, The Chartered Institute of Transport (CIT), the Institute of Travel and Tourism (ITT) and the Association of British Travel Agents (ABTA). In some tourist regions, groups of tourist attractions have combined forces to market their product. For example, in Cornwall 24 centers have formed the Cornwall association of tourist attractions. The general aims of these bodies are to represent the particular interests of their members, to promote certain standards of service, and to act as a lobby to government. Some professional organizations such as the HCIMA (The Hotel Catering and Institutional Management Association), ABTA (The Association of British Travel Agents), and the ITT (The Institute of Travel and Tourism) are concerned about education and training for the industry and the provision of a suitable range of courses to meet the industry's needs.

However, each of these bodies represents an individual sector, and no single organization exists to speak for the interests of the industry as a whole. Even the professional associations are mainly concerned with relatively narrow needs. Thus ABTA is concerned about training for travel agency/tour operations work, HCIMA with catering and hotel or institutional management. There is a clear need for an overall body to integrate the industry, present a single voice to central government, and develop a unified view of the education and training needs of the industry.

The Future of Public Sector Tourism

There are probably more differences than similarities between public sector tourism in the U.K. and the U.S. Both systems have good features and neither could be considered perfect. Certainly the U.S. government, at all levels, lacks a firm, committed, tourism policy. Balanced tourism/travel development is undefined. Planning and financing is left entirely to the private sector unless, if in a city, local zoning regulations and building codes provide some semblance of tasteful control. In rural areas, particularly in the West where large amounts of land are in Federal ownership, these resources are carefully controlled and protected. In the U.K. local authorities exercise such control, but they also have the authority, and with approved aid schemes the ability, to develop resources for tourism. Some of these require large capital investment. Visitor and convention centers are built and operated by local (county) authorities in the U.K. just as they are by local governments in the United States.

There are many similarities between the activities of the individual states and the regional and local tourist boards in the U.K. In both cases, these governmental authorities build and operate parks, museums, visitor information centers, golf courses, highways and airports. The one major difference is that in the U.K. tourism is recognized as an important contribution to the regional and local economy. Financial grants are more readily available for developmental purposes and to voluntary bodies. This is the result of a recognized tourism policy at the national level.

ASSIGNMENTS

1. There are several locations in the United States that have a tourism infrastructure that dates back to Pre-World War II. Some of these locations have recently seen tourist visits stabilized and have become known as retirement areas rather than tourist areas. You have been appointed as a consultant to undertake a feasibility study into the prospects for reviving tourism in order to attract jobs and investment into the local economy. Show how this might be done, taking advantage of government and private assistance, and suggest changes that are needed to improve the administration of the area at a local level. Examples of areas are: Blue Ridge Mountains of North Carolina in the vicinity of Asheville; Tucson, Arizona; Fort Meyers, Florida.

2. You are a Senior bureaucrat and have been asked to produce a memorandum for the Under-Secretary for Tourism, setting out how the public sector should be reorganized and developed for the United States.

Chapter 9

Planning And Development Of Tourism

Learning Objectives: After reading this chapter and the references contained in it, you should have a clear understanding of:

— the role of both the public and private sector in planning for tourism;
— the stages involved in preparing a feasibility study of new tourism developments;
— the financing of tourism developments;
— the main elements in the tourism planning process.

Introduction

Historically, many interests — both public and private — have played a part in the development and provision of facilities for tourism in the United Kingdom. This has ranged from the parks, promenades and piers of the Victorian period, to the hotels, leisure complexes and conference centers of the present-day. This planning and development was generally influenced by speculative developers and entrepreneurs up to the 1930s, but after the 1947 Town and Country Planning Act local authorities, for the first time, were given wide powers to control the development of public and private land and facilities in towns and countryside.

In the United States, tourism planning and development is not subject to stringent public control by the Federal or state government. Local governments have responded to and guided development by enacting planning and zoning ordinances to which developers must adhere. Once a potential developer owns a parcel of land then there is considerable freedom to develop it with minimal government regulation. This freedom is quite different from the United Kingdom as will be demonstrated. The reader is left to decide which cultural system is thought to be the best. Both development and planning systems for tourism have advantages and disadvantages. Knowledge of a variety of cultural systems is essential to the understanding of international tourism development. Good planning is basic regardless of the country. Only policy, financing, and implementation are different.

As tourism grew in scale during the 1930s, and increased rapidly with the advent of mass tourism in the post-war years, this brought with it the recognition that the tourist resources of the community and region needed to be managed so as to reconcile conflicts over the use of land, to meet future needs, and create an environment within which tourists could enjoy both natural and man-made resources without damaging or destroying the very features that attract them in large numbers.

The second decision that both private and public sector organizations must make is to compare the supply of tourist resources (both natural and man-made) with the demand for them, in order to identify short-falls in provision. A public or commercial organization will require an inventory of the supply and distribution of tourist facilities in order to identify potential for tourism development. *Demand* can be defined as the use of existing tourist facilities and the desire to use them either now or in the future. The people who take part in tourist activities make up the *effective demand*. In addition there is the *deferred demand* (that is those who could take part in domestic or overseas tourism but do not, either through lack of knowledge, lack of facilities, or both); and *potential demand* (that is, those who cannot at present participate and require an improvement in their social and economic circumstances to do so).

Tourism Development (Project Appraisal)

Having identified a market, chosen a site, obtained clearance for building and funding for the project, there is a need for the national, regional or local government to assess the impact of tourism developments. Tourism projects cannot be planned independently because they have a wide range of impacts on the cultural, physical and economic environments of the locality. Physical planning (i.e. land use planning) is important as a means of organizing the distribution of facilities, the conservation of natural resources and the integration with other sectors of the economy. The *scale* of tourism development is a critical factor and one that will have the most immediate impact on the environment. This issue is discussed in more detail in Chapter 12.

At national or regional level, the first strategic decision is whether to concentrate developments in those regions or localities which are accessible and most likely to attract tourists, or to disperse facilities so as to ensure that as many areas as possible benefit from tourism developments. Concentrating development projects provides economies of scale but raises problems of environmental impact.

There is a need to study the effects of new facilities on usage rates from within their market area. Supply of new facilities may transform latent demand into effective demand and bring changes within the pattern of effective demand. The degree of substitution between one kind of facility and another should be measured, and depends on the inherent attraction of different recreation resources in relation to centers of demand. The 'drawing power' of tourist resources is linked to individual perception of tourist facilities or landscape resources and the motivation of tourists.

It is essential to have a tourism development plan in the following situations:

(i) in regions that cater for mass tourism;
(ii) in regions with a fragile natural environment;
(iii) in newly-developing tourist regions.

One of the paradoxes of mass tourism is that in particular cases tourists, by arriving in large numbers, may cause overcrowding and congestion which can destroy the very thing they come to see. In any tourist region there is likely to be a range of development opportunities and a series of thresholds for development. Thus for areas that have fragile environments which make them highly sensitive to visitor numbers, access has to be discouraged. Areas that are scenically attractive,

Figure 35: THREE KINDS OF DESTINATION ZONES

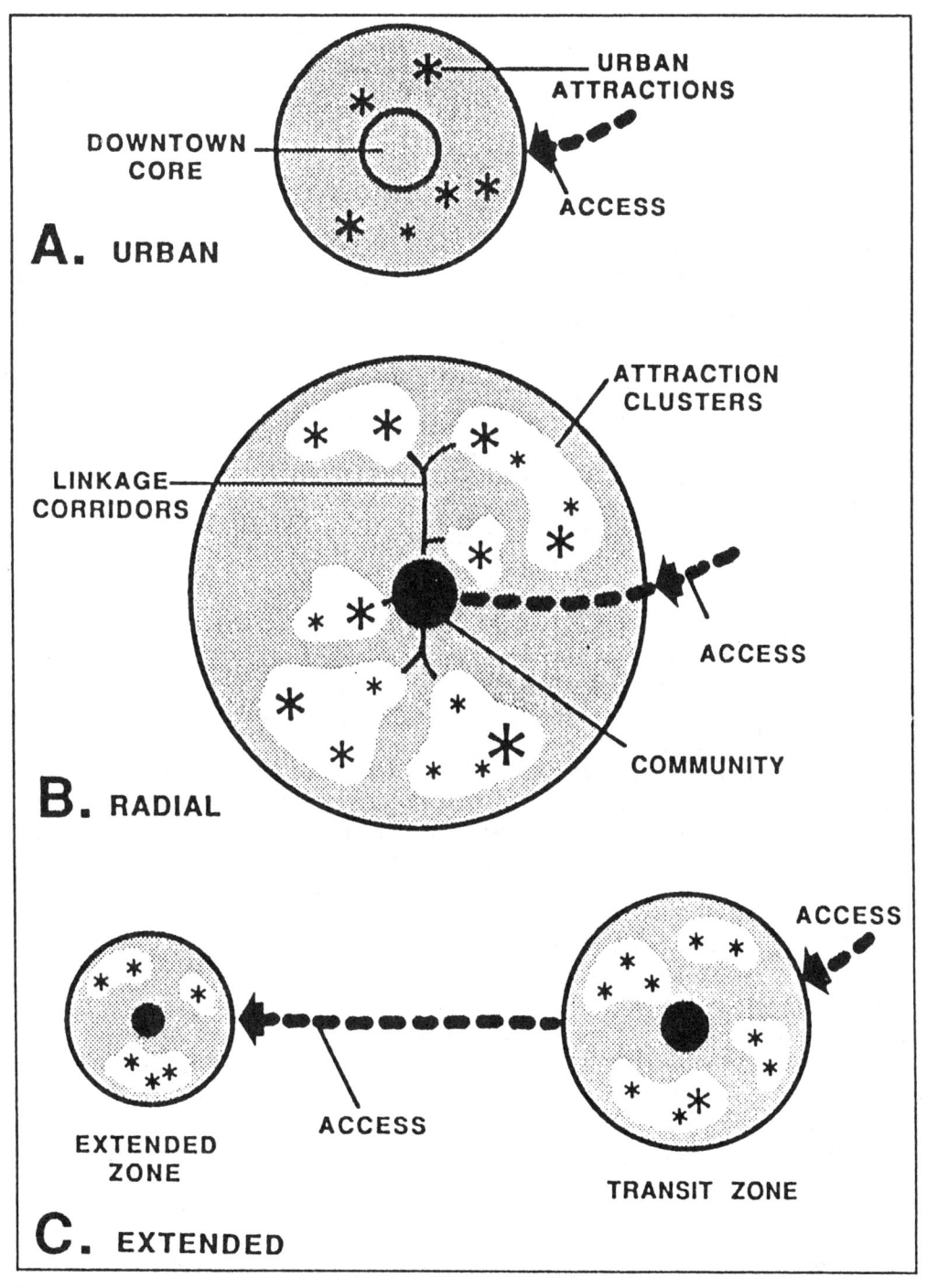

Three Kinds of Destination Zones. Three popular patters of tourism destination zones: (A) urban, (B) radial, and (C) extended.

Reproduced from Tourism Planning by C. A. Gunn with permission of the Author and Pulbisher, Taylor and Francis.

which are wild and relatively remote, should have limited vehicular access. Areas suitable for intensive tourist use should be identified and developed so as to absorb visitors. Development Planning operates at three different levels — national, regional and local. In the United Kingdom, at the national level the National Tourist Board produces strategic plans (usually on a 4 to 5 year basis) which set out the broad framework within which all the agencies involved in tourism can coordinate their activities. This document usually outlines investment plans and policy decisions in tourism development. For example, in its document *Strategy for Growth 1984 – 1988* (BTA 1984) the British Tourist Authority reviews the trends in tourism to Britain 1972 – 1982 and identifies the main strengths and weaknesses of the British market. It then identifies economic and social factors and government policies likely to affect tourism over the plan period. The document concludes by identifying, in the light of BTA's objectives, the target markets and new product development required to translate this strategy into action. Planning of this type does not exist in the United States.

At the regional level, the Regional Tourist Board will produce a coordinated strategy for tourism and this is usually implemented through a Development Panel consisting of both local authority and private sector interests who are members of the Tourist Board. The final part of this chapter outlines two case studies which demonstrate the planning and development process.

Planning for Tourism.

In this context, what does 'Planning' mean? It means several things, and attempts to be an amalgam of the best of them. For the public sector, it means reconciling conflicts over the use of land. In the case of both private and public sector organizations, it means managing resources effectively (both natural and man-made) so that the best use is made of scarce resources. It means identifying features or sites with tourism potential and preparing proposals to develop them to meet an actual or predicted demand. Planning is concerned with relating the supply of tourist facilities to the demand for them, so that public needs are met without under or over-provision. Planning can be pro-active in initiating tourism projects, and should not be seen as a negative approach associated with controls, regulations and restrictions. Planning has increasingly been seen as a means of safeguarding the environment from excessive or ill-thought out tourism development, and there are now several public and quasi-public bodies with an interest in and responsibility for land management. Planning should be a partnership between the public and private sectors and, in recent years, there has been a trend towards more public-private partnerships epitomized in the Tourism Development Action Plans which involve assembling large parcels of land and complex financial packages and creating opportunities for large-scale private investment in tourism projects.

These projects are not only focused on urban areas, but in the countryside also. The 10 national parks and stretches of heritage coast around Britain (Fig 16 on page 48) represent major tourist resources identified over the past 40 years. During the 1960s and 1970s it was recognized that the network of national parks was not sufficient and many country parks were developed around all the major towns and cities, with the aim of encouraging more people to enjoy and use the countryside on their doorstep (Figure 35).

Planning for tourism raises issues related to *resources* and *management*. Resources can be natural (forests, lakes, beaches, scenery) or man-made (theaters or visitor centers) or the financial investment needed to translate plans into reality. Management covers management policy and management action both in the provision of tourist facilities and their day-to-day operation. In other words, the provision of facilities is not enough. They must be managed efficiently so as to maximize the public's use and enjoyment of them while ensuring that the public organization or private business covers its operating costs.

Both the public and private sector have a common approach towards managing tourist facilities. Both are concerned about value for money and effective control of budgets and look at ways of maximizing their income over expenditure. The growth of public and private sector partnerships suggests that each sector needs to understand how the other operates and to share management skills. Public-private partnership for tourism development in the United States, like Britain, is a concept in the formative stage. Development examples in both nations are Baltimore's Harborplace, Mission Bay in San Diego, St. Katharine's Dock redevelopment in Central London and Bristol's transformed historic harbor area.

The public and private sectors should have similar, if not identical approaches towards preparing proposals for new tourism developments. Five main factors need to be considered when preparing a feasibility study for new tourism facilities:

(i) the market for the facility;
(ii) the optimum location;
(iii) the site;
(iv) the management structure of the facility;
(v) the financial appraisal.

A variety of professional talents must be utilized when preparing the feasibility study. Architects, landscape designers, engineers, contractors, and planners normally have input into any type of major development, whether for tourism development, or an industrial plant complex. Tourism developments require additional expertise; wise development at the feasibility and planning stage will consider the human impact once the project is completed. There are two types of influence on people. For the project to be successful the visitor's action space, needs, and desires must be considered to ensure a positive experience. Experienced tourism developers are generally aware of these factors; but frequently, the development's impact on the local inhabitants may not be analyzed carefully. What will be the development's social, economic and environmental consequences? The feasibility planning team should include sociologists, psychologists, and environmental scientists to identify potential human and physical impacts. Without input of this type, the marketing, management and financial appraisal of the project may be well off the mark.

The Market

The principles and practice of tourism marketing are discussed in more detail in Chapter 10, but it is sufficient to say that in planning any tourism project several questions need to be asked:

- what is the target market?
- what facilities/features will attract them?
- is it a growing or declining market?
- how much will people pay to use the facilities?
- how can this market be reached?
- what competing facilities exist and what are their objectives and weaknesses?
- what is the planned capacity?
- what is the planned 'season'?

The answers to these questions can be found by undertaking detailed market research and this is discussed in the next chapter.

The Location

What is the best location for a new tourism development? Clearly this depends on the type of facility being provided and whether or not it needs to be adjacent to a lake, river or the sea. Should it be near a major concentration of population or in a quiet country area? Accessibility is usually a key factor because, unlike other products, the tourist product has to be consumed on the spot and potential customers need to be able to travel to the facility quickly and inexpensively. Is there good road, rail and air access? Does it need to be located adjacent to other tourist resources?

Having identified a location, the next step is to select a site for the development. Is it an established tourist area, or is it a new area with tourism potential? What is the local authority or government policy towards this kind of tourist development?

The Site

At this stage, planning issues need to be carefully considered. Does the site have planning permission for the land use proposed? If not, can this permission be obtained or will there be planning constraints on the site? Are there mains services available or if not, can they be provided? Is the site accessible from the main road? Will the development require extensive landscaping works? Is there sufficient land to provide adequate car parking? Is there room for expansion on the site should the development be very successful? All of these factors need to be considered when the developer applies for outline planning permission, which is the first stage in getting a project approved. This work would lead to an outline site plan, building elevations and sketches showing the main land use layout with details of the function of buildings and range of services to be provided.

The Management Structure

This is a critical element in deciding how a business is to be run and what it will cost to operate. How many permanent and how many seasonal staff will be needed? What tasks will each staff member do? What specialist skills will be needed? Will they have to be recruited nationally or locally? Will a staff training program need to be developed? A typical management chart for public sector and commercial sector organization would probably have a senior management group above the facility manager, and in turn the senior managers responsible to Chief executives and council committees or boards of directors. At the facility level, the main management activities will be planning and forecasting, budgetary control, dealing with the public, organizing work, recruitment, selection and staff training, working computerized systems and industrial relations.

Financial Appraisal

This follows from decisions about the type of tourist facility to be provided and the range of markets to be served. Very often, the financial appraisal will include several forecasts based on a range of assumptions about the management of the project and changes in the financial climate. The assumptions must be based on accurate estimates of the capital cost of the project, the potential operating cost, and the potential revenue. A further factor is the degree of 'risk' if the project is providing a new form of tourist facility, related to the level of capital investment required and the rate of return on capital that can be earned. The element of 'risk' operates at two levels. First, the break even point below which the business will not survive. Secondly, the break even point beyond which investors will get a return on their investment. Potential guarantors will need to have this information. This will need to be set against a time scale which allows for the facility to come into full operation, to build up a 'market', and to produce actual as against forecasted accounts.

There are sophisticated computer models to predict investment returns on potential resort developments based on the cost of borrowing money and the potential return on investment over a period of years. Most developments anticipate a return within five to ten years.

Financing Tourism Projects

(a) Public Sector Finance

In the public sector, finance for tourism projects can be classified under two main headings: *Capital* finance and *revenue* finance. Capital spending is generally financed through borrowing approved by central government and is divided into two categories — key sector and non-key sector projects. The key sector developments reflect national policy, for example, maintaining maximum standards for roads, hospitals etc. and is controlled by agreement with central government departments. Tourism projects are non-key sector and here the local authority has a block allocation each year to be spent as it wishes. Many local authority services such as housing, education and the social services will be competing for this money. In addition, local authority capital expenditure can be funded in several ways:

— direct government grant (e.g. Countryside Commission, or English Tourist Board (Section 4) grants from the regional or national tourist board);
— revenue contributions to capital spending (i.e. from the rates);

- capital receipts from the sale of local authority land;
- loans from commercial concerns;
- income from other sources such as lotteries.

Revenue finance comes from four main sources:

(i) from the users of facilities (income from membership fees, admission charges, hire of facilities, catering);
(ii) grant aid from central government or quasi-public bodies such as the Tourist Boards, Sports Council, or Countryside Commission;
(iii) from the taxes paid by local residents;
(iv) from central government Tax Support Grant.

Public sector financing for private developments in the United States is non-existent. Local governments support the private investor through general sales tax revenues which are invested in public infrastructure. Some states and local governments issue industrial revenue bonds and do assist in financing some private tourism growth, if related to service facilities. Local governments in some states may levy special taxes on lodging and airport passengers, using the revenue for tourism promotion and development.

(b) Private Sector Finance

The scale and type of private sector finance will depend on the scale of the project and the resources of the organization planning the development. If it is a large organization it may have sufficient capital reserves to finance new projects without borrowing, or can raise new capital through a share issue. If capital has to be borrowed there are two types of finance which relate to the timescale of the project. There is *fixed* capital to develop the land and buildings, plant and amenities, and *short-term* capital to provide cash flow when the project is in its early stages of operation.

All tourism businesses, particularly small businesses, will need short-term finance for 1 to 3 years until the business becomes established. The most common source is overdraft facilities provided by the commercial clearing banks. An alternative source is using Hire Purchase Agreements to obtain fixed-term interest to meet the cost of plant and equipment.

Medium-term finance (4 to 8 years) is provided by the clearing banks, the industrial and Commercial Finance Corporation (ICFC), the merchant banks, and the finance houses.

In the United States large banks, insurance companies, savings and loan associations, and pension funds are the primary source of capital financing.

Usually medium-term finance is at a variable rate of interest and this has the benefit of fixing the cost of money for the future and, where operating profits are high, paying for the capital loan out of net operating profit. This type of financing is particularly attractive if inflation increases and general interest rates rise.

Large scale projects involving say, capital investment of over $180,000 will require long-term finance (over 10 years) if the loan repayments are to be of a manageable size. These loans are mainly provided by insurance companies and building societies and some of the clearing banks.

Another source of finance is through sale and leaseback which can realise 100% of the valuation of a property. A case in point is the sea front development at Great Yarmouth, where a $10.25 million indoor leisure development was financed by a 25 year leaseback agreement between the Council and CIN Industrial Investments Ltd (a company wholly owned by the British Coal Pension Fund) for the sum of $8.1 million. The balance was funded by Lloyds Industrial Leasing Ltd.

Other sources of finance are through venture capital provided by the leading merchant banks or funds obtained through the government's Business Expansion Scheme.

Case Studies in Planning & Development

(a) Tourism Development of Languedoc — Roussillon

This development was carried out between 1966 and 1980 by the French Government in close cooperation with local authorities and private interests. Its objective was the overall development of a 100 mile length of coastal strip in order to stimulate the stagnant local economy in the Languedoc-Roussillon area. The impetus behind the project was the growing pressure on the Cote d'Azur and the need to protect the undeveloped stretches of the Mediterranean coast from unplanned development. This region formed an almost uninterrupted stretch of large beaches, often separated from the inland area by a series of lakes and salt marshes. Access was limited and roads were of poor quality.

The Languedoc-Roussillon Development Plan had three main objectives:

— to relieve pressure on the Cote d'Azur and meet the growing demand for mass tourism facilities on the Mediterranean coast.

— to raise the level of incomes in the region and, by attracting both French and foreign visitors, help France's international balance of payments.

— to diversify a predominantly agricultural economy, provide employment for young people, and stem the depopulation of the region.

A government agency was established to coordinate the activities of the State Ministries and to implement and supervise the development decisions. Joint public and private development companies were established, with the state providing the infrastructure needed for mass tourism, local development companies responsible for providing the ancilliary infrastructure, and the private sector responsible for construction and marketing.

Six new resort areas were developed (Fig 36) with a total capacity of over 700,000 beds, capable of accommodating up to 3 million tourists a year. Each resort area has been zoned into areas for villas, apartments, hotels, holiday villages and camp-sites. The whole development has provided moorings for 20,000

Figure 36: **Resort Development in the Languedoc-Roussillon Region**

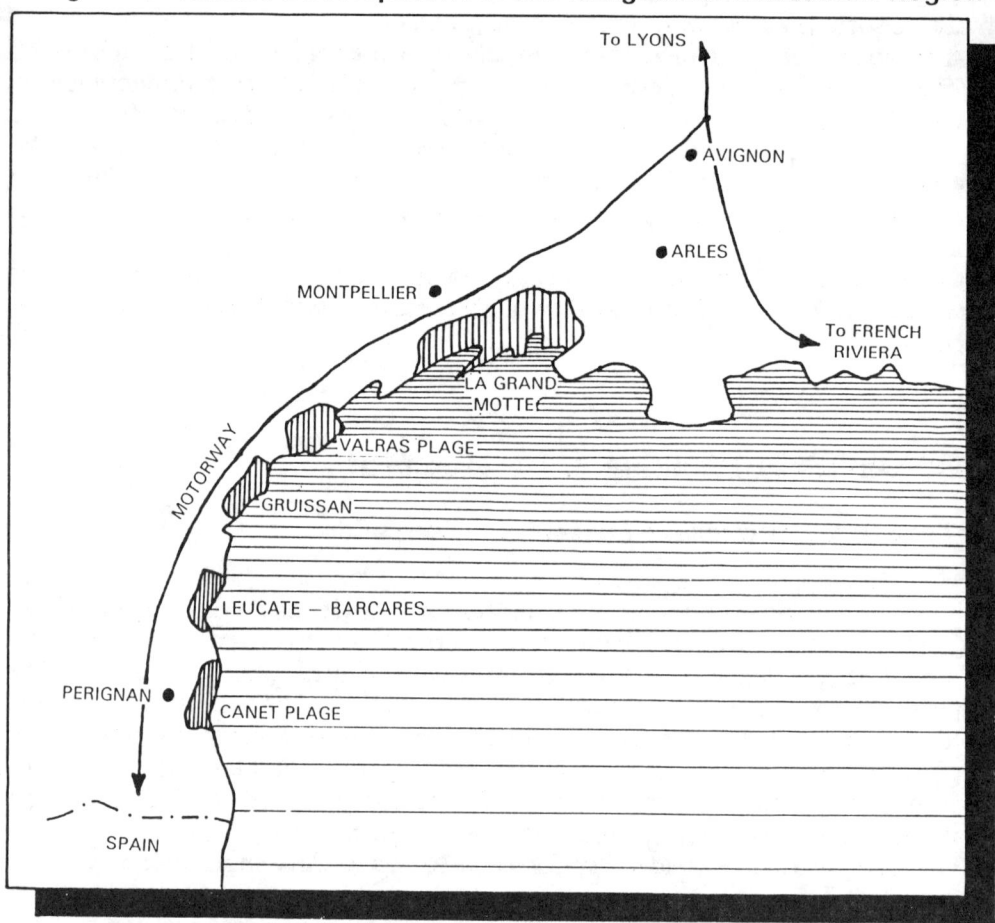

boats and 80,000 new jobs. The construction of the new resorts involved the acquisition of 4,000 hectares of land at a cost (1970 prices) of $24 million. By 1980, The Development Commission, the mixed Development Boards, local authorities, and the private sector had invested an estimated $1,300 million in the whole scheme.

A network of express motorways was created, linking the six new tourist resorts. Seven main marinas and thirteen smaller marinas were developed.

In addition a large-scale re-afforestation programme was implemented in what was a largely treeless region, and about 12,000 hectares has been planted.

Finance for the development companies was provided in the form of low interest loans from the Caisse des Depots and the Fund National d'Amenagement Foncier et d'Urbanisme. They developed improved the plots transferred to them by the State and then offered the improved land to private builders. The development costs were high, ranging from 50 francs to 2,000 francs per square metre. (*The Economist,* 1970).

This project achieved four main aims:

— it created a new tourist region, and provided important employment opportunities in a stagnant regional economy;

- it relieved pressure on the Cote d'Azur by opening up a 100 mile stretch of beaches;
- it controlled the type and location of development on a stretch of coast that had previously been developed in a piecemeal fashion;
- by a substantial program of tree planting it reversed the extensive deforestation that had taken place since the nineteenth century.

One further by-product has been the rapid growth of new industry in the region attracted by the massive infrastructure developments and the attractive location.

(b) Development of a Strategy for Hadrian's Wall

Hadrian's Wall is one of the finest archaeological and historic features in Britain and is unique in Western Europe. It is over 70 miles long and its chain of outer earthworks, milecastles and forts encompasses an area managed by three County Councils and six District Councils. Part of it lies within a National Park: two Regional Tourist Boards are responsible for promoting it and several national agencies have functions within this area. In addition, there are many private interests concerned with the land on which the major remains are located.

From the early 1960s through to the 1970s, there was a gradual but steady increase in the numbers of visitors to the Roman Wall, particularly to the well known and accessible sites. This, in turn, led to problems of visitor pressure at specific locations along the Wall causing erosion of the monument, and the main footpaths leading to it, and creating problems of congestion and access and lack of suitable services.

In 1974, the Countryside Commission appointed, as consultants, the Dartington Amenity Research Trust with the brief to 'appraise the existing and likely pressures on the Wall and its setting, give guidance on the broad planning strategy for their conservation, and to advise on traffic and visitor management and on interpretation and publicity related to the Wall'. In preparing the strategy, it was clear that a wide range of interests had to be accommodated, including landowners, farmers and local residents, local and County planning policies, archaeological and environmental issues, and the many other bodies with an interest in the land covered by the Wall.

Aims of the Strategy

The broad aims of the strategy were:

a) to safeguard the splendid heritage of Roman monuments and all associated remains so that they are not lost or spoilt for future generations;

b) to protect, and where possible enhance, the quality of landscape setting of the Wall sites;

c) to encourage appropriate public visiting of the Wall area, with convenient access and high-quality experience and (for those who seek it) understanding of the Roman monuments and way of life.

d) to ensure that local people derive the best possible benefits from tourism by way of income and employment, whilst ensuring that all appropriate steps are taken to minimize the adverse effects of tourism, particularly on agriculture.

Clearly, these aims may appear to conflict with one another. How can one safeguard the Roman heritage and protect the landscape quality of its setting whilst at the same time improving public access and encouraging the public to visit the Wall? With this in mind, it was clear that any final strategy had to be realistic and practical if it was to be acceptable and capable of implementation.

Preparing a Strategy

The first step in the preparation of a strategy was to make a comprehensive assessment of all the relevant forts, earthworks, and visible parts of the monument in the light of four criteria. These were:

— existing and projected number of visitors;
— environmental constraints;
— the appropriate timescale for proposed developments;
— land ownership.

(i) Assessment of future visitor numbers to the Wall sites

An assessment was made of the potential peak usage at the 9 major sites along the Wall, taking into account development proposals, development of visitor services and increased car parking (Table 26 on page 147).

(ii) Environmental constraints

These estimates were then related to the ability of the major sites to accommodate visitors. Four environmental criteria were used to determine the acceptable number of visitors:

a) the capacity of the landscape in the Wall corridor to absorb the infrastructure which visitors need, e.g. car parks, access roads, toilet blocks, picnic sites;
b) the effect of visitor pressures on farming and the capacity of existing and proposed footpaths, including that along the Wall, and other factors;
c) the implications for nature conservation (a subject of particular concern in the consultation exercise);
d) the protection of the archaeological fabric itself, particularly from the effects of increased visiting.

The Strategy for Major Sites

After reviewing the Dartington Amenity Research Trust's recommendations for each site, and making a site-by-site assessment on the lines set out above, four categories of site were identified:

(i) Sites where no development is envisaged

(ii) Sites where limited development would be acceptable

(iii) Sites with major development potential

(iv) Sites with long-term potential

Since Victorian times, the Roman Wall has been recognized as a major archaeological monument and tourist attraction. By the 1970s, wear and tear caused soil erosion and in parts the foundations of the Wall itself began to erode as the soil was washed away. Visitors found the main sites crowded at peak times, there was a lack of visitor services and interpretive facilities were limited. The DART report highlighted these problems but it was clear that no single organization could provide a solution because the Wall extends over such a large area, with a great number of different landowners, and cuts across several local authority boundaries. For the first time, 32 public and private organizations came together to prepare a single policy framework for decisions affecting the whole length of the Wall.

Table 26
Forecasts of Peak Capacity at Main Sites on Roman Wall

Site	Annual No. Of Visitors	Forecast Peak Capacity At Any One Time
Birdoswald	NA	250 – 400
Carvoran	NA	480
Vindolanda	80,000	600 – 650
Housesteads	113,000	450
Carrowbrough	NA	40
Chesters	101,000	1,000
Corbridge	28,000	1,200
Rudchester	NA	200
South Shields	40,000	450

Source: *A Strategy for Hadrians Wall*. Countryside Commission, 1984

Hadrian's Wall development is an excellent example of the many factors that must be considered in a tourism development scheme. The age of the attraction requires scientific experts to halt and control the erosion and degradation of a historic structure and, at the same time, assure public access to a part of their heritage. The development crosses many governmental jurisdictions. It can be an attraction of enormous economic and social benefit to the population in the vicinity of the Wall. Obviously, there is not a comparable structure in North America. However, National Parks in both Canada and the United States, as well as governments at the Provincial and State level, have faced similar planning and development decisions for significant archaeological and historical sites. Comparable in historic age to Hadrian's Wall would be the pre-historic Indian sites, particularly in the southwestern part of the United States, such as Mesa Verde Pueblo and the Chaco Canyon ruins of New Mexico. Although of more recent age, Indian trading posts, missions, village reconstructions, forts and battlefields are examples of similar New World attractions. Linear examples to Hadrian's Wall might be the Blue Ridge Parkway, the Natchez Trace Parkway and the Appalachian Trail. As yet undeveloped, but with potential for development, are some of the historic trails that were prominent in the settlement of North America — the Oregon Trail, Santa Fe Trail or the route of the Lewis and Clark expedition from St. Louis to Oregon.

(c) Resort Development in the Coastal Zone — The Rockresorts

The resorts developed by Lawrence Rockefeller provide the classic example of tasteful development with an appreciation for the environment. Each resort has been developed in a remote location, requiring expensive infrastructure as well as superstructures. In several locations, such as the Virgin Islands and Wyoming, the Rockefeller fortune was used to purchase many thousands of acres surrounding the resorts. This acreage was then donated to the government for National Parks (i.e. Virgin Islands National Park and Grand Teton National Park). The resorts are very up-scale and popular, too expensive for persons with middle incomes. However, in both Wyoming and the Virgin Islands, the National Parks provide accommodation for people with modest incomes.

Rockresorts have been built at Caneel Bay Plantation on the island of St. John, Dorado Beach and Cerromar Beach in Puerto Rico, Little Dix Bay in the British Virgin Island of Gordo, Mauna Kea on the island of Hawaii, Kapulua Bay Hotel and Club on the Hawaiian island of Maui and, most recently, the Boulders Resort in Carefree, Arizona. A number of these resorts are no longer owned or even managed by Rockresorts. What characteristics make them unique? They are unique because of the concepts used in their development. Each resort has been developed in an undeveloped area to act as stimulus for further tourist growth in the vicinity. In addition, each development has adhered to a strong natural resource conservation idea in conjunction with landscape designs that emphasize natural beauty.

The development, in 1965, of the Mauna Kea Beach Hotel on the Kohala coast of the 'Big Island' Hawaii, the largest island in the Hawaiian Islands, provides a case study of the Rockresort philosophy. The resort hotel was the flagship development of a larger master plan for the Kohala coast region. This dry coast is on the west side of the island, in the lee of the prevailing winds, deficient of a natural water supply but with an ideal sun drenched atmosphere. Offshore deepsea fishing is excellent and there are a number of long, natural sandy beaches. The water supply is provided by a twenty mile pipeline tapping water from the windward side of the island. The region is rich in Polynesian history and missionary activity. Modern settlements were, at the time of development, economically based on the production of Kona coffee to the south and ranching on the gentle slopes of the volcanic mountains, Mauna Kea and Mauna Loa. The master plan was based on a massive community attraction complex including a new city harbor, shopping centers, medical facilities, banks, cultural center, government buildings, single and multiple dwelling units, golf courses and a Hawaiian state park. The hotel itself is said to have cost $80,000 per room, an extremely large amount at the time. No coastal roads were allowed in the plan between beaches and there were many large protective buffer zones planned between development sites. By the 1980s, two additional large resort hotels had been built in the region and condominiums were under construction. This development was privately financed with the obvious cooperation of the Hawaiian government and is a prime example of a public-private resort, real estate development.

In the United States, other developers have followed this example. Sea Pines Plantation on the South Carolina's Hilton Head Island is one example. The United States is fortunate in having sparsely populated and undeveloped areas where developments that emulate the Rockresort example can be attempted. Developers now see the value of a planned unit complex that not only blends with the natural surroundings but conserves the natural resource.

ASSIGNMENTS

1. You are the Director of Tourism Development for a state. You wish to encourage development of a historic trail in your state as a tourist attraction. Develop a plan for site developments, historic interpretation, management structure and financial appraisal. What argument would you use with local governments and businesses to encourage the development? Where might you seek planning and financial assistance? What tourist support services and facilities would be necessary?

2. As a state tourism director, devise a visitor questionnaire to administer to tourists in order to evaluate your state's tourist attractions and services. Your desire is to measure tourist satisfactions and to discuss how developments can be enhanced to increase visitor satisfaction.

Chapter 10
Tourism Marketing

Learning Objectives: After reading this chapter you should have a clear understanding of:
— the difference between selling and marketing;
— identifying the tourist product;
— the elements of market research;
— market segmentation;
— advertising, publicity and promotion as marketing tools;
— the main elements of a marketing plan.

Introduction

Marketing covers a wide range of activities including promoting, selling and developing a product. Marketing is a process which involves persuading a potential buyer that a particular product or service is the most suitable for his or her needs. This is relatively straightforward if the product is a motor car or detergent. It is less so if the product is a tourist product. The demand for the tourism product is entirely discretionary. It is not essential and is influenced by people's tastes, perceptions and preferences and other intangible factors. The tourism product is often seasonal and if 'unsold' by a particular date, is lost. Unlike a manufactured article which can be reduced in price or sold at a later date, an airline seat or hotel bedroom has to be sold by a set date otherwise it has no value/earning potential. In order to overcome these problems, a tourism marketing plan needs to be developed which includes the following stages:

— identifying the existing tourism product;
— undertaking market research to identify the psychology of the tourist, the market segments, the strengths and weaknesses of the tourism product;
— modifying the tourism product in response to the market research (product strategy);
— identifying the marketing mix;
— promotion, including advertising and publicity;
— selling the tourism product;
— analyzing the results of the marketing strategy and modifying it, if necessary.

Each of these elements may be thought of as tourism marketing — but in isolation they are not. Together they make up marketing. It is a cyclical process, with periodic reviews of the product-market mix and the promotional strategy, in order to measure their effectiveness and to decide whether new strategies are needed.

The Tourism Product

In Chapter 3, the tourism product is defined as the resort or historic town, the beaches, scenery, mountains, historic sites, theme parks, museums and other tourist attractions, as well as the accommodation stock. The difference between this and almost any other product is that the consumer (i.e. the market for the product) travels to the place of production and consumes the product on the spot. So tourism marketing must take account of the psychology of the traveler as well as the consumer.

The travel element of the tourism product may simply be a means of getting from home to resort as quickly and as cheaply as possible. Or, it may be an end in itself as with cruising, or the Orient Express, where the journey *is* the product. Again a distinction must be made between discretionary travel (tourist travel) and non-discretionary travel (business travel). The marketing approach is quite different in each case.

A less tangible element of the tourism product, but in many ways the most important, is the quality of service provided to the tourist (the consumer). It is not enough to identify who the customers are and what their needs are. It is important to remember that customer satisfaction depends on the standards of quality and service meeting the expectations of customers. If a charter flight is cancelled or a hotel room is over-booked it can affect the whole holiday experience. Similarly, poor service cannot be retrieved and can lead to adverse publicity and a decline in trade. An emphasis on quality control and staff training in customer relations, are essential elements of a good tourism product.

Seasonality may be a key influence on the tourism product. Sales may be concentrated into four or five months, and the level of sales during that period must be sufficient to make the business financially viable.

Good marketing can help to extend the season, identify new client groups, develop new pricing strategies, and improve the profitability of a tourism business.

As the tourist industry has developed, certain elements such as international hotels or major airlines have evolved a broadly similar product. One jumbo jet is very similar to another regardless of the logo; a 4-star hotel should have similar facilities regardless of its location. This raises the question of how do companies offering a very similar product succeed in persuading the public to choose them in preference to their competitors? The answer is found in their marketing strategy. In order to develop a marketing strategy you need to know as much as possible about the market. In order to obtain this information it is necessary to undertake market research. The following section outlines the principles and practice of market research.

Market Research

This should provide answers to the following questions:

— what is the total size of the tourist market?
— who are the existing customers?
— where are they from?
— what are existing customers seeking?

- what level of pricing (in relation to facilities), will customers accept?
- what are the past and existing trends in the tourist market?
- what factors influence these trends?
- who are the potential future customers?
- what are the strengths and weaknesses of the product compared with competitors?

Market research uses two types of data — primary and secondary.

Primary Data can be obtained from two sources, from in-house data and from field surveys. *In-house data* can provide information about the performance of the business, measured by daily, weekly, monthly figures on:

- occupancy rates
- visitor spending
- sources of business
- profit margins
- revenue costs

This can be analyzed for an individual business, a group of businesses, or a region — if the data is available.

Field surveys

These can take several forms, but the most frequent means of collecting primary data is by using questionnaires. These can be either self-completed or filled in by trained researchers during personal interviews. Self completed questionnaires are commonly used by hotels and airlines but they suffer from two main drawbacks which seriously limit their value for market research. They allow no control over the 'sample' of tourists completing and returning the questionnaires. It is not a representative sample and often consists of people who were dissatisfied with some aspect of the facility/service provided.

In carrying out field surveys, the most valuable results are generally obtained by taking a random sample and using a trained interviewer to complete a structured questionnaire during personal interviews. A *random* sample assumes that it is unbiased and representative of the population being studied. Using random number tables and names drawn from the Electoral Register it is possible to produce a general random sample. However, in doing field surveys with interviews at airports, harbors, or hotels, it is more difficult to produce a genuine random sample, and it may be more practical to produce *a stratified sample* where the data and the sample are related to particular groups, weighted according to the proportion in each group as part of the total population.

The questionnaire generally provides two types of data. First there is the demographic and socio-economic profile of the tourist. That is, the age, family composition, income, occupation and place of residence of the tourist, and his spending patterns on holiday. The second set of data relate to the opinions, perceptions, motivations, and values and lifestyles of the tourist — in relation to a particular tourist product and/or competing tourist products. The way in which these more subjective questions are put and the order in which they are put are critical aspects of questionnaire design.

Secondary-Data can be obtained by undertaking Desk Research using census returns, company reports, local, regional, national or international tourist surveys, general household surveys, studies of leisure trends, and reports from trade associations and professional bodies. This can provide information on tourism trends and changing public preferences over time. In Britain, the National and Regional Tourist Boards regularly publish a wide range of statistics on tourism trends.

In the United States the US Travel Data Center, based in Washington DC, publishes frequent reports on many aspects of travel and tourism. Most of this information is available, at a cost, and may not be found in public libraries.

The Marketing Mix

Having undertaken market research, using desk surveys, field surveys, or a combination of both, the resort or tourist company should have acquired a mass of information about the elements of their tourist product that attract or detract tourists, the preferences and attitudes of the tourist, and an extensive profile of the different types of tourist that together make up the 'market'. Among the first questions requiring an answer are 'What factors influence the tourist to buy my product?' or 'How did he hear of my product?' These, and related questions, enable businesses within the tourist industry to design or modify a product that will improve their competitiveness and ultimately their profitability. The consumer, in this case the tourist, is rarely buying a single product. He or she is buying a set of 'products' that appeal to him or her and the choice of product may be influenced by income, education, age and life-style. The preference may be for exclusive, exotic, cultural tours or low cost self-catering beach holidays with guaranteed sunshine. Between the high cost low volume trade and the low cost mass market there is a wide range of possible products. Ideally, a tourist region, resort, or individual business aims to develop a range of tourism products that will appeal to the widest possible market. This is known as the *product mix*. So, a resort will offer a wide range of types of accommodation and a variety of forms of entertainment. Special pricing packages for hotels or airlines within a range of prices/fares are also examples of product mix.

After the market research is complete, a profile of the tourist can be constructed and the product can be improved or modified to make it more competitive in the marketplace. The next step must be to examine the ways in which the consumer is made aware of the product. Unless, and until, the customer knows of the existence of a product, he or she will not be able to consider buying it. The product is made known to the tourist by a method known as the *communications mix*. This is done in a variety of ways including:

— direct marketing (mailshots, telephone canvassing, etc.);
— media displays (TV ads, newspapers, magazines etc.);
— special events/promotions;
— exhibitions, (trade shows, displays etc.).

The tourism 'product' is often a combination of elements including transport, accommodation, amenities and entertainments. The way in which these products are sold to the consumer is known as the *distribution mix*. This mix can include inclusive tours bought through travel agents, direct sell holidays, or special promotions carried out by the airlines or selected hotels. There is a great variety of possible distribution channels, and the aim of a marketing strategy should be to use these as cost-effectively as possible, so as to reach the greatest possible number of potential tourists. Every tourist business, resort, or region is in competition with other tourist destinations, and it is the firm or organization that keeps its distribution costs (and hence its product costs) down that will be the most competitive. Price/cost is not the only criterion, although it is important. The product must be attractive and marketed in an effective way if tourists are to be persuaded to buy it.

Product Life Cycle

If the sales of the product are plotted on a graph, a successful product — in this case a hotel resort or airline — will show an upward curve on the sales chart. This will continue until the market is saturated and the number of consumers (tourists) will either remain static or even decline, showing a downward curve (Figure 37). This cycle, from the introduction of a product through to its demise or saturation, is known as the *product life* and may be measured in years or decades. The life of the product can be extended in two principal ways:

(i) by finding new markets for the product; or
(ii) by redeveloping the product to meet changing tastes and preferences.

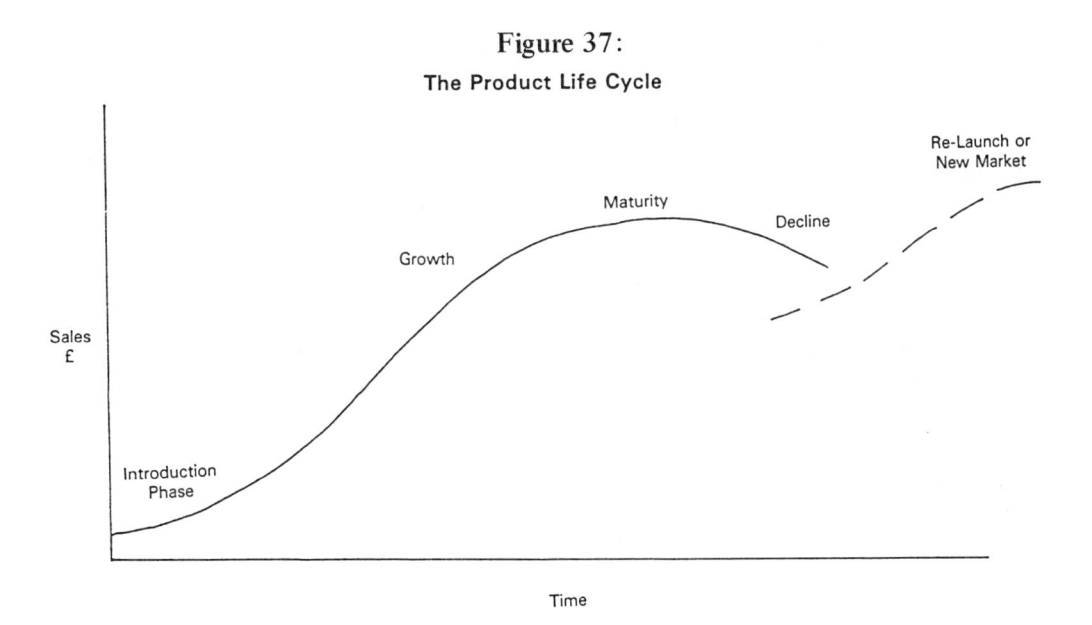

Figure 37:
The Product Life Cycle

Market Segmentation

This is a term for the process where companies or organizations will identify particular groups within the population who are potential buyers for the tourist product, and the marketing strategy will target these market segments. Market research should help to identify these target markets. These segments are made of four broad groups:

(i)   the youth market;
(ii) the family market;
(iii) the senior citizen market;
(iv) the special interest market.

The tourist market can also be grouped by region, with a concentration of marketing effort on the main tourist generating regions. The main markets are those countries or regions who provide say over 30% of the main tourist flows. Pricing policies, promotional campaigns and advertising will focus on these areas. Then there are the secondary markets who provide some tourists to a particular destination, but who have considerable potential traffic which is, at present, going to other destinations. Finally there are targets of opportunity, new, rapidly growing economies which are historically of little significance as generators of tourists. However, these emerging markets may be attracted to existing tourist destinations.

Pricing Policy

This is a further crucial element in any marketing strategy. In order to arrive at the most effective price, the following information is needed:

(i)   the cost of producing the product;
(ii) the planned volume of sales;
(iii) the prices charged by competitors;
(iv) other external factors such as interest rates, fuel surcharges etc.
(v)   consumer's views on prices;
(vi) the level of investment required to produce the target sale to achieve a marginal rate of return on that investment.

A number of pricing policies may be used, varying according to the nature of the tourism product and the forecasted life cycle of that product. Where a tourist business or region is trying to break into an established market, a policy of lowering prices, and hence profit margins, may be introduced, with the longer term aim of gradually increasing prices once a market share has been established. This is known as *penetration pricing*.

Promotional pricing may be used to attract customers for a new product or to revive flagging sales of an old product. Here a lower price than normal would be introduced.

Where there is high initial investment, and an early recovery of this is needed, the organization may introduce high prices and then progressively lower them as competition increases. This is known as *skim pricing*.

Pricing policy can also be used as a planning tool. If, for example, a region, resort or hotel wishes to concentrate on an up-market clientele it may deliberately choose to impose high prices as a means of controlling the influx of tourists.

Selling the Product

Having done the market research, developed a product, identified market segments, established a pricing policy, and made customers aware of the product, it must be sold to them. Making a sale is the final part of the communications mix. If the seller is a retail travel agent, he or she has to identify the client's needs and suggest the best destination for that tourist. If it is an inclusive tour, does it provide the right kind of accommodation, at the right price and in the right location? Are the travel arrangements satisfactory? If the seller is promoting/selling a particular product he needs to convince the particular customer that the product will meet his needs at a price he can afford. He needs to know the product in detail and the strengths and weaknesses of competing products. Selling the benefits of a particular product is an important part of the sale. As soon as the seller is aware that the customer is willing to buy, he should seek to close the sale and ask for the business.

Preparing a Marketing Strategy

The first step in preparing a marketing strategy is to establish the main goals and objectives of the firm or organization. In the case of tourism marketing, there is generally a combination of:

(i) increasing the market share of the product;
(ii) increasing the profits from tourist spending;
(iii) developing new tourist markets;
(iv) reviving declining tourist products.

These are general long-term objectives and there is often a difference in objectives between those of the national or regional tourist organization and the individual business who is usually selling a specific product to a specific segment of the market. Small tourism businesses often do not have a marketing plan and usually have not undertaken any market research. These are the most vulnerable elements in the tourism industry.

There is an element of risk in any marketing strategy in that expenditure has to take place on developing a tourist product and marketing that product *before* the business or organization is in a position to measure the success of the strategy. Forecasting the outcome of particular strategies is an important element in market research and can be used to predict not only the probability of success of a strategy, but also the degree of risk involved.

There are six main stages in preparing a marketing strategy. These are:

(i) *identify the target market segments.* This relates to the age, socio-economic profile and region of origin of consumers (tourists) and decisions on whether a high volume mass market or low volume high spending exclusive market is desired.
(ii) *identify the consumer's profile for these market segments.* Market research among the target population can identify the preferences of the target market and those aspects of the product mix which have most appeal.
(iii) *identify the key factors which influence the segment's decision to buy a holiday.* Is it price? Is it conditioned by the image of the product? Is it the

availability of distribution channels? Is it influenced by socio-political factors?

(iv) *establish the pricing policy*. This has already been discussed, but it is important in relation to whether the strategy is aimed at new markets, fighting off competition from other tourist regions, optimising income year-round, or changing the image of the product.

(v) *Relate the marketing mix to the factors which most influence the client's decision-buying process*. This may involve a review of the product mix, the distribution mix and the communications mix in the light of factors that persuade the consumer to buy a particular tourist product. If he or she knows little about the product there is clearly a case for looking at the effectiveness of the communications mix.

(vi) *identify the main groups of clients*. There are usually two or three groups of client. In the first stage of the distribution mix, there are the retailers (travel agents) and the wholesalers and general tour operators. They will require particular discounts or special offers in order to promote and sell the product. In the second group, there are the tourists themselves and the marketing strategy must cater for them also. Finally, there are the business travelers who are influenced by differential pricing but more concerned with factors such as reliability, comfort, frequency and quality of service.

Measuring the Performance of a Marketing Strategy

In any marketing strategy, it is necessary to build in a control and evaluation mechanism so that the oganization can measure the success of its policies and, if need be, change them in the light of new information. One effective method is to keep weekly and monthly sales (and booking) figures and plot them on a graph to show:

(i)   weekly and monthly sales compared to previous years;
(ii) cumulative sales to date showing performance over the year up to the present (perhaps against target figures);
(iii) deviations from a regression line which shows long-term trends.

If these sets of indices are plotted, the graph will show a Z shape (Figure 38 on page 159). This provides a clear picture of this year's performance compared to last year when measured by monthly sales and cumulative sales, and should show that the long-term trend is up, static, or in decline. Clearly this technique is readily applicable to an individual business and less so to a tourist resort or region as a whole, *unless* there are detailed statistics available on tourist numbers and spending over a period of years.

An alternative method is to tabulate the weekly/monthly budget forecast of sales and the actual sales for the same period, to measure the shortfalls or surpluses that occur, and, if necessary modify the marketing strategy. *Analysis of variance* is a commonly used statistical method, and for more detailed consideration of this see Gregory, 1971.

The tourist industry is continuing to grow as new firms, new destinations, new kinds of tourist product and new markets are developed.

For example, Chapter 6 discussed the impact of deregulation of coach and air transport and forecast changes in aircraft technology in the 1990s. Both of these

Figure 38: A Typical 'Z' Graph

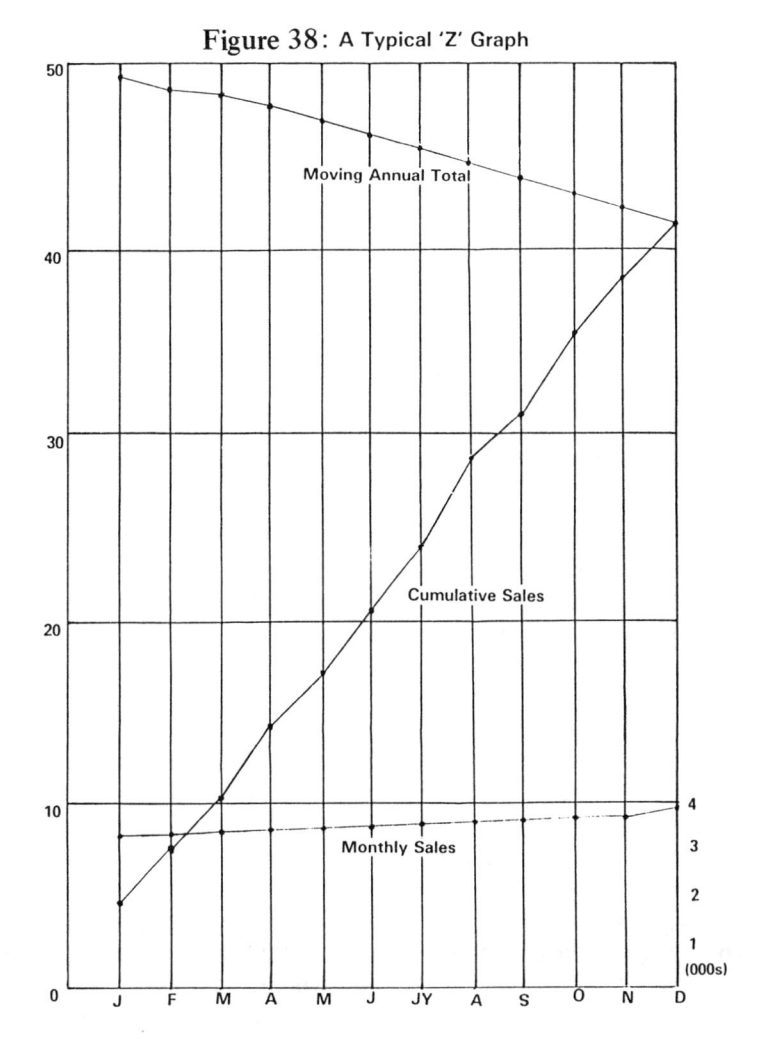

developments are already having a significant impact on the tourism industry. Chapter 13 includes references to time-share, theme parks and inner city tourism. All the evidence points to the dynamic and fast-changing nature of travel and tourism and underlines the need for effective marketing. This growth in activity brings with it increasing competition as businesses seek a greater market share. It is clear that any tourist business — from the largest company or national tourist office to the small family business — must develop a marketing strategy if it is to survive and prosper.

Any marketing plan should include the following elements. In developing a tourism product it should be evaluated for its:

Strengths (i.e. how does it compare over other similar products?)

Weaknesses (i.e. where is it deficient compared to competing products?)

Opportunities (i.e. what new markets or market segments exist for this product?)

Threats (Who are the main competitors and what are they doing in the marketplace?)

In addition to the acronym SWOT which sums up the evaluation process, the business of marketing revolves around four P's:

Product This can be summed up as the scenic, climatic, cultural, historic features that attract tourists; the range of services to transport them to and from their destination, and the facilities to accommodate them during their stay here.

Price This is of crucial importance in marketing tourism because of the high level of competition between many tourist products. Pricing may be used as a marketing tool, to establish a niche in an existing market, to fight off competition, to retain market share, or to present an image of exclusiveness. Pricing policy is usually not static and can vary according to the nature of the tourist product.

Place This is not only the resort or tourist attraction, it means all the locations where the potential tourist can buy the tourist product. Thus high street retail travel agents and direct sell tour operators who are selling tourist products are a key factor in the marketing process. Tourist Information Centres and other points of sale are also included under 'Place'.

Promotion This includes advertising, production of brochures, public relations, sales promotion and is the most recognizable of the four P's. It is often taken to be synonymous with marketing but is only *part* of the marketing process.

Each of these P's has a key role to play in evolving a marketing strategy. However, to be successful they must be seen as part of an overall decision-making process which aims to match the needs and wishes of market segments with particular tourist products, to sell the product as effectively as possible, and to maintain or increase market share for the firm or organization concerned.

Conclusions

The tourist industry is continuing to grow as new firms, new destinations and new markets are developed.

The growth of deregulation of transport (see Chapter 6) and the emergence of new tourist generating countries underline the continual need for effective marketing. This growth in activity brings with it increasing competition as businesses seek a greater market share. It is clear that any organization in the tourist industry, from the National Tourist Organization or the multi-national company to the small tourist business, should have a marketing strategy if it is to prosper.

Certain acronyms have evolved to summarize the key elements of any marketing plan. Two are of particular value:

— **SWOT** — which stands for Strengths, Weaknesses, Opportunities, and Threats. This sums up quite effectively the important elements in evaluating the tourist product.

— **Four P's** — Product, Price, Place and Promotion. These are the four main components of marketing.

ASSIGNMENTS

1. You are a marketing consultant, charged with preparing a marketing plan for a new company seeking to develop exclusive package holidays to selected long-haul exotic destinations. Prepare a proposal, setting out your choice of destinations and market segments. Identify the strengths and weaknesses of existing competitors.

2. You are the owner/manager of a large hotel in a downtown location in a major resort. Your room occupancy is below average and you have a suite of large rooms on the ground floor that are greatly under-used. Suggest how you might develop a marketing plan to increase your occupancy levels and the usage of your ground floor rooms.

Chapter 11

Tourism Impact Studies
1: The Economic Impact of Tourism

Learning Objectives: After reading this chapter you should understand:

— the way in which tourism affects the economy of a town or region;
— the 'multiplier effect';
— the main methods of measuring economic impacts of tourism;
— the impact of tourism on the national economy.

Introduction

Tourism as a phenomenon has two kinds of impact. In the first place, tourists bring income to a region through their spending on goods and services there. Secondly, wherever it occurs, tourism has an impact on the environment both through the infrastructure that is part of the tourism development process, and the impact of tourists themselves on the culture and society of the tourist region. This chapter and the following one will look in detail at these different kinds of impact and, in particular, consider:

— What is the nature of these impacts?
— How can we measure them?
— What are the consequences of these impacts?
— What are the implications for future planning and development of tourism?

This chapter attempts to examine the economic impact of tourism and looks at ways of measuring this.

Tourist Expenditure

Tourist spending is made up of several components related to the different stages in the holiday package. If it is an inclusive tour, the tourist will have paid for the holiday in his home country and the bulk of this money will remain with the operator, retailer, and carrier. A proportion will go to the hotel in the tourist regions.

The main spending in the tourist region will therefore tend to be on:

— Meals and drinks out;
— Entertainment;
— Car hire or travel in the region;
— Gifts and souvenirs.

However, measurement of economic impacts is more complex than this, in that income comes not just from visitor spending, but also from wages and salaries of those working in the tourist industry, profits that tourist businesses make, and interest on capital borrowed to develop tourist projects.

Methods of Measuring the Impact of Tourism on the Economy

1. On Regional and Local Economies

The concept of measuring the economic benefits on regional economies of particular activities, by means of particular models, is not new and appears in books and articles on regional economic analysis going back over the past 40 years. However, the application of these models to tourism as an economic activity is much more recent. For a general introduction to methods of regional economic analysis, two useful references are W Isard — *Methods of Regional Analysis* (1970) and H Richardson — *Elements of Regional Economics* (1970).

There are three main methods generally used and these vary in their applicability and effectiveness.

These are:

— the economic base method;
— input-output analysis;
— the multiplier method;

(a) The Economic Base Method

This method divides the economic activities of a region into those that are *basic* and *non-basic*. The *basic* activities are considered to be those exported to other regions and which bring income and generate jobs in the area in which they are based. The *non-basic* sector depends on and services the basic sector and the size of the *non-basic* sector is dependent on the level of economic activity in the *basic sector*.

It is therefore a very simple model, which is based on 3 assumptions:

— all economic activity is either basic or non-basic;
— economic performance can be measured by the performance of the basic sector;
— there is a constant relationship between the size of the basic sector and the size of the non-basic sector.

If the number of jobs provided by the basic and non-basic activities can be identified, then it is possible to establish the ratio between them and to calculate the number of new jobs created in the non-basic category, following a growth in exports (in this case tourism).

However, this method is limited in its application, not least because it is difficult to identify all the basic and non-basic activities. It overlooks the fact the firms may have activities that are both basic and non-basic, and that there may be linkages between basic and non-basic operations. Also, it is questionable whether the non-basic sector *is* entirely dependent on the basic sector and whether the ratio between the two sectors remains constant. In the case of tourist activity, as a region grows, a proportion of the domestic population may consume the local tourist product and alter the basic/non-basic ratio.

(b) Input-Output Analysis

This is based on the concept that the economy of a region (or place) can be divided into producing sectors and consuming sectors. Input-output analysis attempts to model the inter-relationships between the producing and consuming sectors of the economy.

A detailed account of the methodology of input-output analysis is provided in Isard (1970), but the broad concept is developed by producing a matrix of transactions between the producing and consuming sectors. As Table 27 shows, the producing sector forms the rows on the vertical axis and the consuming sector the columns on the horizontal axis. It is possible, by using this matrix, to discover how much each industry purchases from other industries and how much of the output of each economic activity is allocated to other industries in the region. Although Table 27 shows three main sectors, these could be disaggregated into individual industries within each sector to produce a much more detailed and complex transactions matrix.

Table 27:
A Transactions Matrix

Producing Industry	Consuming Industry					
	Sector 1	Sector 2	Sector 3	Sector 4	Final Demand	Total Output
Primary	20	130	20	10	20	200
Manufacturing	80	50	70	150	50	400
Services	30	10	10	10	180	240
Other	30	20	100	100	200	450
Value Added	40	190	40	180		
Total Input	200	400	240	450		

The main problems associated with applying this method to regional economic analysis generally, and to the tourism industry in particular, are that it is dependent on identifying the representative set of industries and calculating constant coefficients to explain the transactions between them. It is also dependent on having available extensive data sets on regional income and employment levels in a sufficiently disaggregated form to identify particular facets of the tourist industry, at a local or regional level. In many tourist regions, the economic theory is in advance of the data needed to apply it.

(c) The Multiplier Method

The concept of a *multiplier* has been used by economists since the 1930s at least, but it was Keynes who provided a much more precise application of this approach. The *multiplier concept* is based on the premise that initial spending within a region will inject additional cash into the flow of income in the regional economy, and thus increase the regional income. The size of the income multiplier is based on the proportion of the additional income that is spent *within* the region to be received as income by other businesses who, in turn, will spend a proportion of this income within this region, and so on. The more that the intitial injection of cash is re-spent within the region, the greater will be the rise in total income.

However, not all this income will be spent or, if spent, remain within the region. There will be 'leakages', for example savings or spending on goods and services from other regions. With each successive iteration there will be a certain amount of 'leakage' out of the system and the amount of additional income generated will decline.

The application of the multiplier method to estimates of the regional economic benefits of tourism was developed during the 1970s by B H Archer (1973), D R Vaughan (1977), and others. These studies identified visitor spending by carrying out extensive on-site questionnaire surveys, together with information from particular local businesses that were thought to be either representative of the local tourist industry or related to/dependent on the local tourist industry.

— *generated spending,* which is indirect spending resulting from the further purchase of goods and services by the tourist businesses in which visitors have spent their money;

— *additional spending* by local residents of the income they have earned, directly or indirectly, from visitor spending.

For each type of visitor, a profile was prepared showing the impact of spending and the successive stages that this income progressed through as it circulated in the local economy. For example, if a family spend $500 in a local hotel, the hotel will in turn use this income to pay the wages and salaries of staff, buy food and supplies, pay laundry bills and bank the profit. Some of these purchases, or services, will be provided by local businesses who will, in turn, use this income to pay wages, meet other costs and keep as profit the residue. Table 28 on page 167 gives a hypothetical example and shows that, by using the multiplier method in this way, for every $500 spent by a visitor $145 is generated as additional income. So, in this case, the multiplier would be 0.29.

In addition to direct visitor spending in hotels and local facilities, such studies have attempted to survey the main business activities related to tourism in order to produce a coefficient which will reflect the additional income generated. After both types of survey have been completed, the end result is a composite multiplier as an index of all three types of income generated.

The approach, developed by Archer (1973) and others, is based on a concept that is in itself simple, but which requires extremely complex data collection and analysis to apply in practice. For multiplier analysis to be used in a meaningful way, the economic data must accurately reflect the range of monetary transactions that take place within the local economy. The previous chapter discussed data collection in the context of market research. The same principles apply. The first stage is to identify what local economic data already exists and in what form. Any new data should provide information that will clearly show the impact of tourism spending within the local economy. Such surveys must cover a representative sample of the visitor and local business population and be undertaken over a sufficiently long time-scale to reflect any seasonal or cyclical elements in spending patterns.

Table 28:

The Tourism Multiplier in Action

	Action	Expenditure	Income
1.	*A family spends in a hotel*	$500	
2.	*The hotel in turn spends this money on:*		
	Purchases of goods and services	255	
	VAT	75	
	Taxes	45	
	Rates	10	
	Wages and profit locally	**115**	Direct Income
3.	*The suppliers spend their income on:*	65	
	Goods for resale, and	30	
	Other services	15	
	Taxes	5	
	Rates	5	
	Wages and profit locally	**10**	Generated Spending
4.	*Direct and Generated Income*	125	
	of this $105 is re-spent	105	
5.	*Additional Income*	20	Additional Income
	TOTAL INCOME =	145	
	For every $500 spent by a visitor, $145 is generated as additional income so in this case the multiplier would be 0.29.	145 / 500	

These surveys generally attempted to identify three separate sets of data on:

— *direct spending,* that is expenditure of visitors on services/facilities provided by hotels, restaurants, shops and other local businesses/facilities;

Because of the need for highly accurate data at a disaggregated level, such studies using multiplier analysis are usually confined to a local or sub-regional level. They involve time-consuming interviews and visitor surveys and would be expensive to replicate on a larger scale. For this reason, studies of the economic impact of tourism at a national or supra-national level have used different measures.

2. Tourism Impacts on National or Supra-national Economies

Tourism, as an economic activity at national level, is generally measured using three criteria:

— its contribution to overall economic activity;
— its contribution to overall employment;
— its contribution to the Balance of Payments.

(a) Contribution to Overall Economic Activity

The two most useful measures are the ratio of tourist receipts (income) with Gross Domestic Product and tourist expenditures with Private Final Consumption. The tourist receipts of a country generate economic activity and are therefore a measure of economic production of that country. Tourist expenditures (i.e. consumption) are part of the overall consumption (Private Final Consumption). Not all countries or tourist regions possess economic data that accurately measures these components, but the annual reports of the OECD on *Tourism Policy and International Tourism* contain a wide range of economic data for the member countries, that can be used to calculate the proportion of tourist income and expenditure compared with total income and expenditure.

Between 1975 and 1985, the proportion of international tourist receipts in the GDP of the OECD member countries increased steadily, particularly in the United States, Germany and Spain. Within the Common Market countries, total tourist receipts were of most importance in France (over 5% of GDP), Greece (over 4%) and West Germany (over 4%).

International tourist expenditure as a component of Private Final Consumption was most important in Germany (over 4%), Denmark (4%), Ireland (4%) and the Netherlands (over 4%) and least important in Greece (1.1%), (OECD 1985). However, the income and expenditure from international tourism is only part of total tourist activity. In order to calculate the total contribution to overall economic activity it is necessary to collect data on:

— international tourist income and expenditure;
— intra and extra-regional tourist income and expenditure;
— domestic tourist income and expenditure.

Moreover, estimates based on direct contributions of tourist spending do not provide a complete picture. Tourist spending makes an indirect contribution to economic activity as initial incomes are re-spent within the national economy.

(b) Contribution to Employment

It is difficult to measure the total number of jobs dependent on or generated by the tourist industry, as the effects of spending by tourists are seen across a wide range of occupations and are felt directly and indirectly. There are three particular problems when relating tourism to employment:

(i) The tourist product is very diversified and covers a wide range of economic activities, many of which provide services used by the local population. Thus, censuses of employment usually include hotels with restaurants and other catering and do not distinguish between those firms mainly servicing the tourist and those which do not. Transport is often put as a single category, without the tourism element being identified.

(ii) Employment statistics tend to cover employees only and often fail to register employers or self-employed. Many tourism businesses are small businesses run by families or owner-managers and they make up a major proportion of total employment in the industry.

(iii) Tourism is a seasonal activity and its importance as an employer will fluctuate with seasonal changes in visitor numbers.

Most studies linking tourism to employment are based on expenditure data for three sectors of the economy:

— direct employment in businesses that sell goods and services directly to the tourist;
— indirect employment in manufacturing and wholesale distribution firms that supply goods and services to tourism businesses;
— employment in construction industries (investment-related employment). (A. Smaoui).

(c) Contribution to the Balance of Payments

A country such as Britain receives a significant income from spending by overseas tourists. For example, in 1985 14.5 million overseas visitors spent $6.4 billion. This is known as an 'invisible export', as it contributes to the national economy. However in the same year around 6.5 million Britons took holidays abroad spending money on tourist goods and services in other countries and, therefore, 'importing' these services. The contribution of tourism to the overall balance of payments of a country is the *difference* between the amount which overseas visitors spend in the country and the amount that the country's residents spend overseas, and shows the net surplus or deficit on the tourism account. Figure 39 on page 170 shows the contribution of tourism to the balance of payments between 1978 and 1987.

The United States is not as fortunate as Britain in this respect. Since 1978, the United States has had only one year (1981) in which the receipts from foreign visitors to the United States exceeded the travel payments of U.S. travelers in foreign countries. In 1985, payments by U.S. travelers in foreign countries were $15.4 billion while receipts from foreign visitors to the United States were $11.7 billion, creating a dollar drain of $4.8 billion. In 1986 the net differential was only $4.7 billion as a result of the dollar's depreciation against the currencies of European countries and the fear of terrorism. These factors slowed the flow of tourists to Europe and the Mediterranean by 1.3 million. Foreign visitors to the United States from overseas increased by 1.3 million in 1986 compared to 1985. This visitor increase was not of magnitude needed to offset the travel dollar drain (*Survey of Current Business,* June 1987).

In developing countries with limited potential for exporting manufactured goods, and reliant on low cost primary products and imported high-cost products, the development of tourist facilities can greatly improve the balance of payments position by bringing a considerable inflow of spending into the local economy. In this context, tourism can have a stabilizing effect by decreasing a deficit on the overall balance of payments.

Most Communist bloc countries have tried to encourage the inflow of Western tourists while placing restrictions on the foreign travel of their own nationals, with the aims of improving their balance of payments and 'importing' much needed hard currency.

As well as influencing the creation of jobs and general trade balance at national level, tourism can make an important economic impact at regional level. 'Region'

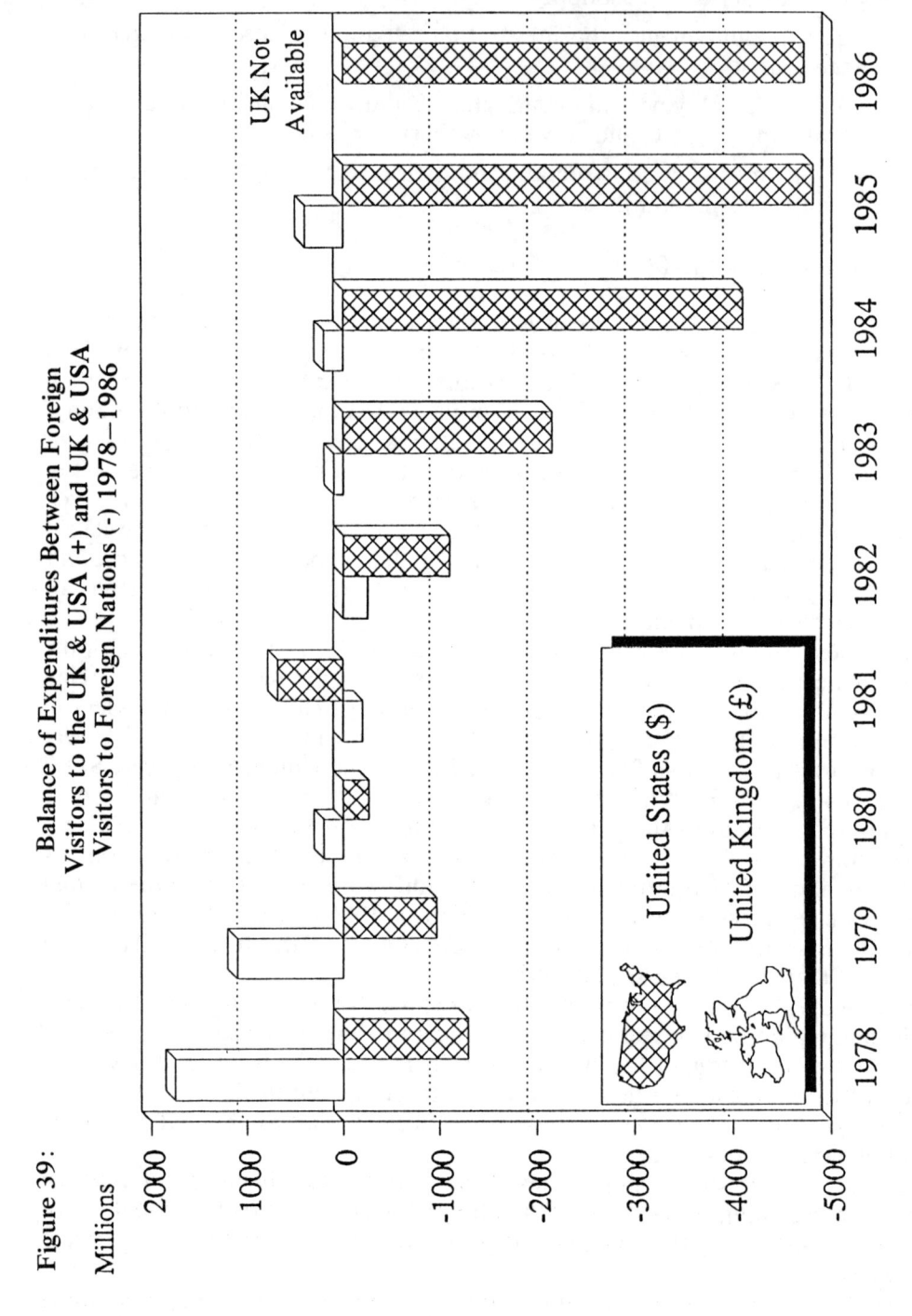

Figure 39: Balance of Expenditures Between Foreign Visitors to the UK & USA (+) and UK & USA Visitors to Foreign Nations (-) 1978–1986

SOURCE: United Kingdom - International Passenger Survey
United States - Survey of Current Business

in this context can mean part of a country, or an individual country that is part of an economic trading bloc. In regions with scarce national resources and limited manufacturing potential, and where agriculture may be marginal, tourism is often seen as a major catalyst in the development process.

The case of Languedoc-Roussillon in Chapter 9 is a good example of the way in which tourism development can transform a hitherto under-developed region. The economy of the region was mainly agricultural, largely low quality wine production, and rural depopulation was occurring at a rapid rate. Over $1,300 million was invested in a tourism development program during the 1970s and 1980s. 30,000 year round and 20,000 seasonal jobs were created in providing direct tourist services, ancilliary services, and construction/public works. Over 8 million visitors a year spend over $119 million in the region.

ASSIGNMENTS

1. Using sets of data from a recent OECD annual report on tourism policy and international tourism:
   (a) Assess the impact of tourism on the economies of 4 contrasting member states.
   (b) Plot the balance of payments 1975—1985 for two member states.

2. Using the further reading referred to in the text, critically review the application of multiplier analysis to the study of at least *one* local economy.

Chapter 12
Tourism Impact Studies
2: The Impact of Tourism on the Environment

Learning Objectives. After reading this chapter and the references contained within it you should have a clear understanding of:
— the types of impact that can occur;
— the methods of measuring the impacts of tourism development upon the environment;
— policy measures that have been developed to conserve the environment;
— methods of planning and managing tourism to reconcile conservation and development.

Introduction

There has been a growing awareness of the socio-cultural and environmental impacts of tourism on a region, and that disbenefits can occur through developments which are often overlooked in the search for economic benefits of tourism. The large-scale seasonal influx of visitors can mean that, by sheer pressure of numbers, the visitors to fragile environments risk destroying the very attractions that they come to see. In coastal regions, the rapid growth of a tourist infrastructure in the form of hotels, condominiums, shopping malls and roads, can transform a landscape in a short space of time. Because any discussion on the environmental impacts of tourism can risk being influenced by value-judgements, it is necessary to adopt an objective approach when measuring impacts. This chapter therefore seeks to describe and explain the types of impact that can occur, the methods of measuring these impacts, the public policy response (in the form of planning and control measures) that has evolved to conserve the environment, and management approaches designed to reconcile the inherent conflict between conservation and development.

Types of Environmental Impact

Tourism impacts on the environment in a number of ways. There is the visual intrusion of large numbers of parked and moving vehicles; the presence of large numbers of people on beaches, footpaths, or lakesides. There is noise, pollution and overcrowding. There is destruction of vegetation, visual intrusion of new buildings; developments out of scale with existing buildings. There is the impact on vegetation and wildlife and on the ecological system as a whole. Overall, there is a very real risk that, if unchecked, tourism development will lead to conflicts over the use of land.

For example, in the coastal dune areas of North West England, and on the coasts of Holland and Denmark, trampling has caused the loss of stabilizing vegetation leading to sand blows inland, the collapse of a fragile ecosystem, and the inundation of farmland. In the Dutch dune system, because of its importance as a sea defence, no public access is allowed to beaches except on a few board walks. In Norway and Sweden, the increasing spread of second homes in the mountain areas which lack sewage systems has led to pollution of local rivers and streams, (Council of Europe 1971).

The nature of the tourism impacts is associated with the nature of the tourist resources. With natural resources i.e. beaches, national parks, lakesides or forests, it is the ability of the resource to absorb the tourist that is the first measure of impact. This has been measured in relation to the *capacity* of the resource. There are three different kinds of capacity: physical, environmental and ecological.

Physical Capacity is the easiest concept to grasp because many tourist facilities/resources will have absolute limits on the number of tourists they can accommodate. Usually other constraints will intervene before this is reached. For example, the approach roads will become congested or car parks full before the beach reaches its maximum capacity.

Environmental Capacity. This is the maximum level of tourist use that an area can accommodate before visitors perceive a decline in their attraction to that place and move on elsewhere. This is the most abstract and least tangible measure of capacity, but is an important influence on visitor behavior. This level of capacity is very personal and varies with the season, prevailing weather, and type of tourist activity — so a wide range of capacity levels exist using this as a measure. Burton (1974), in her work on Cannock Chase, established that 10 to 50 cars in sight represented a critical level of use at which people first perceived the environment was crowded.

This concept has been studied in different tourist environments to produce national standards of capacity. Dower and McCarthy (1967), in their study of Donegal, identified a range of resources critical to the development of tourism and estimated the capacity of each to take people at any one time. Using studies by Furmidge (1969), Houghton-Evans and Miles (1970), it is possible to produce a range of estimates of environmental capacity. See Table 29 below:

Table 29:
Suggested Space Standards for Environmental Capacity

Type of recreation area	National environmental capacity
Major scenic route	20 persons per mile
Minor scenic route	4 persons per mile
Major scenic feature	20 persons per mile
Major historic site	30 persons per mile
Woodland area	100 persons per square mile
Picnic area	60 persons
Enclosed land	50 persons per square mile
Rough or hill land	5 persons per square mile
Coast or lake shore (basic level)	50 persons per mile
Attractive and accessible coast/beach	400 persons per mile

Ecological Capacity is the maximum level of tourist use that an area can accommodate before ecological damage or decline occurs. It is affected by geology, soils, vegetation cover and terrain of an area, and the seasonal intensity of tourist use. A person on horseback has more effect than one on foot. When people come in vehicles, especially the 4-wheel drive variety which gives them much greater accessibility to fragile landscapes, the wheels of these vehicles can destroy the vegetation cover and expose heath and stone. This has happened in parts of the New Forest where damage to the vegetation and to trees has occurred, and access to water and food for wild animals has been restricted.

In her work *The Recreational Carrying Capacity of the Countryside* (1974), Rosemary Burton points out that because the concept of carrying capacity is little understood, and because it has not been translated into a set of practical planning guidelines, attempts to manage environmentally sensitive areas are often frustrated. Although this work was undertaken over 14 years ago, the findings are just as relevant today because of the continuing need to understand and plan for the impacts of tourism on the environment.

Case Studies of Environmental Impact

1. Spain

In the 1950s and 1960s, Spain was developed as a major destination for mass market package tours. By the late 1970s, the growth of domestic and international tourism produced a seasonal influx of over 56 million tourists, concentrated in parts of its Mediterranean coast.

The Spanish authorities, when faced with this huge inflow of seasonal visitors, took two policy decisions. First, they sought to maximize the income from tourism. Secondly, they wished to minimize the damage to the environment. In order to assess the nature, scale, and distribution of tourism impact, several studies were carried out during the 1970s to measure:

— the capacity of the tourist regions;
— the existing levels of tourist use of these regions (i.e. their market share).

The aim was to identify those tourist regions with the greatest pressures of visitor use.

The tourist capacity of the leading holiday regions was calculated using the following formula:

$$\text{Tourist Capacity} = \frac{\text{No. of Beds} + \text{No. of Restaurants} + \text{No. of Commercial Licences}}{\text{Normal Population ('000's)} \times \text{Land area (Km}^2\text{)}} \times 100$$

This index produced the following table of leading tourist regions:

Region	Tourist Capacity	Rank			
Costa Brava	27.7	1	Madrid	4.5	6
Majorca	13.6	2	Murica-Alicante	3.6	7
Costa del Sol	10.5	3	Tenerife	2.3	8
Grand Canary Island	8.0	4	San Sebastian	2.0	9
Barcelona	6.7	5	Santander	1.0	10

This can then be related to the market share of the various regions as a proportion of total tourists to Spain.

Region	Market Share (%)	Rank
Majorca	35.2	1
Murica-Alicante	7.4	2
Madrid	7.5	3
Barcelona	6.8	4
Costa del Sol	6.4	5
Costa Brava	5.5	6
Tenerife	5.1	7
Great Canary Islands	4.7	8
Santander	0.8	9
San Sebastian	0.7	10

It can be seen from this limited example that some regions with a more limited tourist capacity (such as Murica-Alicante) had a greater market share than other regions such as Grand Canary which possessed greater capacity. Certain localities, such as Murica-Alicante or the Costa del Sol, were faced with a substantial influx of tourists over a limited period in the year and this led to a range of problems including acute congestion, especially on the coastal strip, inadequate infrastructure, environmental damage, and overloading of local services. Recent publicity has highlighted the response of the Spanish authorities to the spread of development, especially on the coastal strip of the Costa del Sol, where no new development is to be allowed within 100 metres of the shoreline and buildings erected without planning permission may be demolished.

2. Languedoc-Roussillon

The development of this stretch of the South of France was described in detail in Chapter 9. Over a period of 20 years, a 180 kilometre stretch of the French Mediterranean coast was transformed from a remote rural region of lakes, salt marshes and uninterrupted beaches, into the second most important tourist region in France. There were few roads and the local infrastructure was limited. Six new resorts were built, with a total capacity of 2 million visitors and moorings for over 20,000 boats. A network of major roads and water supply installations were developed. Between the six resorts, the natural vegetation and original landscape was to be preserved and protected so that the local flora and fauna would remain.

However, tourism development on this scale will have a considerable impact on the environment. How do we measure this impact? Is it a beneficial impact or a detrimental one? Was the original environment worth preserving? How can we best plan for tourism development so as to minimize its impact on the environment? How can the remnants be best conserved? In any assessment of the impact of tourism on the environment these are some of the questions that must be answered.

Methods of Measuring Environmental Impact

The original work on environmental impact studies was developed in the United States, the stimulus being the National Environmental Policy Act (1972) which required Federal Authorities to identify and measure the environmental impacts of proposals and to disclose the results to State and local bodies and the public. Several methods of environmental impact analysis have been developed, and three of those most adaptable to measuring tourism impacts are outlined below.

(i) Overlays

This is the most simple method of EIA and consists of a series of map transparencies overlaid to show the geographic extent and intensity of impact of proposed developments. An area can be divided into grid squares and, within each square, information can be displayed showing the potential impact of development proposals on environmental factors. This can bring out significant conflicts between development and the environment. At a manual level, there is a practical limit to the number of overlays that can be effectively superimposed upon one another. However, the use of computer graphics could overcome this problem and a wide range of overlays could be interrelated to identify interactions.

(ii) Matrices

A matrix can be constructed to show the impacts of the proposed developments (on the horizontal axis) on the individual characteristics of the existing tourist region (on the vertical axis). Within each cell of the matrix, it is possible to assess the level of the individual impacts (Fig 40 on page 178), with a score ranging from 1 to 10 representing the increasing size or magnitude of the impact. For example, a proposed hotel complex or condominium development might lower the existing water table by several inches, or introduce the risk of pollution within the network of local rivers and lakes. This would produce a high score as a measure of environmental impact. One criticism of this method is that it only takes account of the *immediate* impacts and is not sufficiently sophisticated to account for secondary and successive levels of impact.

An impact matrix should take account of both the development and the operational phase of a tourism project and the scale of individual impacts may vary between these two phases. If at all possible, impacts should be measured objectively using quantitative analysis so that the end product of an impact matrix would be a summary indicating that a proposed tourism development would produce:

— gains or losses;
— short-term or long-term effects;
— reversible or irreversible effects;
— local or regional impacts.

Models

The view that matrices are cumbersome to construct, and only measure first order impacts, led to the construction of dynmamic simulation models. The environ-

Figure 40: Environmental Impact Analysis Matrix

CONSTRUCTION PHASE

CHARACTERISTICS OF EXISTING SITUATION	Land Needs	Population Changes	Noise from plant	Traffic Noise	Transport of material	Pollution	Increased Traffic	Water Discharge	Transport of Employees	Labour Needs	Site use
SCENERY											
LAND USE											
RESIDENT POPULATION											
TOURIST POPULATION											
TRAFFIC MOVEMENT PATTERNS											
NOISE AND DISTURBANCE											
ECOLOGICAL CHARACTERISTICS											
ARCHAEOLOGICAL CHARACTERISTICS											
POLLUTION											
POWER SUPPLY											
SERVICES											
SEWERAGE											
EXISTING SETTLEMENT											

OPERATIONAL PHASE

CHARACTERISTICS OF EXISTING SITUATION	Land Needs	Population Changes	Noise from plant	Traffic Noise	Transport of material	Pollution	Increased Traffic	Water Discharge	Transport of Employees	Labour Needs	Site use
SCENERY											
LAND USE											
RESIDENT POPULATION											
TOURIST POPULATION											
TRAFFIC MOVEMENT PATTERNS											
NOISE AND DISTURBANCE											
ECOLOGICAL CHARACTERISTICS											
ARCHAEOLOGICAL CHARACTERISTICS											
POLLUTION											
POWER SUPPLY											
SERVICES											
SEWERAGE											
EXISTING SETTLEMENT											

ment is seen as an open or closed *system* and models are constructed which predict the effects of changes brought about by tourism developments on this environment. The system can be seen at successive intervals of time, as a series of calculations are carried out to predict successive impacts on the environment. The construction of such models generally requires considerable data about the environment and the proposed development, and this may require time and technical expertize that is not available. Provided such data is available, it is possible to construct complex mathematical models to deal with large complex development proposals.

Policy Responses to Environmental Impact

With the growth in tourism on a world scale, not only are more people using the coastal and inland regions for tourism, they are travelling greater distances, impacting on a greater area and spending more time there. Over the past 40 years, there has been increasing concern for the quality of the environment and the need to conserve scenery and wildlife in areas of great natural beauty. At the same time, there have been growing demands for more land for urban development, roads and factories, water supply, mineral extraction and many other land uses. The remaining land must also be used for farming, forestry, and many other needs.

In order to meet these conflicting demands on the use of land, and to conserve areas with fragile ecosystems or of great scenic value, most countries have developed a hierarchy of planning controls. The major landscape resources are conserved in *National Parks,* with the Yellowstone National Park in the USA the first to be established, in 1872. The US *National Park Service Act* of 1916 sums up the role of National Parks *'to conserve the scenery and natural objects and wildlife therein, to provide for the enjoyment of the same, in such a manner and by such means as will leave them unimpaired for the enjoyment of future generations'*.

The Netherlands has three National Parks, similar in concept to those of the United States. In Britain and West Germany, by way of contrast, most of the land in the National Parks is in private ownership and they have the normal land uses of farming, forestry and mineral extraction. In England and Wales, the designation of an area as a National Park enables special planning legislation to be used to control use and development of this land. The National Park authorities have powers to plant trees, clear eyesores and provide facilities for tourists such as car parks, camp sites and information centers. Following the National Parks and Access to the Countryside Act of 1949, 10 National Parks were established in England and Wales. The 1949 Act also provided for the designation of Areas of Outstanding Natural Beauty (AONB's) of which 33 have now been recognized (Fig 9 on page 37). Following the 1968 Countryside Act, local authorities in England and Wales have the powers to establish country parks and picnic sites. These are much smaller, but nevertheless attractive, recreational facilities and are sited in pleasant countryside within easy access of the major conurbations. One underlying reason for their establishment was a belief that they would help to relieve pressure on the National Parks which were faced with a growing influx of car owning visitors who could reach, with ease, the remoter more fragile landscape areas.

The most successful examples of conservation are in the United States and Holland where land ownership and management are in the hands of one Authority. In Britain, a quasi-public body, the National Trust, has acquired many thousands of acres of countryside and coast and protects them in the face of development pressures. Otherwise in Britain the National Parks have a chequered history as a means of controlling land use, especially mineral extraction.

The most successful measures to reconcile tourism development with environmental conservation have come about through the development of management plans for tourist regions. Conservation is the sensible use of resources and is concerned with the quality and quantity of many resources. Underlying this is a general view that if the natural resources are not conserved, they will deteriorate or be destroyed and then the tourists will leave, perhaps never to return. This could have disastrous effects on a local, regional, or national economy.

Planning for Tourist Environments

The ecological, scenic and social impacts of tourism can be both positive and negative. The key to successful integration of tourism in the environment lies in planning and management of any proposed development. The aim must be to use rural and coastal resources so that as many demands as possible can be provided for. A number of management techniques must be used to minimize existing conflicts and to conserve the environment for future generations to use and enjoy.

In order to protect those regions with scarce or fragile environments, a threefold planning program needs to be agreed. This consists of:

(i) increasing the capacity of regions/resources already committed to tourist use;
(ii) creating new resources for tourism using reclaimed or undeveloped and disused land around our cities;
(iii) developing multiple use of the same resource.

(i) Increasing the Capacity of Existing Sites/Regions

Wherever possible, the aim should be to improve the capacity of existing resorts and holiday areas to accommodate more tourism. This will involve a reappraisal of the use and effectiveness of existing resources and the development of management measures outlined later in this chapter. The advantage with this approach is that these destinations are already well known to the public and are likely to receive the first impact of any increase in demand for tourism. As demand, and therefore use, is often seasonal, measures to extend the season can also help to minimize peak season congestion.

(ii) Creation of New Tourist Resources

This can take 2 forms:
(a) the reclamation of land from the sea by means of polder or barrage schemes;

(b) the development of derelict or under-used land around our major towns and cities, especially in or adjacent to the main tourist destinations.

The reclamation of the Ijsselmeer and the Delta scheme in Holland have created a great number of new tourist opportunities for camping, water sports and natural history. The proposed barrage schemes for Morecambe Bay and the Wash, in England, and in Southern France would also provide new resources for water-based tourism activities.

Throughout Europe, there are many thousands of hectares of disused mineral workings, former railways, derelict canals and disused airfields that can be reclaimed/redeveloped for tourism uses. Sand and gravel workings can be reclaimed for water-based tourism. Many of the country parks in Britain and the regional parks in France include derelict mineral workings or industrial land that has been reclaimed. In Britain, disused railways have been converted into long-distance footpaths and bridleways and disused canals have been restored and now provide facilities for cruising, walking and other activities. Much of the derelict industrial land and mineral workings is within easy access of major towns and cities, and if it can be reclaimed and put to tourist uses, this will help to relieve the pressures on more distant, perhaps more fragile, environments. Recent developments in some of Britain's inner city areas are a case in point. In London, the 9-mile stretch of former docklands is being transformed as part of a major development project to provide a wealth of man-made and water-based tourist attractions. Similar, but smaller scale, schemes are under way in the dockland areas of Bristol, Liverpool, Swansea, Hull and Newcastle. In North America, similar schemes, varying in size, have been completed for Montreal, Quebec EXPO '67; Vancouver, B.C. for EXPO '86; the Waterside in Norfolk, Virginia; Brightleaf Square in Durham, NC; and South Street Seaport in New York City. However, reclamation of underused land or restoration of derelict land is not the only answer, and may not be possible in every case. In order to protect and conserve the environment, it is also necessary to integrate tourism with other land uses especially water supply, afforestation and nature conservation.

(iii) Multiple Use

Reservoirs and their catchments in upland Britain can serve as visitor attractions and provide opportunities for walking, sailing, camping and fishing. The Kielder scheme is a good example, where a major new tourism development is under way. Eight projects are planned in a 2-year program centered on Kielder water and the surrounding forest area. Additional sports facilities, provision of more accommodation, and improvements to existing facilities are part of an ambitious development plan jointly sponsored by the Forestry Commission, the Sports Council, the Water Authority and the local authorities.

There are several large and scenic reservoirs, parks and forests in the United States in the vicinity of major tourist destinations. Lake Mead in Utah and Arizona, which has flooded the arid valley of the Colorado River above Hoover Dam, is near Las Vegas and Grand Canyon National Park. Everglades National Park in southern Florida is managed for multiple use, as are all National Parks and National Forests in the United States. These Parks and Forests are in themselves major tourist attractions.

In Britain, the Forestry Commission has successfully integrated tourism with forestry and now provides opportunities for many activities including scenic drives, picnic sites, camping and fishing. Britain now has seven Forest Parks where these activities are encouraged, and in parts of upland Britain the Forestry Commission has developed and built holiday villages. In the Netherlands, over 10% of the holdings of the state forest service are managed for tourism and the service has built roads, camp-sites, viewpoints and picnic areas. In the United States many of the forest areas play a similar role and see no conflict between the need for timber supply and the provision of amenities for tourists.

Managing Tourist Environments

The most effective means of resolving potential conflicts between tourism and the environment is by applying good management practice. In this context three aspects of management are involved:

(i) traffic management;
(ii) land management;
(iii) visitor management.

(i) Traffic Management

Tourists often travel by car to or within their holiday destination, and the large numbers of moving and parked cars are one of the most immediate impacts of tourism on the environment. For many years traffic management has been recognized as a necessary means of controlling the movement and access of vehicles in major towns and cities. In tourist regions, the same principles will need to be applied if the impact of traffic is to be minimized. This should take the form of traffic design and highway engineering. Traffic design includes the provision of one-way systems, speed limits, limits to access to the remoter areas. In some areas cars may be banned altogether. In the Peak District National Park an experiment was carried out in the Goyt Valley, where rural roads were closed at weekends to all vehicles except minibuses carrying visitors into the valley from car parks located around its perimeter (Miles 1972). This scheme was possible because the valley had limited access by road and had no resident population.

To compensate for restrictions on motor vehicles the planning authorities should provide scenic drives, picnic areas and viewpoints at other locations. In some cases new roads may need to be built by-passing environmentally sensitive areas. The Susten Pass in Switzerland, between Innertkirchan and Wassen, and the Deutsch Weinstrasse from the French border to Mainz are good examples of such purpose-built routes.

(ii) Land Management

This concerns aspects of design and maintenance and, by a mix of persuasion and financial incentives, encouraging private bodies to provide amenities for tourists on their land. A circulation pattern may be necessary to direct and control the flow of visitors through a site and this may involve the erection of signs, fences and barriers, additional landscaping and planting schemes. It may be necessary to change the visitor access points and circulation routes on an annual basis to minimize the effects of trampling on the vegetation and to introduce a program of planned maintenance of the site. It is important to know the number of visitors the site can support before the services, in the form of car parking, access, water and sewage disposal risk becoming overloaded. There is a need, therefore, to monitor visitor numbers so that controls can be introduced if overcrowding or congestion are to be prevented. Good visitor management techniques are essential in order to control the impact of tourism on the environment.

(iii) Visitor Management

The most effective techniques of visitor management are usually unobtrusive but persuasive. Visitor management involves two actions — preventing or restricting access to environmentally fragile areas and directing visitors to those areas that can accommodate them. The most immediate control on site usage can be by limiting car parking provision, since in Europe and the USA most tourists will use their cars to visit the coast or countryside and most stay close to their cars when they arrive there. In the Huron-Clinton system of regional parks around Detroit, there is a system of notifying potential visitors that a park is 'full' and most Americans appear to be prepared to move on when they know a park is full.

Management by price is another control mechanism particularly for the private sector. A variation of this approach is to have a variable system of pricing related to the seasons and prevailing visitor numbers.

The use of barriers such as ditches, screens of trees, or mounds can deter people and, when combined with direction signs to attractions, control the spread of visitors in a recreational area. A scheme for the interpretation of the site is an essential element in the approach to visitor management. Guided tours or walks, exhibitions, self-guided trails or leaflets can all be used to guide visitors to those parts of the site that can accommodate them. If the tourist resource is sufficiently large, it may be possible to zone different localities for a range of uses — from the intensive gregarious activities around the main beach/lakeside area — to the less gregarious scenic drives or small picnic areas and the remoter parts, accessible on foot and some distance from the main visitor facilities.

In order for these planning and management measures to succeed, there is a need for continued coordination of efforts between central and local government and between the public and private sector. In many cases, the works needed to conserve the natural environment and to manage it effectively require capital investment from central government if they are to succeed. This raises issues related to the capital cost of financing of tourist developments, especially in National Parks and scenically important countryside and coastal areas, and the revenue costs of managing them. Should the tourist generating areas (i.e. the major towns and cities) pay for the upkeep of the rural recreation areas that they use and rely on? In the public sector, should site management costs be financed by admission charges so that the burden of maintaining and conserving sites rests on those who use them? In the not too distant future we may have to find answers to these and other difficult questions if our environment is to be preserved for future generations. The popularity and success of many private sector visitor attractions does indicate the ability and willingness of people to pay. These are complex issues and no clear cut solution has as yet emerged.

ASSIGNMENTS

1. Using a country park, stretch of coastline or beauty spot in your locality attempt to measure the following:
   (i) the impact of visitors on the area;
   (ii) the types of visitor amenities/facilities provided and their location;
   (iii) the local policies for visitor management.

2. Select two State or National Parks; compare and contrast the approaches to their planning and management.

Chapter 13

New Developments in Tourism

Learning Objectives: After reading this chapter and the additional references you should have an understanding of:

— innovations in tourism development;
— the factors influencing the changing preferences of tourists;
— the tourist potential of our industrial heritage;
— new approaches to the tourist market.

Innovation is perhaps the one word that best describes the development of tourism in the 1980s and which separates this period from the main phases of expansion in the late 19th Century or the 1950s and 1960s. In North America and Europe the traditional tourist market is approaching saturation point and major companies are competing for a share of a relatively static market. In this kind of business environment it is the innovative entrepreneur who can identify new resources and/or new preferences for tourists, who will become the market leader. This chapter attempts to identify new and emerging trends in tourism and discusses the lessons to be learned from them.

Innovations in Tourism Development

The traditional image of a tourist destination is a resort town set amidst attractive scenery with a variety of day-trip opportunities within easy access. The resort has been usually on the coast and has relied on sun, sea and sand to attract its clientele. During the 1970s and 1980s new types of tourist destinations have emerged. These are based on several types of product and demonstrate new approaches to tourism marketing.

This chapter examines how new tourism products have been developed and their role in helping to promote new tourist destinations, particularly areas not traditionally associated with tourism.

Examples of these products and changing innovation concepts include:

1) Inner city rebirth of riverfronts, harbors, and ethnic and commercial neighborhoods;
2) Theme parks — Shopping — Theme Park/Malls;
3) Attractions based on historical/cultural restoration including living history interpretation;
4) Continued growth in Second Home/Condominium Development and Use-Time Sharing;
5) Rapid adoption of high-technology innovations in the travel and tourism industry at all levels;

6) Increased public-private cooperation and partnerships in developing and fostering travel and tourism growth.

1. The Inner City as a Tourist Attraction

Major cities of the world have long been focal points for visitors whether for commerce or for leisure. The leisure attraction has been based on historical, regal and cultural events. London and New York City are recognized for the theater, while London, Paris, and Washington, D.C. as capitals are recognized for historical governmental structures, and national museums and galleries. For every city, regardless of size, shopping and dining in pleasant places are primary attractions. Inner city redevelopments capitalize on these factors. In the United States, Baltimore, Atlanta, Detroit, Dallas, Denver, San Antonio, and Seattle are just a few of the areas that have redeveloped significant parts of their inner cities into pleasing locals for shopping, dining, offices, hotels, conferences and residences.

Cities in the United States are not alone in revitalizing the inner city. In Britain, London, Bristol and Liverpool have initiated redevelopment schemes of the decayed and unused dockland areas. In London, the regeneration of Docklands involves an ambitious project covering over 9 miles of riverside land and four main sites — the Surrey Docks, Wapping, the Isle of Dogs and the Royal Docks. The government is spending over $807 million to provide a new infrastructure including a light railway, new roads, riverbus services and a short take off and landing (STOL) London City Airport. The private sector is expected to invest about $3.8 billion. The existing waterscape of the docklands will be used as a backcloth for a mix of commercial, residential, retail and leisure development. New museums are planned for the area including a Victorian Life Museum and the Great Eastern Railway collection in the Royal Docks. There will also be a 25,000 seat Sports Stadium, an education center and a leisure complex. Marina developments will encourage sailing, windsurfing and waterskiing. The planting of thousands of trees, the development of riverside footpaths and new retail/leisure complexes will transform this part of London by the year 2,000.

2. Theme Parks — Malls

These are perhaps epitomized by the Disneyland developments in California and, more recently, in Florida where, on several hundred acres of land, a series of fantasy worlds has been created, together with rides and amusements and a wide range of fast food outlets capable of meeting the needs of tens of thousands of visitors in a single day. The development of a park on this scale is usually designed around a theme or themes. In Disneyland, the themes are Adventureland, Main Street USA, New Orleans Square, Frontierland, Fantasyland and Tomorrowland, and the phenomenal success of this concept, since its development in the late 1950s, has spawned many imitations.

The forerunners of the theme parks in the USA were the seaside amusement parks such as Coney Island and Santa Cruz Beach boardwalk. In its first year of operation, in 1956, Disneyland attracted almost 4 million visitors and current visitor numbers are 12 million a year.

There are about 30 theme parks in the USA with a combined visitor level of 100 million per annum (Figure 41). The three Disney developments – Disneyland (California), Epcot Center (Florida) and Walt Disney World (Orlando, Florida) dominate the theme park market and between them account for over one-third of all visitors to USA theme parks.

Most USA theme parks were built in the period between 1950 and 1970 with only two pre-dating this period of rapid growth. The situation has remained fairly static since the mid 1970s and visitor numbers have not grown substantially since then. The theme park market would appear to have reached saturation point, and many of the existing theme parks have concentrated on reinvestment, together with the development of indoor attractions.

USA theme park ownership is highly concentrated, with 21 of the 29 largest attractions owned by six companies. With corporate ownership they have been able to achieve levels of capital investment generally not available in Europe. Most US theme parks are visited by day trippers with most of their catchment coming from a 150 mile radius. In 1986, the US Travel Data Center carried out a survey of 2,000 people regarding their frequency of visits to theme parks.

On the basis of this study, the International Association of Amusement Parks and Attractions estimated that 235 million visits would be made to major theme parks, smaller theme parks, and amusement parks in 1986. This study also showed that visiting a theme park is an important element in holiday planning and two thirds of the sample said that such tourist attractions played a part in selecting a holiday destination.

Unlike the USA, in Europe theme parks have been going through a boom period in the 1980s. They are of much more recent origin, most having been created in the last 17 years. Most are concentrated in Northern Europe, reflecting the concentration of populations and higher levels of car ownership and disposable income in countries such as Britain, Holland and West Germany.

The largest European theme park is De Efterling in the Netherlands which is a fantasy-based park with themes based on well known fairy tales. In recent years several 'white knuckle' rides have been added. De Efterling attracts over 2 million visitors a year. The leading European theme park is Europa Park in West Germany between the Black Forest and Alsace. The park has a European theme with Italian and Dutch villages and French, German and Scandinavian themed areas. The 40 hectare site also has about 30 rides and facilities for entertainments in a 800 seat theater.

The European theme parks, like their counterparts in the USA, predominantly attract day trippers. Between 70 and 95 percent of all visitors to the main European theme parks are day visitors, and most have come from places within 2 hours journey time of the park.

Most of the new theme park developments are taking place in France, in part encouraged by Disney's announcement of plans to open a theme park near Paris in 1991 (See below).

Two of the most recent developments: Mirapolis (opened in 1987, 25 miles north of Paris, and costing $37 million), and Asterix Land (opened in 1989, also north of Paris, and costing $145 million) are seasonal operations. Only the Euro-Disney project will have a significant covered element to support year-round opening. The initial season for Mirapolis was disastrous and only a major reorganization of its management and better budgeting and control have over-

Figure 41:

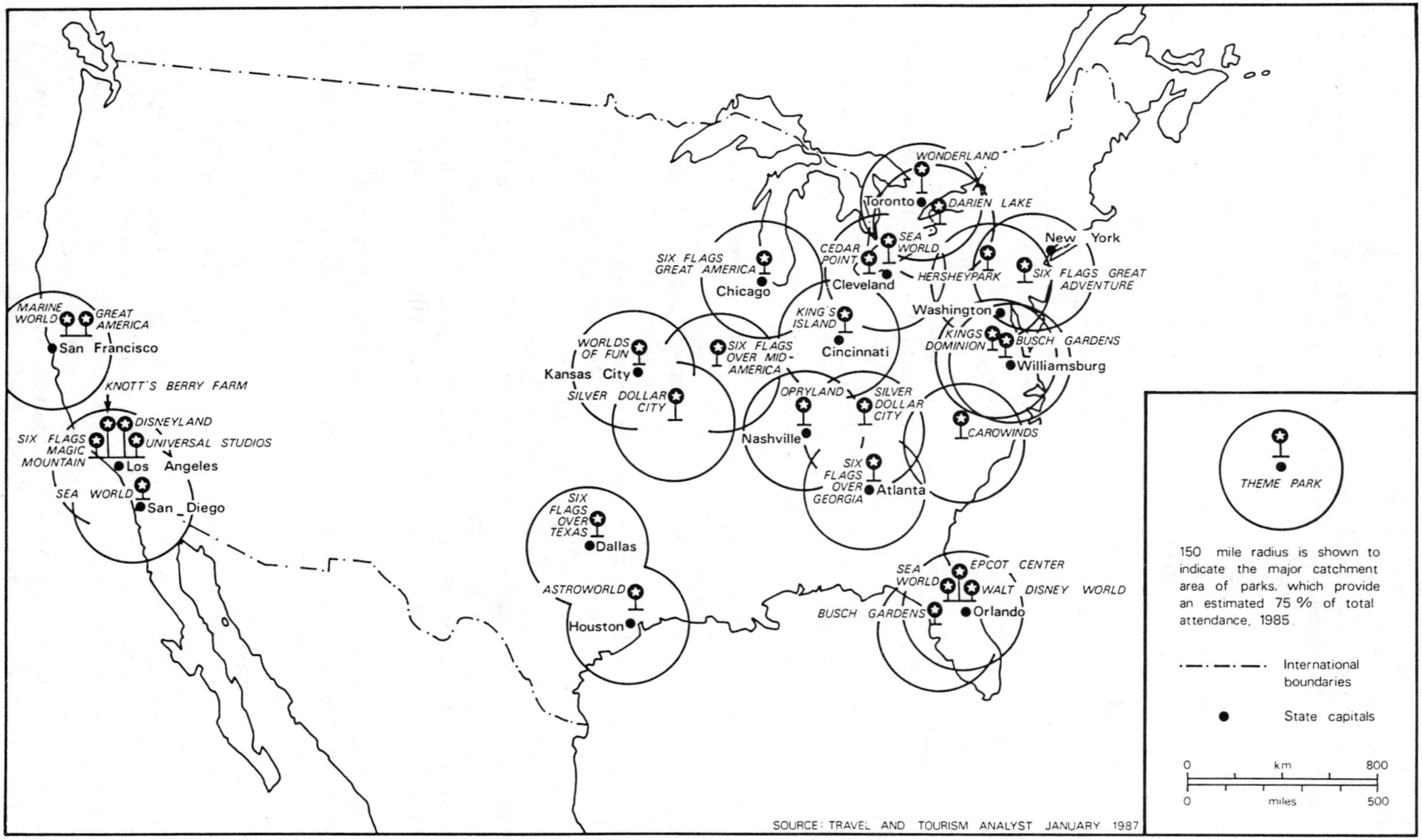

LOCATION OF MAJOR THEME PARKS IN NORTH AMERICA

SOURCE: TRAVEL AND TOURISM ANALYST JANUARY 1987

come a difficult start. (*Leisure Management* — January 1988). This experience does highlight the highly competitive nature of the theme park market and the need to exercise all round quality control and to ensure that the standards of the product, the landscaping and the rides are maintained as new theme parks come on to the market.

The imitation of Disneylike parks has frequently been successful but Disney parks are still the favorite of most visitors. In the 1980s a Disney park opened in Japan. The first Disneyland in Europe is currently being developed at Marne la Vallee, just 25 miles from Paris, and the battle for the contract saw competing bids from Barcelona and Alicante in Spain. The reason for the fierce competition can be seen in the impact of a Disney theme park on the regional economy. The construction phase, from 1988 to the year 2000, will create 20,000 jobs and the running of the park another 30,000. Ten million visitors a year are expected, more than half of them Non-French (*The London Times)*. The new French Disneyland will have a French flavor alongside the planned Wild West and New Orleans Jazz areas.

The largest and best known theme park in Britain is Alton Towers in North Staffordshire which attracts over 1½ million visitors a year to the 700 acre site. There are over 200 acres of gardens and lakes, 300 acres of woodlands and a series of rides and attractions. Over $7 million was invested in new rides for the 1987 season. The original house — Alton Towers is being restored and renovated and acts as a backcloth to the main fairground activities of the theme park. Alton Towers is located mid-way between the M6 and M1 motorways and has over 20 million people within 2 hours journey-time of the park.

These theme parks act as tourist 'honey pots' and, by their sheer size and drawing power, can attract visitors from a catchment up to a day's journey time away. Often, as has happened in the United States, the presence of a major theme park will act as a spur to related tourist development, particularly accommodation provision. The major drawback with Alton Towers as a tourist destination is the lack of adequate good quality accommodation in the immediate vicinity of the park.

By careful planning and design, a large number of tourists can be managed and guided through the theme park in ways referred to in the previous chapter. The spread of rides and distribution of gift/craft shops, restaurants and fast food outlets can be built into the overall design of the theme park so that organized routes can be developed in an unobtrusive way.

Most theme parks are limited to seasonal operations. The success of the Edmonton Mall, which is totally enclosed, will undoubtedly encourage developers to imitate the theme park — shopping mall concept in other northern cities.

3. Historical/Cultural Restoration — Living Museums

In the United States the restorations of colonial or westward expansion towns, forts and trading posts significant in the nation's development have been popular travel attractions. Recent innovations have included the living history concept with individuals conducting activities that were actually carried out by former residents. In Williamsburg, Virginia, one can watch a cobbler make footwear with the tools and technology of the 1700s. The craftsman at Williamsburg are in Colonial dress and include printers, weavers, bakers, farmers, etc. The National Park

Service has restored many significant properties in the United States and, like Williamsburg, operate many as living museums. Attractions of this type provide visitors with a better understanding and appreciation of daily living a century or more ago and have proven to be extremely popular. Privately operated living history museums will probably increase in the future, using successful ventures such as Colonial Williamsburg, the Polynesian Cultural Center in Hawaii, and Mystic Seaport in Connecticut as examples.

In Britain, the same concept is used. The label is different such as open air museums, or industrial heritage areas. The North of England Open Air Museum at Beamish in County Durham is a case in point. This was one of the forerunners of a new museums movement designed to be a living museum recreating an industrial and social environment present in the region between 50 and 100 years ago. The museum occupies 300 acres and has a farm with live exhibits, an adit mine, a working tramway, steam railway and a village made up of buildings rescued from demolition from various sites in North East England. In a row of miners cottages on the site, there are reconstructions of interiors common 50 years ago. In the West Midlands, in 1967, the Ironbridge Gorge Museum was set up to preserve the industrial artefacts of Coalbrookdale which was one of the leading centers of the early industrial revolution. Now the Ironbridge Museum has an extensive open air site at Blists Hill, together with exhibits on several other sites in the locality.

Although each of these innovations has produced a new major tourist attraction on its own, it is not sufficient as a catalyst for tourist development. Recent trends in tourism have included more short-break holidays and second and third holidays. In order to attract this potential market the tourist authorities associated with industrial heritage projects need to develop the tourist product as a whole. Because they are not traditional tourist regions most of these areas lack a range of adequate accommodation and lack centers to provide a network of information. This means investment in major hotel schemes, development advice schemes for small businesses and establishing a network of information centers.

4. Second Homes — Condominiums — Time Sharing

In the past the tradition has been for more prosperous individuals to buy or build second homes and certain parts of New England, the Great Lakes States in the United States and Canada, and the mountainous regions of these countries became synonymous with widespread second home development. In the last three decades many new resort hotel developments in the 'Sunbelt' have included condominiums as a part of the development scheme.

However, as these properties are often empty for part of the year they are costly to maintain and require payment of taxes and risk being vandalised. As an alternative to this, developers hit upon the concept of multi-ownership or time-sharing as a way of selling holiday apartments during the recession in the United States in the early 1970s. For a single capital outlay, the buyer gets one or more weeks of fully furnished and equipped holiday accommodation for a given period of years. The cost of purchase varies with the holiday season, the most expensive weeks being at the optimum time of the season. There is also usually an annual maintenance charge.

Timeshare

Timeshare is one of the fastest growing sectors of the holiday market in the 1980s with much of the growth concentrated in the USA (850,000 timeshare owners) and Europe (320,000) especially in the UK, France, Italy and Switzerland. It represents a current investment of over $9 billion by 1.2 million owners worldwide *(Travel and Tourism Analyst)*.

Table 30 shows the growth of timeshare ownership over the period 1975 to 1985. In Asia, it is almost entirely concentrated in Japan.

Table 30: Growth of Timeshare Ownership 1975 – 1985

Nationality of Owner	1975	1980	1985
USA/Canada	5,000	260,000	650,00
Europe	15,000	70,000	220,000
Asia	35,000	50,000	160,000
Mexico	1,000	20,000	75,000
Africa	2,000	4,000	30,000
Caribbean	2,000	10,000	25,000
Central/South America	—	10,000	20,000
Australasia	—	5,000	20,000

Source: UK Tourism Advisory Group

The concept was further refined in the mid 1970s when salesmen found that, while potential clients were attracted to particular timeshare accommodation, they did not wish to be tied to holidays in the same location year after year.

This led to the introduction of timeshare exchanges between different individuals in different resorts. There are now two main international timeshare exchange companies, Interval International and Resort Condominiums International which is by far the largest, with 560,000 members in 1,200 resorts in 70 countries. It was the emergence of these two companies which encouraged the rapid growth of timeshare developments from the mid-1970s onwards. The most recent development has been that of entire timeshare resorts. The Marriott Corporation have five timeshare resorts and is planning more. Club Hotel (a subsidiary of Club Mediterannee) in France, with over 40 resorts, is the market leader in Europe. Most of the timeshare properties in Europe are located around the shores of the Mediterranean and, in France and Italy, most of the timeshare owners are nationals from within the domestic market. In Italy, there are about 40,000 owners in 45 resorts — either in the skiing regions of the Alps or along the beaches of southern Italy. In the UK, about 40,000 of the total 60,000 timeshare owners have bought weeks outside the UK, mainly in Spain and the Canaries. Table 31 outlines the major European timeshare companies.

Table 31:
Major Companies Developing Timeshare in Europe

Club Hotel (Club Mediterannee)	French	40,000 owners	40 resorts
Hapimag	Swiss	30,000 owners	48 resorts
Barratt	UK	10,000 owners	7 resorts
Incorporated Investments	UK	10,000 owners	2 resorts
Wimpey	UK	3,500 owners	5 resorts
Kenning Atlantic	UK	3,000 owners	4 resorts

Source: *Travel and Tourism Analyst,* June 1986

Although timeshare in the UK went through a cautious period of investment in the mid-1980s, these developments can bring spectacular rewards for the firms investing in them. For example, the Palm Beach Club in Tenerife has 7,000 timeshare owners who have invested $62 million in 311 units. (TTA, 1986).

The main timeshare developments have tended to be in those locations of the world where large volume tourism flows are already established, where there is a good year-round climate (so avoiding the problem of selling weeks during unseasonal periods), and where there are good links with the main tourism-generating countries. One good example is Fairfield Communities of the USA which is the world's largest timeshare developer. They have had timeshare sales of over $120 million in 5 years at Vistana, Florida, which is close to Disneyland in Orlando.

In Europe, future timeshare developments are likely to focus on Greece, Spain and Portugal which are the least represented timeshare destinations. The main markets for timeshare sales will be West Germany (which is at present very underdeveloped) the UK and Scandinavia. All three countries are among the main users of the Mediterranean tourist destinations.

In the United States, new timeshare developments have declined in number since the boom years of the early 1980s, although more recent developments have been on a much larger scale, and several major corporations are investing in timeshare, including Marriott, Sheraton and ITT. The major concentrations of timeshare resorts in the USA are in Florida, the Carolinas, and the California coast.

(vi) Leisure and Speciality Shopping in Indoor Resort Complexes

The future will see the development of large-scale mixed retail and leisure developments with tourism as the unique selling point. In northern latitudes all-weather complexes of this type will become the indoor resorts of the future. Shopping is an important adjunct to tourism. In 1986, tourist expenditure by overseas visitors to the UK on shopping accounted for 37 per cent of their total expenditure, emphasizing the synergy of tourism investment with mixed development schemes.

West Edmonton Mall in Edmonton, Alberta, Canada provides a model for indoor resorts of the future. In 1981, it was originally intended to be a standard shopping center but the owners decided to develop a theme park, an amusement park and shopping complex — all under one roof. It contains 836 shops, covers over 5 million square feet and cost over $600 million (U.S.) to build. At the center is a 2½ acre lake with a replica Spanish galleon and 4 submarines (more than the Canadian Navy) that take visitors on an underwater ride through waters with live sharks and octupuses. The roof is 16 stories up. A 10 acre water park is now being built with a Fantasyland hotel. The whole complex employs 15,000 people and, in 1985, brought in over $500 million (U.S.) revenue a year. There is parking for 30,000 cars. It now acts as a major visitor attraction in its own right and on autumn weekends, over 400,000 visitors come to the Mall, nearly half of them from outside of Alberta. Many come from the United States on short break holidays. A third of visitors are now specifically attracted to Edmonton from the United States and the rest of Canada because of the West Edmonton Mall. In 1988 it attracted over 8 million visitors.

In London Battersea Power Station is being transformed into a family entertainment center with high tech and heritage attractions on 8 floors. Being in the heart of London, it goes beyond the traditional leisure park concept by providing a year round air conditioned weather-proof environment containing entertainments, restaurants and retail shops in one enormous complex. Over half the available space will be given over to rides, shows, attractions and arcades. Food and retailing will occupy about one-third of the space. It will cater for about 4.5 million visitors a year and will employ 4,000 people.

Europe's largest indoor shopping complex is the Metro Centre on Tyneside with 10,000 free car parking spaces and its own rail link to the center of Newcastle. This huge shopping and entertainments complex is another indication of the type of development that can transform urban areas and lead to the emergence of the most unlikely tourist destinations.

For cities in northern latitudes with limited sunshine, large population concentrations and cheap land, this may be the new type of tourist destination. Accessibility to large urban populations and new kinds of tourism product in an all-weather themed indoor environment will be the unique selling proposition that will enable those cities who invest to compete with the more traditional resort destinations.

5. Technology and New Technology

Industrial science has already provided the tourism industry with numerous ancient and modern structures to interest the curious. The Pyramids, the Great Wall of China, the Eiffel Tower, the Golden Gate Bridge and the Panama and Suez Canals are a few examples of man's creativity and industrial fortitude. Electricity, automobiles, airplanes, the telephone and television are accepted amenities in developed nations. Air conditioning helped foster the development of the American Sunbelt. The computer has been the prominent growth catalyst of the last decade. It has been influential in every sector of the travel and tourism industry. For example, SABRE, the computer travel information network of American Airlines, provides travel agents with a communication system for the efficient and economic access to over 1,700 travel service suppliers worldwide. Suppliers include 650 airlines, 17,500 hotel properties, more than 35 tour companies and 39 car rental firms (*U.S.A. TODAY,* Sept 19, 1988).

In the past 10 years, Computer Reservation Systems in the United States have grown to such a scale that 88% of U.S. airline tickets are sold through them. The growth of U.S. air travel in the 1960s and 70s, and its deregulation in 1978, encouraged these processes. Airlines discovered that computer technology could help them keep up-to-date reservations and fares more accurately, quickly and cheaply than by taking on more clerical staff. The airlines quickly realized that an industry-wide reservations and fare system could be extended to retail travel agents especially the larger multiples developing the business travel market.

During the 1960s and 1970s, there were several attempts to set up a single industry system but these largely failed because the two largest airlines — United and American said they would expand their own internal reservation systems and related products — Apollo and Sabre and market them to travel agents. From 1976, the race was on to install CRS terminals at travel agent locations thus getting greater sales exposure. However the impact was relatively limited in a largely regulated market and the three largest airlines United, American and TWA also handled other carriers' transactions.

However, after deregulation in 1978, these joint activities ceased, particularly when the airlines began to realize the competitive edge they had in the form of their computerized reservation systems. A huge database was needed in order to process deregulated fares and routes and the major carriers exploited their CRS's. For example, fees per booking for smaller airlines were raised from 35 cents to $2.75 per booking.

A wide range of incentives was offered to agencies to sign up with the main systems — hardware, software, free lines and so on. The percentage of agencies with CRS went from 5% in 1977 to 95% as of May 1987. In theory, use of automated airline systems didn't mean that agents had to lose their neutrality, but in practice they often did as the airlines, through financial penalties or pressure, wrote contracts that precluded multiple systems.

In the 1980s this has resulted in growing interdependence between travel agents and airlines, high fees for previously very cheap services, and agent favoritism. Other non-vendor airlines and agents began to complain on three major issues — fees, display bias and subscriber contracts. Fees were higher for CRS participants who competed with the vendor airlines and lower with CRS participants who didn't compete. Even where fees were paid, there were charges of display bias in that the less competitive airlines were allegedly given less obvious display positions. There was also the 'halo effect', that is higher revenues for airlines from their agents than from non-vendor agents, which led to some substantial incentives being offered to agents. (In a 1985 Congressional hearing Northwestern cited an example of the incentives offered to an agent in its territory: $500,000 in cash, a 10% override (on top of the standard commission) for sales on United, and five years free use of Apollo, including telephone line charges if the agent would switch from Sabre to Apollo. In 1986, Northwest resolved this by buying a half share in TWA's PARS system.

However, there are a number of lawsuits pending against United and American and, to date, the U.S. Government has not acted. Sabre and Apollo between them now account for three quarters of automated revenue from airline ticket sales and CRS is clearly the primary form of marketing airline seats. (Table 32).

The 'halo effect' of CRS sales is certainly significant and the stronger airlines have found that the system dominating sales has the ability to affect sales. For example, American's Chairman Robert Crandall has said that American gained 8 – 12% in incremental revenue from display preference from Sabre Agents over non-Sabre automated agents.

Vast sums of money are involved in setting up CRS and they are now a major feature of airline strategic planning. American and United have spent about $750 million on Sabre and Apollo development and United has talked about $1 billion worth of new investment in computer systems and personnel. Texas Air is spending $200 to $400 million to make the System 1 CRS more competitive. In fact, System 1 has been selected by the AMADEUS Consortium in Europe as the basis for their CRS. Each of the other main CRS's is investing heavily in order to increase, or at least maintain, their market share.

The impact of both deregulation and CRS's on travel agents in the U.S. has been considerable. The major CRS's are looking for retail outlets that can bring them a large amount of business in the fastest possible time and that often means agents producing a lot of business travel. However, although there are over 30,000 travel agents in the U.S., only 7% of these accounted for 28% of agency sales and the picture has been one of fewer agents doing more business. In many cases dwindling profits have led to consolidation, and many agents have joined or formed chains that are able to offer good national coverage and the kinds of discounts on air tickets, hotel rooms and car rentals that come with volume of business. All CRS vendors are now offering agents PC's and three offer IBM's new PS/2 as standard. These smart terminals offer a variety of accounting and administrative backup as well as the reservations system.

Table 32:
Airline Computer Reservation Systems in the United States

Airline	American	United	Texas	TWA	Delta
CRS	Sabre	Apollo	System 1	Pars	Datas II
Revenue ($ millions)	490	325	210	160	140
Profits ($ millions)	190	125	50	40	20

In transportation, on-board computers can take-off and land our most modern airliners, control fuel consumption, navigate to a destination and make flight service for the passenger more efficient. On the ground, flight control is expedited by computers and reservation systems are made and monitored by computers. The tunnel now being constructed by Great Britain and France under the English Channel will be a major engineering accomplishment and will provide a medium of spatial interation to link a prominent island nation economically and socially with the rest of Europe. As an attraction and monument demonstrating man's creative skills, 'the chunnel' as it is called will attain equal stature with other structures that have become synonymous with man's ingenuity.

Tourism attractions, particularly theme parks, increasingly rely on computers, not only to operate animated shows and rides but for inventory/accounting control. Lodging and food services are rapidly adopting new technology as well. At many hotels one can now check in and out by credit card. Indeed the credit card industry worldwide would not function as efficiently as it does without the new technology. As we move toward increased travel market segmentation, new products and services that appeal to specific groups and individuals will be furthered by computerized information and reservation systems. These marketing systems may eventually be common in our homes with viewdata systems.

6. Public/Private Cooperation

As the travel and tourism industry continues to grow, increased public/private partnerships and cooperation, particularly in the United States, will be more common in order to foster the industry's growth. Many of the urban redevelopment schemes discussed above provide evidence of public/private cooperation. Chambers of Commerce and Visitor and Convention Bureaus in most political entities have embraced a spirit of public/private unity in order to build convention centers, refurbish historical/cultural areas and even promote other types of leisure amenities that benefit visitors and local citizens. The travel and tourism industry has become a dominant economic and social catalyst to encourage public/private cooperation.

Conclusion

Travel is a major characteristic of the changing lifestyle of people in the developed nations. Travel for leisure is now considered a right, not just for the privileged few as in the past. As our leisure time increases and we seek more specialized travel experiences, market segmentation will intensify. The desire for an individually-designed travel experience will require more knowledge of the customer, and of the supply of travel services and products available, in order to design a satisfying and personally-enriching experience. The vacation traveler will become astute in seeking those travel destinations that provide maximum satisfactions and benefits. The information sources and communication networks will become more specialized and abundant. The printed brochure will eventually be replaced by videos that allow the potential traveler to see accommodations, vistas, currency, and hear languages as a step in the selection of a vacation experience. Consumerism will become a more powerful force in the industry.

According to *The Futurist* (July – August, 1988) the travel industry can be expected to increase between now and the 21st century. Air travel for business and pleasure is predicted to be twice that of 1985 and one out of every 10 people in the United States will be employed in the hospitality industry. This article also foresees the number of international visitors to the United States increasing as this country and Canada become major destinations for world travelers. The London-based Economist Intelligence Unit, in a recent study, predicts that the Germans and British will overtake U.S. citizens as foreign travelers in the year 2000 (*U.S.A. Today,* August 10, 1988). U.S. travelers, according to this study, will not equal the Japanese and French in the number of nights spent abroad.

There will be some downsides to tourism and travel growth that must be anticipated and planned for in advance. Societies in the developed world are changing rapidly. Some of the changes may at times work against the travel and tourism industry as social problems resulting from income and social differences in some segments of society create undesirable influences. Development projects for the industry may degrade the natural and/or cultural environment, increase congestion and create considerable controversy as local citizens question the benefits and costs of a tourism project. These residents may resist change as they envision their own vulnerability economically, politically, socially and environmentally.

Both public and private developments will be vulnerable to citizen and industry protest groups. The same people who have become astute consumers will be just as vocal as citizens protecting their lifestyles, social welfare, and environments on the basis of principle rather than economic gain.

Travel is still an adventure and heart beats are increased by reports of riots, coups, and acts of terrorism in the world. Televised scenes of street riots in Korea prior to the Olympic Games in 1988 deterred many sports enthusiasts from attending the Games. Bolder acts of international terrorism can have a profound effect on tourist travel, as the events of 1986 and 1988 proved. Incidents in the Mediterranean, highjackings and bombings, significantly reduced travel by North Americans to Europe. Political strife in some countries for extended time periods can destroy the tourism industry as demonstrated in Lebanon and, to some extent, in Northern Ireland and Israel. Tourism holds great promise as a means to understanding and peace in the world. Unfortunately, it is an imperfect world in which optimism, compassion, communication, trust and compromise are desirable and necessary traits to achieve world harmony.

The United States, as other developed nations, has witnessed the birth of a relatively new and viable industry. Tourism has progressed, in a few decades, from steam power to kerosene, from telephone and radio to satellite and electronics, from tourist rooms to upscale hotels and a return to bed and breakfast lodging. It has grown rapidly as a result of the consequences of many social and technological innovations.

This diversified industry bridges the public and private sectors, but has been troubled by disunity, disorganization, and conflicting policy development and implementation. Still, the industry has prospered because it has responded to human needs and satisfactions for travel and recreation experiences. The industry has been characterized by some 'as frivolous, patrician, consumption oriented, anti-culture, and environmentally insensitive' (Committee on Commerce, 1978). Some of these characterizations are true but, if one accepts certain basic national goals such as economic development, freedom of travel, and national resource preservation and protection, then one may wish to accept the challenge of participating in this viable industry. The goal should be to view the industry from the eyes of the traveler and question what is a satisfactory travel experience. The traveler is seeking satisfactions and benefits and the motivation to travel provides the energy to generate and sustain the travel industry. The prospects are bright for the tourist industry in the 21st century. Many parts of the world have yet to realize their tourism potential and many new markets/new products are awaiting discovery.

ASSIGNMENTS

1. Identify what you think are the two most significant innovations in tourism during the 1980s. Give a measured justification for your choice.
2. Using your library, look at a tourist guide for the 1950s and compare it with one written in the 1980s. What are the main differences? What are the most significant changes that have taken place over the past 30 years?

Glossary

Accommodation	Lodging facilities
Bank Holiday	Legal holiday
Building Society	Savings and Loan Association
Caravans	Camper vehicles or trailers
Car Hire	Automobile rental
Catering	Food and drink (non-alcoholic) services
Coach	Bus
Courier	Tour Guide — attendant hired to make arrangements
D of T	Department of Transport — National Government
D of E	Department of Environment — National Government
Dual Carriageway	Divided highway — unrestricted access
Estate	Subdivision/housing or industrial development
Flat	Apartment
Foot Path	Sidewalk or path
Holiday	Vacation
Local Authorities	Refers to Town or City form of government. Can also be used for County government bodies
Motorway	Freeway — restricted access
Petrol	Gasoline
Pound (£)	British currency
Quay	Dock
Rates	Property taxes
Redundancies	Unemployment
Reception	Front desk (hotel)
Return	(Ticket) round trip
Subway	Underpass — Vehicle or pedestrian
Tailback	Line of traffic (congestion)
VAT	Value added tax (sales tax)
Venue	Location of an event
Viewdata Terminal	Computer reservations (Most common PRESTEL (UK))

References

CHAPTER 1

British Tourist Authority, (1984). *Annual Report.*
British Tourist Authority, (1986). *Annual Report.*
British Tourist Authority. *British National Travel Survey.* Annually.
British Tourist Authority *et al.* (1981) *Tourism in the UK — The Broad Perspective.*
Chicago Tribune, Graph, April 18, 1988.
Clawson, Marion and Carlton S. Van Doren. *Statistics on Outdoor Recreation.* Resources for the Future. Washington, D.C. 1984.
Department of Employment. *Pleasure, Leisure and Jobs — The Business of Tourism,* HMSO 1985.
Development of Tourism Act (1969) HMSO 1969.
English Tourist Board, (1986). *Annual Report.*
English Tourist Board. *Annual Reports and Regional Facts Sheets.*
Frechtling, Douglas. 'U.S. Domestic Holiday Traffic,' Travel and Tourism Analyst. *The Economist* Publications. London. 1986.
The Henley Centre. *Leisure Futures,* Published quarterly.
International Union of Official Travel Organisations (IUOTO). *UN Conference on International Travel and Tourism,* Rome 1963.
International Passenger Survey. (Published annually, usually reported in *British Business).*
League of Nations. *Report on Tourism by Committee of Statistical Experts,* January 1937.
Lickorish, L.J. *The Travel Trade.* 1958, Appendix III.
National Tourism Resources Review Commission, Report: *Destination USA.* Six Volumes. Washington, D.C. 1973.
Organisation for Economic Cooperation and Development. *Tourism Policy and International Tourism.* Published annually. ECD Paris.
Time Magazine: 'Travel--A $260 Billion U.S. Industry on the Move,' Business Edition, May 18, 1987.
Travel Weekly. *Travel Market Yearbook, 1987.* News Group Publishing. 1986.
U.S. Department of Commerce. International Travel and Passenger Fares, 1982, *Survey of Current Business* 63, No. 5, May 1983.
U.S. Department of Commerce. International Travel and Passenger Fares, 1986, *Survey of Current Business,* 67, No. 6, June 1987.
U.S.A. Snapshots, *U.S.A. Today* December 5, 1984.
U.S.A. Snapshots, *U.S.A. Today* May 5, 1986.
U.S. Travel Data Center. *National Travel Survey*--Full Year Report 1986. Washington, D.C. 1987.
U.S. Travel Data Center. *The 1986–87 Economic Review of Travel in America.* Washington, D.C. 1987.
U.S. Travel and Tourism Administration. *Recap of International Travel to and from the United States in 1986.* U.S. Department of Commerce, Washington, D.C. 1987.
Waters, S.R. *Travel Industry World Yearbook*--The Big Picture. (1987). Child and Waters. New York. 1987.
Waters, S.R. *Travel Industry World Yearbook*--The Big Picture. (1988) Child and Waters. New York. 1987.
White, K. and M. Walker. 'Trouble in the Travel Account' *Annals of Tourism Research* 1982.

World Tourism Organisation. *Annual Reports.*
World Tourism Organisation. *Economic Review of World Tourism,* WTO 1986.
World Tourism Organisation. *World Tourism Statistics Annual Yearbook.*

CHAPTER 2

Bennett, E.D. (Ed.) *American Journeys-An Anthology of Travel in the United States.* Convent Station, New Jersey: Travel Vision. 1975.
British Travel Association. *The British Travel Association 1929 – 1969,* British Tourist Authority 1970.
Brittain J. and E. Wedlake Brayley. *The Beauties of England and Wales,* (Cumberland) London 1802.
Brunner, E. *Holiday Making and the Holiday Trades,* OUP 1945.
Burnet, L. *Villegiature et Tourisme sur les Cotes de France,* Paris 1963.
Clawson, Marion. 'The Crisis in Outdoor Recreation'. *American Forests* 65(3):22 – 31, (1959).
Defort, P.P. 'Quelques Reperes Historique du Tourisme Moderne'. *The Tourism Review,* January/March 1958.
De Santis, Hugh. 'The Democratization of Travel: The Travel Agent in American History'. *Journal of American Culture* 1(1):1 – 17, (1978).
Dulles, Foster Rhea. *A History of Recreation-America Learns to Play.* New York: Appleton-Century-Crofts. 1965.
Howell, Sara. *The Seaside.* Cassell, Collier, MacMillan, London. 1974.
Lennard, R. *Englishmen at Rest and Play,* Clarendon Press. Oxford, 1931.
Lickorish, L.J. and A.G. Kershaw. *op. cit.* Chap. 1.
Lundberg, Donald E. *The Hotel and Restaurant Business.* CBI-Van Nostrand, New York. 1984.
Lundberg, Donald E. *The Tourist Business.* Cahner Books, Boston. 1974, 1985.
Patmore, J.A. *Land and Leisure,* David and Charles 1970.
Smollett, T. *Humphrey Clinker,* Dent.
Stephenson, R.L. *Travels with a donkey in the Cevennes,* Dent 1986.
Swinglehurst, Edmund. *Cook's Tours-The Story of Popular Travel.* Blandford Press. Poole, Dorset. 1982.
Travel Weekly. (May 31) 1983.
Travel Weekly. Park Data Show RV's Top Choice. (September 3) 1984.
Ullman, Edward L. 1954, 'Amenities as a Factor in Regional Growth'. *The Geographical Review* 44(2):119 – 132.
U.S. Bureau of the Census, *Statistical Abstract of the United States.* Washington, D.C. Various years.
Van Doren, Carlton S. 1981, 'Outdoor Recreation Trends in the 1980s: Implications for Society'. *Journal of Travel Research* 19:3 – 10.
Van Doren, Carlton S. 1983, 'The Future of Tourism'. *Journal of Physical Education, Recreation and Dance* 54:27 – 29. 42.
Van Doren, Carlton S. 'The Consequences of Forty Years of Tourism Growth,' *Annals of Tourism Research,* 12, 1985.

CHAPTER 3

Cohen, Erik. 'Rethinking the Sociology of Tourism,' *Annals of Tourism Research.* 6 No. 1, Jan/March 1979.
Caribbean Tourism Research and Development Center, 1987. *Travel and Leisure's World Tourism Overview 1987/1988,* The Annual Review of the Travel Industry World Wide, American Express Publishing Company, NY. 1987.

Education and Training Advisory Council. *Hotel and Catering Skills — Now and in the Future,* Hotel and Catering Industry Training Board, London 1983.

Gearing, Charles E. *et al. Planning for Tourism Development,* Praeger Publishers. 1976.

Gunn, Clare A. *Vacationscape-Designing Tourist Regions,* Second Edition. Van Nostrand. 1988.

Gunn, Clare A. *Tourism Planning,* Second Edition. Taylor and Francis. 1988.

Institute of Manpower Studies. *Jobs in Tourism and Leisure,* English Tourist Board 1986.

Mayo, Edward J. and Lance P. Jarvis. *The Psychology of Leisure Travel.* CBI Publishing. 1981.

McIntosh, Robert W. and Charles R. Goeldner. *Tourism--Principles, Practices, Philosophies.* Wiley & Sons, New York. 1986.

Plog, Stanley. 'Why Destination Areas Rise and Fall in Popularity,' *Cornell HRA Quarterly* 14 No. 4. 1974.

Ritchie, J.R. Brent and Charles R. Goeldner. *Travel, Tourism and Hospitality Research.* New York: John Wiley and Sons. 1987.

Stengel, Richard. 'Ah, Wilderness!' America's parks have become too popular for their own good,' *Time,* July 11, 1988.

Time Magazine, 'Travel--A $260 Billion U.S. Industry on the Move,' Business Edition, May 18, 1987.

Travel Weekly. *Travel Market Yearbook, 1987.* News Group Publishing. 1986.

Travel Weekly. *Waikiki Beach and Oahu--1988 Reference Guide* (Supplement). July 11, 1988.

U.S. Department of Interior. *National Park Statistical Abstract.* 1987. Denver, Colorado.

U.S. Travel Data Center. *Tourism's Top Twenty* (1987). Washington, D.C. 1987.

Waters, S.R. *Travel Industry World Yearbook*--The Big Picture. (1987). Child and Waters. New York. 1987.

Waters, S.R. *Travel Industry World Yearbook*--The Big Picture. (1988) Child and Waters. New York. 1987.

CHAPTER 4

Working group of the National Trust Organisations of the EEC, Fifth Report *The Economic Significance of Tourism within the European Economic Community.* British Tourist Authority, 1983.

Organisation for Economic Cooperation and Development. op. cit.

Waters, S.R. (Ed). *op. cit.* Chap. 1.

World Tourism Organisation. *Economic Review of World Tourism,* WTO 1986.

CHAPTER 5

American Society of Travel Agents. *ASTA. STAT.* Various issues.

Beaver, A. *Mind Your Own Travel Business,* Beaver Travel 1979.

Business Travel News, 1988 Business Travel Survey, Issue 113, CMP Publications, June 6, 1988, I.

Economist Intelligence Unit. *The British Travel Industry — A Survey, London 1968.*

Lickorish, L.J. and A.G. Kershaw. The Travel Trade. 1958.

The Times, Article in the Business section 12.1.87.

Travel Trade Gazette, Article, January 1987.

'The 1988 Louis Harris Survey.' *Travel Weekly,* June 29, 1988.

Travel Weekly Focus, '1987 Profit Guide,' July 31, 1987.

CHAPTER 6

Beeching Report. *The Reshaping of British Railways.*
Department of Trade. *Report of Official Inquiry into the collapse of the Court Line,* HMSO 1975.
Daube, Scott. 'Daylight Rockies Service Debuts,' *Travel Weekly,* July 21, 1988, 24.
Lickorish, L.J. *op. cit.* Chap. 1.
Official Airline Guides (OAG). *Worldwise Cruise and Shipline Guide* (bi-monthly).
Pryke, Richard. *Competition Among International Airlines.* Brookfield, VT: Gouver Publishing, 1987.
The Travel Agent, 'More Americans Take to the Skies,' October 19, 1987.
Time Magazine, 'Travel--A $260 Billion U.S. Industry on the Move,' Business Edition, May 18, 1987.
Transport Act 1980.
Transport Act 1988.
Transport Statistics, HMS (Annually).
Travel Agent Magazine, 'ABA's Top 100 List Rounds Up Cream of North America's Crop,' March 3, 1988.
United States Travel Data Centre — Annual Surveys of Airline Travellers to US.
Waters, S.R. *Travel Industry World Yearbook--The Big Picture.* (1987). Child and Waters. New York. 1987.
Waters, S.R. *Travel Industry World Yearbook--The Big Picture.* (1988) Child and Waters. New York. 1987.

CHAPTER 7

Brown, B. and P. Lavery. *A survey of serviced and self-catering accommodation in South East Dorset,* Southern Tourist Board 1986.
Department of Employment. *Action for Jobs* in Tourism HMSO 1986.
Education and Training Advisory Council. *Hotel and Catering Skills — Now and in the Future,* Hotel and Catering Training Board 1983.
FOA/ECE Working Party on Agrarian Structure and Farm Rationalisation (Several papers on Farm Tourism contained in) *Report of the Symposium on Agriculture and Tourism,* Government of Finland, Helsinki 1982.
Horwath and Horwath. *World Wide Hotel Industry.* 1987.
Laventhol and Horwath. *U.S. Lodging Industry* 1986. Philadelphia. 1986.
Travel Weekly, 'Study Cites Need for More Hotel Rooms.' November 11, 1985. 44 No. 103, 1985.
U.S. Department of Interior. *National Park Statistical Abstract,* 1987. Denver, Colorado.
U.S. Travel Data Center. *National Travel Survey*--Full Year Report 1986. Washington, D.C. 1987.
Waters, S.R. *Travel Industry World Yearbook--The Big Picture.* (1987). Child and Waters. New York. 1987.

CHAPTER 8

British Tourist Authority, 1970.
Beekhuis, Jeanne V. *World Travel Overview.* Travel and Leisure 1987 – 1988.
Department of Employment. *Pleasure, Leisure and Jobs* (Ch 4) *op. cit.*
English Tourist Board. *Annual Reports.*

Hewett, R, and L.J. Lickorish et al. The British Travel Association 1929–1969, London 1971.

National Tourism Resources Review Commission, Report: *Destination USA.* Six Volumes. Washington, D.C. 1973.

Organization for Economic Cooperation and Development, *Tourism Policy and International Tourism.* Paris. 1984.

United States Congress. National Tourism Policy Act. 97th Congress 1st Session (Public Law 97–63). 1981.

U.S. Travel Data Center. *The 1986–87 Economic Review of Travel in America.* Washington, D.C. 1987.

CHAPTER 9

British Tourist Authority. *Strategy for Growth 1984–88,* 1984.
English Tourist Board, *Financing Tourist Projects,* 1980.
Lundberg, Donald E. *The Tourist Business.* Cahner Books, Boston. 1974, 1985.
Murphy, Peter. *Tourism A Community Approach.* Methuen. 1985.
Tourism U.S.A. Guidelines for Tourism Development. U.S. Department of Commerce, U.S. Travel and Tourism Administration. 1986.
Travel Weekly. Waikiki Beach and Oahu--1988 Reference Guide (Supplement). July 11, 1988.

Further developments on the Languedoc Rousillion development, see:
Lavery, P. et al. *The Strategy for Hadrians Wall,* Countryside Commission 1984.
Loudry, R. 'Tourism development of Languedoc Rousillon'. Paper given at International Seminar *Physical Planning and Area Development for Tourism,* IUOTO Geneva 1973.

CHAPTER 10

For further reading on Tourism Marketing, see:
Foster, D. *Travel and Tourism Management,* Macmillan 1985.
Krippendorf. *Marketing et Tourisme,* H. Lang & Co 1971.
Wahab, S. et al. *Tourism Marketing,* Tourism International Press 1976.

CHAPTER 11

Archer, B. & C.B. Owen. Towards a Tourist Regional Multiplier 1971.
Isard, W. *Methods of Regional Analysis,* MIT (1960).
Organisation for Economic Cooperation and Development. *Tourism Policy and International Tourism.* Published annually.
Richardson, H. *Elements of Regional Economics,* Penguin (1970).
U.S. Department of Commerce. 'International Travel and Passenger Fares', 1982. *Survey of Current Business* 63, No. 5, May 1983.
U.S. Department of Commerce. 'International Travel and Passenger Fares', 1986, *Survey of Current Business,* 67, No. 6, June 1987.

CHAPTER 12

Burton, R. *Recreation Carrying Capacity in the Countryside,* MSc Thesis, University of Birmingham, 1974.

Ceton, Marvin J., *et al.* 'Into the 21st Century, Long Term Trends Affecting the United States.' *The Futurist,* Vol. 22:4 July-August, 1988.

Davis, Robert S. 'Tuttle Cites the Importance of Regional Structure,' *Travel Weekly,* Vol. 45:96, November 3, 1986.

De Santis, Hugh. 'The Democratization of Travel: The Travel Agent in American History', *Journal of American Culture,* 1(1):1 – 17, 1978.

Dower, M. and P.E. McCarthy. 'Planning for Conservation and Development', *Journal of the Royal Town Planning Institute,* 53, No. 1, 1967.

European Information Centre for Nature Conservation *The Management of the Environment in Tomorrow's Europe,* Council of Europe, Strasbourg, 1971.

Furmidge, J. 'Planning for Recreation in the Countryside'. *Journal of the Royal Town Planning Institute,* 55, No. 2, 1969.

Houghton-Evans, W. and J.C. Miles 'Environmental Capacity in Rural Recreation Areas', *Journal of the Royal Town Planning Institute,* 56, No. 10, 1970.

Kotler, Philip. 'Dream Vacation—The Booming Market for Designing Experiences'. *The Futurist* 18:5, 1984.

Organisation for Economic Cooperation and Development. *The Impact of Tourism on the Environment,* General Report OECD, Paris 1980.

Ragatz, Richard L. Trends in the Market for Privately Owned Seasonal Recreational Housing. Proceedings — 1980 National Outdoor Recreation Trends Symposium, Volume 2, U.S. Department of Agriculture, Forest Service, Northeastern Forest Experiment Station, Broomall, PA, General Technical Report N.E.—57, 1980.

Van Doren, Carlton S. 'Outdoor Recreation Trends in the 1980s : Implications for Society'. *Journal of Travel Research* 19:3 – 10, 1981.

Van Doren, Carlton S. 'The Consequences of Forty Years of Tourism Growth,' *Annals of Tourism Research,* 12, 1985.

INDEX

AA	112
AAA	112
ABTA	67, 71
Accommodation sector	108, 113
Accommodation, self catering	110
Activities, recreational	44
Africa	62
AHMA	107
Air traffic controllers	102
commerical air carriers	96
growth, figure	95
world scheduled, figure	96
Air travel	65, 103
Aircraft	65
Operational Characteristics, table	97
Airlines Reporting Corporation	70
Airports, major	107
Air Transport Association of America	131
American Automobile Association	112
American Bus Association	89
American Express	76
American Hotel and Motel Association	107, 131
American Plan, for meals	28
American Society of Travel Agents	131, 70
Amtrak	82
Annual Economic Review of World Tourism	58
Arrivals, international tourist, Europe	62
Ask Mr Foster	76
Association of British Travel Agents	67
ASTA	76, 70
Atlantic City	25
Attractions sector	39
City	49
classification	41
classification of travelers, figure	43
Cultural-Social-Entertainment	41
natural	44
New York City	49
Resource dependency of, figure	42
Washington	49
Automobiles Association	112
Automobils	35, 85
British Coachways	89
British Commonwealth Institute of Travel Agents	77
British Tourist and Holidays Board	124
British Tourist Authority	127, 124
British Travel Association	124
Bucket shops	72
Bus industry, commercial	29
Bus Regulatory Reform Act, 1982 (UK)	88
Business Travel	73
News	76
growth, UK	74
US	74
Butlin, Sir Billy	117
Caravans	111
Caribbean	53, 55
CARTO	131
Center Parcs	117, 118
Certified Travel Counselor	77
Channel Tunnel, impact	94
Charter Flights	99
Civil Aeronautics Board	101
Civil War	24
Coastal Zones	54
Commerical Aviation Industry, US	98
Commercial Jet Aircraft, table	97
Commission, rates of	72
Competition, airline	102
Computers, in hotels	113
Cross Channel Ferries	92
Cruise Ships	90
CTC	77
Data Sources, US tourism	14
Day excursions	22
Denmark	111
Department of Commerce	120
Deregulation of Express Services, 1980	90, 100
Destination USA	120, 12
Development of Tourism Act	125, 124
Disneyland	50
Domestic Tourism	3
Britain	7
US	
Earnings, Tourism industry	3
East Asia and the Pacific	62
Economic Base method	164
Employment, travel industry	37, 121
English Channel	91, 94
English, Welsh, Scottish Tourist Boards	127
Entertainment	44
Environment, tourism impact	173, 178
capacity	174
methods of measurement	177
Spain	175
types of	173
Equal Rights Amendment	30
Expenditure, Foreign Visitor, figure	170
International Tourist, growth in EEC	61
tourist	163
Expressways, congestion	87
Federal Economic Recovery Tax Act (ERTA), 1981	109
Field Surveys	153
Finance	141
private sector	142
public sector	141
Flights, chartered	35
Florida winter resort	26
Foreign Visitors, USA, table	5
France	110
Gambling meccas,	53
Government, US	119
Hadrian's Wall	145
Hawaiian Islands	53
Highways	87
Historical/Cultural restoration	189
Hogg Robinson travel agency	74

Holiday Camps	117	Report	120
Holiday Corporation	107	National Bus Company	89
Holiday Inn Corporation	107	National councils, US	131
Holidays with Pay Act, the	29	National Park	49
Home exchange schemes	112	Service, US	45
Horizon Holidays	78	England and Wales	49
Hotel Chains, major UK, table	108	Seashores, lakeshores, US, figure	47
Hotel Development Incentives	125	National Railroad Passenger Corporation	82
Hotel Industry, US 1986, table	116	National Restaurant Association	131
Hotel Marketing Consortia Operating, UK	109	National Tour Association	89,131
Hotels, statutory registration	112	National Tourist Boards	125
US Market share, table	116	National Travel Survey, Bureau of	
worldwide, table	106	Census Regions, figure	17
		U.S.	1
IATA	70	NCSTD	131
members' rankings, table	98	NCTA	131
Indoor resort complexes	192	NCUTO	131
Industrial Revolution	19	New Deal, depression	29
Inner city	186	New World, the	21
Input-Output method	165	North Sea, crossing	94
Institute of Certified Travel Agents	77		
Inter-City Rail Network, figure	83	OECD	57
Intercity transport, bus	88	Operation Off-Peak	113
travel by modes, figure	86	Operation Stabiliser	72
International Tourism, development	64	Organization for Economic Cooperation and	
International Air Transport Association	70	Development	57
International Association of Convention and		Overseas Visitors to US and UK, table	12
Visitor Bureaux	131	UK, table	7
International Exhibitions, North America	28	US states, figure	14
International Leisure Group	78		
International Thompson Organization	78	Parks, AONB's, UK, figure	48
International Tourism	11,57	Passenger Ferries	91
International Tourism Demand, figure	60	transport Sector	81
reports	58	travel, train	28
data sources	57	Pickfords Business Travel	74
International Tourist arrivals, table	59	Pontin, Fred	117
receipts, table	59,63	Post-mobility adjustment	32
Ireland	111	Pricing policy	156
		Private trailers, growth in ownership	111
Japan	62	Product Life Cycle, figure	155
		Product, selling	157
Languedoc-Roussillon	144, 171	Psychology of travelers	41
Legislation, US	124	Public/private cooperation	196
Leisure, attractions, all-weather	55	Puritanism, age of	21
travel, 20th Century	28		
Lodging industry		RAC	112
jobs, US and Britain	105	Rail Transport	81
recent trends	115	Railroad mileage, US, 1870	24
structure	107	Railroads, US	82
table	114	Railway transport system	22
US	109	for the masses	25
Luxury resorts, The resort	26	Europe	25
		US, Canada	25
Market research	152	Receipts from foreign Visitors, US, figure	13
segmentation	155	Recreation, Vehicle Industry Association	131
Marketing mix	154	visitor days, National parks	45
strategy	157	hours of, National Parks, roads and street	87
tourism	151	Regional Tourist Boards	127
Mass Mobility (1958-1974)	30	England's	128
recreation (1946-1958)	30	Rental car business, US	87
tourism	81	Reservations, airline, table	195
Motel, highway	29	Resort development, Languedoc-Roussillon,	
Multiplier method, economics	165	figure	144
National Tourism Policy Act, 1979	120	hotel centers, US, figure	52
National Tourism Resources Review Commission		Hotels and Areas, US, evolution of, figure	27

American invention	26
Britain	53
Retail Travel Sector	67, 71
Road Transport	85
Rockresorts	148
Roman Wall, capacity, table	147
Royal Automobile Club	112
Sea bathing	20
Sealink route map, figure	93
Seaside resort, schematic diagram, figure	23
Victorian England	22
Second Homes	190
Spas, resort towns	20
Standard Industrial Classification, Travel and Tourism	40
State Park systems	49
Statistics, dearth of	15
Stock Market Crash, 1929	29
Surveys, International Tourism	15
National Tourism	16
SWOT analysis	161
Technology, new	193
Theme parks and New Malls	50
malls	186
North America, figure	188
Thomas Cook travel agency	67, 74
TIA	131
Timeshare	190, 191
Europe, table	192
growth of ownership, table	191
Tour and Charter business, growth	89
Tour operations, integrated	78
Tour Operators	77
direct sell	77
general tour contractors	77
wholesale	77
Touring caravans and campers	87
Tourism data, measurement	16
Tourism Development,	
historical/cultural restoration	189
inner city	186
innovations	185
second homes	190
theme parks, malls	186
Tourism Employment, table	4
Tourism impact, balance of payments	169
economic activity,	168
economies,	167
employment	168
Tourism multiplier, table	167
Tourism, Product, attractions	37
British, post 1945	34
development of mass	19
development, project appraisal	136
development, US	135
economic impact	163
farm	110
local authorities and	129
national policy, Britain	35
planning	138
planning, US	135
Public Sector	132
the market	139
Tourist, Activity, share of Economic Activity	63
definition	1
generating Countries	58
industry, development	19
industry, The	2
resources	180, 181
Tourist Board Structure, Britain, figure	126
Board, roles of	127
Boards	125
Tourist Environments	182
management of	182
planning for	180
visitor management	183
Trade Professional Organizations, US	131
UK	132
Transactions matrix, table	165
Transit facilities, US	102
Transport, Act, 1980,	89
Act, 1985	89
air	94
coach	88
maritime	90
road	88
Transportation, mode of, Table	11
Travel, Act 1961	120
Agency Operations	75
Agency, costs	77
Agency turnover	73
Agency, establishing a	69
Agent, services	69
Expenditures, US Domestic	123
Industry Association of America	131
Industry World Year Book	58, 76
Americans overseas	120
Trends, International Travelers, US	33
Trips 72-86, figure	8
characteristics, table	9
United Kingdom	111
United States, ferries	92
US Travel Data Center	131
US Travel Service	120
USTDC	131
Vacation Centers, US, figure	46
Vacation Days	9
abroad, US citizens	31
farm and ranch, US	111
VFR	111
Via Rail	82
Victorian Resorts, North America	23
Visiting Friends and Relatives	111
Visitors, Mexico	32
top 20 US states, figure	38
West Germany	64, 111
Woodside Management systems	74
Workforce, tourism	65
World Tourism Organization	57
Yellow Pages	79
Yosemite National Park	49
Z graph, figure	159
Zones, destination, figure	137

ELM PUBLICATIONS
12 Blackstone Road
Stukeley Meadows Industrial Estate
Huntingdon
Cambs
PE18 6EF

We also publish textbooks on the following subjects:

Managing People

Business Management

Travel and Tourism

Library and Information Studies

Languages

PEG series (Practical Exercises for Groups)
(Computer simulations - multi media packs)

Elm also specialises in educational resources for history

If you would like further details about our publications,
please write to us at the above address.

Our distributor in the United States is:

State Mutual Book & Periodical Service Ltd
521 Fifth Avenue
New York
New York 10175
USA